THE
LITTLE BOOK OF
BIG
IDEAS

DANIEL SMITH

Michael O'Mara Books Limited

For Lauren and Luke — Dream big!

First published in Great Britain in 2017
by Michael O'Mara Books Limited
9 Lion Yard
Tremadoc Road
London SW4 7NQ

A CIP catalogue record for this book is available from the British Library.

Papers used by Michael O'Mara Books Limited are natural, recyclable products made from wood grown in sustainable forests. The manufacturing processes conform to the environmental regulations of the country of origin.

ISBN: 978-1-78243-829-8 in hardback print format
ISBN: 978-1-78243-883-0 in trade paperback print format
ISBN: 978-1-78243-830-4 in ebook format

2 3 4 5 6 7 8 9 10

Designed and typeset by Design 23, London

Printed and bound by CPI Group (UK) Ltd, Croydon, CR0 4YY

www.mombooks.com

Contents

PART TWO: MATHEMATICS

PART THREE: SCIENCE

PART FOUR: MEDICINE AND PSYCHOLOGY 89

PART FIVE: PHILOSOPHY 121

PART SIX: POLITICS

PART SEVEN: ECONOMICS 209

PART EIGHT: ARTS, ARCHITECTURE AND MUSIC 243

INTRODUCTION

'A pile of rocks ceases to be a rock pile when somebody
contemplates it with the idea of a cathedral in mind.'

Antoine de Saint-Exupéry

It is sometimes said that love or perhaps money makes the world go
round, but ideas have a much better claim to keeping us all spinning
on our axis. Ideas are the great currency of life, driving progress and
nurturing understanding – of ourselves and of the world around us – and,
arguably, are the defining characteristic that elevates our species above
all others. We may not be the only creature to entertain ideas – one need
only glimpse a squirrel striving to liberate a feast of nuts from a bird
feeder to see that – but we have the biggest and best ideas, not to mention
the wherewithal to bring them to fruition. As the great architect Frank
Lloyd Wright put it 'An idea is salvation by imagination.'

This book explores 150 of the most significant ideas of all time,
those that have moulded societies and epochs, many of them as
relevant today as they ever were. Over eight parts covering different
aspects of science, art, politics, economics, philosophy and religion,
we will immerse ourselves in the thoughts of great minds spanning
antiquity to the present day. Some are ideas that evolved slowly,
sometimes over a period of millennia – for example, the idea of
democracy – while others represent dramatic paradigm shifts – think
Einstein's General Theory of Relativity. It is also notable how many
great ideas emerged from or fed off others. Human thought clearly
thrives by cross-fertilization. In the words of the American writer

Ursula K. Le Guin: 'It is of the nature of idea to be communicated: written, spoken, done. The idea is like grass. It craves light, likes crowds, thrives on crossbreeding, grows better for being stepped on.'

PART ONE

THE COSMOS
AND RELIGION

'In all chaos there is a cosmos, in all disorder a secret order.'

Carl Jung

The cosmos describes the universe as seen as an ordered whole, as opposed to an amalgam of bewildering chaos. Since the dawn of time our species has sought to make sense of our world and, crucially, how we fit into it. We have utilized different mechanisms to do so, perhaps most notably religious faith and scientific investigation, both of which are considered in the chapter that follows. Yet religion and science have often seemed at odds with each other in this quest. Richard Dawkins, for example, calls faith 'the great cop-out, the great excuse to evade the need to think and evaluate evidence.' Others, though, have believed there is space for both. Einstein took a nuanced approach. While rejecting the idea of a personal god, he once wrote: 'Try and penetrate with our limited means the secrets of nature and you will find that, behind all the discernible concatenations, there remains something subtle, intangible and inexplicable. Veneration for this force beyond anything that we can comprehend is my religion. To that extent I am, in point of fact, religious.' That greatest of science communicators, Carl Sagan, meanwhile, summarized our deep fascination with matters of the universe in *Cosmos*: 'The Cosmos is all that is or ever was or ever will be. Our feeblest contemplations of the Cosmos stir us – there is a tingling in the spine, a catch in the voice, a faint sensation of a distant memory, as if we were falling from a great height. We know we are approaching the greatest of mysteries.'

THE UNIVERSE

The universe comprises all that may be sensed, measured and detected – although, of course, in actuality we know that the vast majority of it remains unsensed and uncharted. It includes all living things, all physical and celestial objects, atmospheres, galaxies, vacuums and voids, as well as concepts such as space and time.

The idea of a physical universe governed by basic scientific laws (as opposed to the notion of a personal universe the nature of which is subject to individual consciousness) was in circulation among, for example, ancient Chinese, Greek and Indian thinkers. Although the descriptions of its origins and nature were largely speculative, human thought was nonetheless unleashed from the shackles of introspection and localization and directed outwards into the unknown of the cosmos. Man, in other words, could begin to perceive of himself within the 'Big Picture'.

There have been long-running fundamental debates as to whether the universe is essentially unchanging or in constant flux, whether it is finite, whether time is linear, or not, and if there is other life like us out there. Most of these 'big questions' remain up for grabs.

Yet even as the mysteries of the universe abound, we have been able to calculate (although we still lack definitive empirical evidence) its rough age (13.8 billion years) and size (at least 93 billion light years across). We have some understanding of how our own galaxy is organized, how time and space may be bent, how black holes are created, how the Big Bang may have birthed the universe – all immense achievements of intellectual imagination. We have much more to find out, of course, but humanity may never have a bigger idea than that which acknowledged, thousands of years ago, that there is more to the universe than what we can see and feel ourselves.

CREATION MYTHOLOGY

There are, perhaps, two questions above all others that have preoccupied humanity from the moment we could cognitively formulate them: where did we come from and why are we here? Despite our rapid advances in scientific understanding, the answers remain as elusive as ever – for all that the likes of Copernicus, Newton, Darwin, Einstein and their ilk have progressed knowledge. For instance, even if you accept the Big Bang theory of cosmological creation (see page 28), who can say with any certainty what, if anything, existed prior to the Big Bang, much less whether we now inhabit the world as a result of pure cosmological chance or with some higher purpose attached to our existence?

All of this doubt leaves room for myriad possible explanations. Traditional narratives that have attempted to explain the origins of the world and our species come under the umbrella term of 'creation myths'. Most are the products of distinct cultural and historical perspectives, striving to express profound truths and explain the 'meaning' of our existence. In terms of content and structure, they tend to fall into two distinct categories: those that claim to be literal, historical accounts of creation and those that are metaphorical stories full of symbolic meaning.

The story as told in Genesis, the first book of the Bible, is among the most famous of all creation myths. It depicts the wise and loving creator-God making the world and everything in it out of nothing over a period of six days (with a day of rest on the seventh). Often creation myths have shared characteristics, making it possible to categorize them under a few broad headings. The biblical story described above might be considered an '*ex nihilo*' narrative, in which a divine figure creates the cosmos (i.e. an ordered world) out of 'nothing' or out of formless chaos. Such a theme is evident in other cultures, including ancient Egyptian mythology, the classical Indian Vedas and the Qur'an.

Popular creation motifs

Other popular motifs include creation by:

- the dismemberment and dispersal of a primordial being
- the division of a primordial union into 'world parents' (e.g. Mother Earth and Father Sky)
- the metamorphosis of a progenitor, usually over the course of a journey through several worlds before eventual arrival at our own
- the disturbance of matter (sand, mud etc.) at the bottom of a primordial sea caused by a divinely sent diving creature, resulting in the creation of terrestrial order
- the cracking of a primordial egg

All these stories attempt to impose a sense of order on our existence. For many cultures, creation myths have offered a sense of solace, a notion of how the individual fits into the world, and even a framework for how we should behave.

POLYTHEISM

Polytheistic belief systems express belief in more than one god. Ancient Egypt and Greece, as well as pre-Christian Roman civilization, all had polytheistic traditions, and polytheistic belief was also widespread across other African, Asian and pre-Columbine American societies.

In polytheistic traditions, gods and goddesses are often delineated by different character traits and functions. In the Greek tradition, for example, Zeus was god of the sky, Aphrodite the goddess of love, Athena the goddess of wisdom, Hades god of the underworld and so on. In Egypt, meanwhile, the characters or functions of gods were typically reflected in an association with a particular animal or natural phenomenon. (Ra, king of the gods, was, for instance, associated with the sun.)

It may be that some polytheistic systems arose out of earlier animist beliefs, in which supernatural powers are attributed to animals, plants, natural phenomena and inanimate objects as a way to rationalize the world and events that occur within it. Thus, polytheism is sometimes seen as an evolutionary step from primitive animism to more sophisticated forms of organized religion. Some academics also argue that polytheism evolved out of aspects of ancestor worship and totemism, developing ideas of clan- or tribe-based spirits into a more complex system that seeks not only to explain natural phenomena but also to establish a cosmological framework in which believers may function.

Polytheism retains a foothold in the modern world, for instance in the many millions of Hindu adherents spread across the planet. The less prescriptive nature of much polytheistic teaching in comparison to the doctrines of monotheism (see next section) has an enduring attraction for some. Consider the wry words of one great American cultural critic: 'It is impossible to imagine the universe run by a wise, just and omnipotent God, but it is quite easy to imagine it run by a board of gods' (H. L. Mencken).

MONOTHEISM

Monotheism is a belief system based around the notion of a single god. Most modern-day religious adherents hold monotheistic convictions. The 'Abrahamic religions' (those that share the Hebrew stories featuring Abraham) – Christianity, Islam, Judaism and Sikhism – are all monotheistic.

In most monotheistic faiths, the divinity shares certain characteristics, including omnipotence and omniscience. The divinities tend, also, to be creator-Gods imbued with benevolence towards their creation and who seek a personal relationship with each individual. Monotheism has sometimes been used as a marker of social progress away from earlier polytheistic beliefs, yet the evidence to back up this assertion is disputed. Indeed, many cultures flirted with the notion of monotheism many centuries before the emergence of the Abrahamic religions.

The Abrahamic religions

Among the Abrahamic religions, Judaism is the oldest (dating back about 3,500 years), then Christianity (about 2,000 years) and then Islam (about 1,400 years). In 14th-century-BCE Egypt, meanwhile, the Pharaoh Amenhotep IV (better known as Akhenaten) dispensed with the traditional pantheon of Egyptian deities in favour of devotion to a single supreme deity: Aten. And in the 5th century BCE, Xenophanes of Colophon wrote of the 'one God, always still and at rest, who moves all things with the thoughts of his mind.'

The monotheism of the Abrahamic religions has been challenged at various points. Some scholars believe that early Judaism elevated the 'God of Abraham, Isaac and Jacob' as the most powerful of an array of deities. Similarly, some early Christian sects are believed to have entertained the notion of multiple (though not equal) gods, while some Islamic scholars consider the Christian notion of the Holy Trinity as being inherently un-monotheistic. Nonetheless, monotheistic belief so came to dominate Western thought that there was historically little room for polytheistic faiths – as reflected in the modern Western dichotomy between monotheism and atheism, with little else on the table.

There is a necessary conflict at the heart of virtually all monotheistic belief: if a single, benevolent, omnipotent and omniscient deity created the universe and everything within it, why does he permit the existence of evil? While there has never been an entirely satisfactory answer, monotheism remains the dominant mode of religious faith across the globe today.

BUDDHISM

Buddhism is different to most other religions in that it does not involve worship of a deity. Indeed, it is sometimes described as a philosophy rather than a religion – albeit one claiming between 300 and 500 million adherents around the world. Focusing on personal spiritual development, Buddhists aim to achieve a state of perfect enlightenment.

Buddhism is based on the teachings of Siddhartha Gautama, more commonly called Buddha – 'the one who is enlightened' – who was born around the 6th or 5th century BCE in what is now Nepal. When, as a young man, he saw first-hand the hardships ordinary people faced in relation to old age, ill health and poverty, Gautama concluded that suffering was the direct result of unsatisfied wants and desires – failure to fulfil them brought disappointment, while fulfilment itself only provided fleeting satisfaction. In response, he strove to live a life free of the burden of fulfilling one's desires, instead adopting an ascetic lifestyle, eschewing all personal indulgence and rigorously practising meditation.

Buddha began to follow a 'Middle Way' between sensual indulgence and asceticism as the most likely path to enlightenment – something he is said to have achieved when he was around thirty-five years old. This involved breaking the chains bonding the self to the desires of the self by recognizing the individual as part of an eternal and vast reality that may be termed the 'non-self'. Through this process of becoming one with the eternal non-self, he taught, it is possible to reach nirvana (see page 22).

Buddha declared that enlightenment is only to be gained through understanding of the four noble truths: *dukka* – suffering is a part of life; *samudaya* – suffering is caused by desire for worldly things; *nirodha* – suffering stops when the self is detached from desire; *magga* – there is an Eightfold Path to achieving detachment comprising right action, right intention, right livelihood, right effort, right concentration, right speech, right understanding and right mindfulness. Gautama's philosophically rooted code for living – and personal tranquillity – continues to attract followers some 2,500 years after his life and enlightened death.

REINCARNATION

Religion, philosophy and science offer various possibilities as to what might happen to us when our earthly lives end. Some believe this life to be our 'one shot' – one that ends with our expiration – while many religions offer the hope of eternal life in the hereafter. An alternative theory, particularly popular among Eastern religions, is the idea of reincarnation – that the human spirit returns after death to live again in a new form or body, as part of a cyclical pursuit of perfection.

Reincarnation (from the Latin for 'entering into flesh again') was an idea entertained by many cultures of the ancient world. Socrates and Plato were among several of the giants of Greek philosophy who gave serious consideration to it. Socrates, for instance, wrote: 'I am confident that there truly is such a thing as living again, that the living spring from the dead, and that the souls of the dead are in existence.' There is also evidence to suggest it formed a significant part of Druidic belief. Today, though, it is a notion that is most commonly associated with the major religions of the Indian subcontinent – Buddhism, Hinduism, Jainism and Sikhism. As it is stated in the *Bhagavad Gita*: 'The end of birth is death; the end of death is birth: this is ordained!'

The endless cycle

Each of these four great Eastern religions shares variants of the doctrine of *samsara*, which dates back to at least the 1st century BCE. Samsara suggests that each human is destined to remain in an endless cycle of death and rebirth, repeatedly drifting through an earthly existence – sometimes envisaged as a suffering-laden 'wheel of existence' – unless the cycle is broken by the acquisition of profound spiritual insights (accessible, variously, through ethical and virtuous living and the observance of ritualistic practices such as meditation and yoga). Spiritual awakening then results in liberation from the cycle and the achievement of a superior transcendent state (a process characterized, for example, as *moksha* in Hinduism and Jainism, and as *nirvana* in Buddhism).

The idea of reincarnation, however, has not been confined to Eastern faiths. There was a spike in interest among Western philosophers in the late 19th and early 20th centuries, particularly in light of a burgeoning fascination with the idea of psychical phenomena and the theory championed by some psychologists (notably Théodore Flournoy) of past-life recall.

'It is the secret of the world that all things subsist and do not die, but only retire a little from sight and afterwards return again. Nothing is dead; men feign themselves dead, and endure mock funerals . . . and there they stand looking out of the window, sound and well, in some strange new disguise.'

American transcendentalist and man of letters,

Ralph Waldo Emerson (1803–82)

ATHEISM

The counterpoint to belief in a deity or deities, atheism is the absence of belief in any gods. Instead of looking to supernatural entities for meaning and structure, atheism instead charges humans (as individuals and as part of wider communities) with finding alternative frameworks. While many religious adherents correlate 'godlessness' with immorality, atheists argue that humans themselves are best placed to devise moral codes free of the burden of religious dogma.

Atheists may cite many grounds for their religious non-belief. These include a lack of empirical evidence for the existence of a god or gods, the conviction that a well-meaning deity would not allow bad things to happen, or the sense that alternative systems of knowledge and understanding – such as science – provide a viable alternative to religious belief.

The rise of scientific rationalism since the 17th century has prompted a steep rise in atheism, with individuals seeking answers to the big questions of life and the universe in science. Indeed, many major scientific discoveries seemingly ran contrary to traditional religious teachings. For instance, geological research into the age of the Earth has undermined traditional biblical timelines that suggest the planet is just a few thousand years old. Charles Darwin's theories of evolution, meanwhile, challenged faith in the biblical account of creation as being a literal narrative. As Richard Dawkins, the arch-proponent of atheism, has said: 'Darwin made it possible to be an intellectually fulfilled atheist.'

Atheism, however, is not a modern invention. The ancient Greek philosopher Epicurus, for instance, adopted an essentially atheist position when he argued that the soul dies with the body and does not enjoy an afterlife. Lucretius, meanwhile, wrote of religion in terms of its ability to bring unhappiness upon humanity, a sentiment echoed millennia later by Karl Marx, who regarded religion as merely a social construct used to maintain the social hierarchy. By the late 19th century, Nietzsche was proclaiming the 'death of god', as humanity liberated itself from religion's shackles. Freud, meanwhile, suggested we are driven towards religious belief not because it is true but because of a psychological compulsion.

HELIOCENTRISM

The branch of science that traditionally considers the nature of space, the universe and celestial objects (e.g. planets, stars and asteroids) is astronomy. Arguably the single most significant breakthrough in the history of the discipline was the establishment of the Heliocentric Model of the universe by Nicolaus Copernicus in the 16th century. Copernicus showed that the centre of the universe is not the Earth, as had previously been thought, but the Sun.

The geocentric model

Since antiquity, the Geocentric Model – with the Earth at the centre of the universe – had been the predominantly accepted view of cosmological reality. The theory was most famously laid out in the 2nd century CE by the Greek polymath Ptolemy, who himself built upon the earlier work of such noted thinkers as Aristotle. The evidence available to the ancients appeared clear-cut – our Earth appears to be stationary while the celestial objects seem to revolve around us. The obvious conclusion was that our planet is the fixed focal point of the universe. Ptolemy developed his theory further to explain why the planets moved at varying speeds and on specific arcs.

The Ptolemic Model returned reasonably accurate predictions of the motion of the planets and became the accepted standard for a millennium and a half. Yet even before Ptolemy, there had been rival theories. Around the 5th century BCE, for example, Philolaus had proposed that the Earth, the Sun, the Moon and the planets circled a fire in the middle of the universe. Then, in the third century BCE, Aristarchus of Samos put forward an early version of the Heliocentric Model, although his supporters seem to have been few and far between.

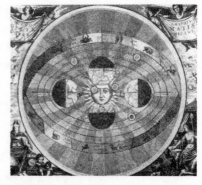

Helciocentrism

So, it fell to Copernicus – building upon the teachings of Aristarchus and a number of medieval Islamic scholars – to establish a more definitive model in 1543's *De revolutionibus orbium coelestium* (*On the Revolutions of the Heavenly Spheres*). He showed, for example, how the changing nature and varying course of the planets could be explained within the context of their passage around the Sun when set against our own planet's elliptical path. The Italian astronomer Galileo Galilei (1564–1642) – armed with his powerful telescopes – was able to corroborate many of Copernicus's ideas as well as resolve certain problems with his model. Galileo's close contemporary, Johannes Kepler, made further refinements to the basic hypothesis.

The impact of Copernicus's work was immense. In terms of science, he undermined previous assumptions and laid down a path for the likes of Newton to follow. The spiritual impact was no less – not only did Copernicus seem to go against the teachings of the established Church (1 Chronicles in the King James Bible talks of the world that 'shall be stable, that it be not moved'), but he forced humanity to re-evaluate its position within the cosmological order. From being the fixed point around which all else revolved, our planet was suddenly just another celestial object, spinning around with all the others.

The shock of Copernicus's ideas was summed up by the great German writer Johann Wolfgang von Goethe:

Of all discoveries and opinions, none may have exerted a greater effect on the human spirit than the doctrine of Copernicus. The world had scarcely become known as round and complete in itself when it was asked to waive the tremendous privilege of being the centre of the universe.

CELESTIAL MECHANICS

A sub-field of astronomy, celestial mechanics strives to calculate the motion of celestial objects, with recourse to generally accepted scientific principles. Practised since antiquity, celestial mechanics has evolved and adapted to new scientific understanding, providing us with a picture of our evolving understanding of the nature of the cosmos.

At the very heart of celestial mechanics is the question of what drives the motion of the universe. The ancients often imagined the universe as a collection of celestial spheres, with the Earth at the centre and all the celestial objects projected within the inner surface of the spheres. The composition of the spheres was a subject of much debate. Plato believed that fire was the dominant material while Aristotle favoured a mysterious substance known as Aether. The primary cause of celestial motion was equally disputed. Plato suggested a sort of universal soul that operated according to mathematical principles to govern activity. The idea of celestial objects imbued with souls was a notion later taken up by Ptolemy. Aristotle opted for an external 'unmoved mover' – a God-like figure from which all else follows and whose perfection is reflected in the uniform orbits of the planets.

The modern age of celestial mechanics

It is notable that much of the debate in ancient times revolved around qualitative rather than quantitative assessments of celestial activity. The modern age of celestial mechanics began in the 17th century, thanks to the leaps forward made by Johannes Kepler and Isaac Newton. In his *New Astronomy, Based upon Causes, or Celestial Physics* (published in 1609), Kepler robustly applied principles of physics to reliable astronomical data (much of it generated by the Danish astronomer Tycho Brahe) to model the motion of the planets, the accuracy of which was proven by the reliability of his astronomical predictions. He elucidated the elliptical nature of planetary orbits and sought to understand the force that held them in these orbits.

In 1687 came Isaac Newton's *Principia*, building on Kepler's work and expanding it to describe the orbits of the planets within the context of the laws of universal gravitation. Allied to the work of Copernicus (see previous entry), certain fundamentals of the cosmos were slowly coming within the grasp of modern scientific comprehension. The great 18th/19th-century Italian astronomer Joseph-Louis Lagrange would further refine and expand upon Newton's and Kepler's ideas.

Through the medium of celestial mechanics, the narrative of the relationship between Man, the universe and God was being rewritten. In the 20th century, Einstein would add a further chapter with his General Theory of Relativity (see page 76), which showed that Newton's universal principles were not quite as universal as they once seemed.

THE BIG BANG THEORY

The Big Bang theory is a wide-ranging, and as yet incomplete, explanation of how the universe came into being that holds sway with a large part of the modern scientific community. In broad terms, it describes how – some 13.8 billion years ago, according to the most accurate current calculations – the cosmos was born when a tiny 'primordial atom' exploded, setting free a vast quantity of energy and undergoing a phase of rapid super-expansion. Then a period of cooling brought about the appropriate conditions to begin the long evolution of our universe as we know it today.

In terms of popularizing the Big Bang theory, there has been no greater figure than Stephen Hawking. His work since the late 1960s (and his capacity to communicate it) has helped consolidate the idea of a period of cosmological super-expansion in the nano-seconds following the creation of the universe – a phenomenon that helps to explain why physically distant regions of the sky look similar, since they were originally in close contact with each other.

Along with James Hartle, Hawking also developed the 'no-boundary theorem' that draws on quantum theory and Einstein's General Theory of Relativity in a bid to show that it is senseless to talk of time before the universe began (not least because the General Theory proved space and time are not absolutes). Querying what predated the Big Bang, Hawking has suggested, is like 'asking for a point south of the South Pole'.

Hawking may be the poster boy of the Big Bang theory but he is just one of an army of scientists who continue to labour to understand better its exact nature.

Birthing the big bang

The man usually considered to have come up with this extraordinary thought was, somewhat unexpectedly, a Belgian priest by the name of Georges Lemaître. He was working in the 1920s, a period in which scientific observations (notably by the British astronomer Edwin Hubble) strongly indicated that the universe is expanding, and at pace. As it became clear that galaxies are hurtling away from us in every direction, Lemaître pondered the existence of a primeval atom as the point of origin of everything. It was an idea that other scientists eagerly seized upon, developing and elucidating the theory. They envisaged a massively dense and ferociously hot mass of energy and matter no more than a few millimetres across but which contained the building blocks of the cosmos – a sort of cosmological flat-pack kit, if you like.

Yet not everyone was convinced. One significant alternative school of thought championed the Steady State Theory, which suggested that as the galaxies travel apart, new matter is created in order to maintain a constant average density across the universe. If this idea was right, the universe must stay basically the same (on the large scale) across all of time – making the Big Bang moment an impossibility. However, by the mid-1960s the pendulum was swinging towards the Big Bangers. In particular, in 1965, cosmic microwave background radiation was recorded for the first time – confirming a phenomenon long predicted by adherents of the Big Bang.

'The Big Bang is our modern scientific creation myth. It comes from the same human need to solve the cosmological riddle.'

Carl Sagan

DARK MATTER AND DARK ENERGY

As we learn more about the nature of the universe, so too we achieve a greater understanding of what we do not know. Scientists now believe that baryonic matter – those atoms that we know comprise our own planet, the Sun, the stars and whole galaxies – makes up perhaps no more than 5 per cent of the universe. It is widely postulated that the rest (and to be clear, that is a lot of universe to account for) is comprised of some 27 per cent dark matter – a mysterious, non-light-emitting material – and 68 per cent dark energy.

Although dark matter is now widely accepted among the scientific community, since astronomer Fritz Zwicky first suggested its existence in 1933, there are currently no devices that allow for it to be observed. Not only is it invisible, it does not emit any known type of electromagnetic energy. However, while dark matter appears to impose a gravitational effect on galaxies, dark energy (which was only putatively discovered in the 1990s) is thought to contribute to the accelerating expansion of the universe in apparent contravention of the expected effect of gravity.

Some scientists argue that dark matter consists of an as yet unknown type of particle, and others suggest that it is better understood if we accept a fundamental revision of traditional gravity. As to what dark energy is, there is even less consensus, although one suggestion is that it is a type of hitherto unknown force filling the universe in the manner of a fluid.

While scientists literally flail around in the dark, the prospect of bettering our understanding of dark energy and matter is an exciting one, opening up vast swathes of the universe that have until now been intellectually off-limits. As Stephen Hawking has observed: 'The missing link in cosmology is the nature of dark matter and dark energy.'

SPACE EXPLORATION

Space exploration is humanity's ongoing investigation of the physical conditions of space. The ability to send humans into space, first achieved in the 20th century, is regarded as one of the crowning achievements of our species and has raised the possibility that we may eventually set up permanent homes elsewhere in the universe.

Exploring the cosmos was until recently only achievable from an earthly base, using technologies such as the telescope. Yet our desire to physically interpose ourselves in space is an old one, stemming directly from our desire to fly.

Back in 1640, the English clergyman and natural philosopher, John Wilkins, had ruminated:

> *I do seriously and on good grounds affirm it possible to make a flying chariot in which a man may sit and give such a motion unto it as shall convey him through the air . . . 'Tis likely enough that there may be means invented of journeying to the moon; and how happy they shall be that are first successful in this attempt.*

Despite primitive rockets having been invented in China by at least the 13th century, it was only in 1903 that the Russian rocket scientist Konstantin Tsiolkovsky published an influential paper that laid the groundwork for the modern era of spacecraft engineering. 'Earth is the cradle of humanity,' he once said, 'but one cannot remain in the cradle forever.'

He, along with Robert H. Goddard in the USA, Hermann Oberth in Germany and Robert Esnault-Pelterie in France, put space travel on a sound theoretical basis in the early decades of the 20th century. The development of new armaments during the Second World War – most notably Wernher von Braun's V2 rocket – gave impetus to space programmes in the war's aftermath. Then came the Cold War, which provided the political climate for a 'space race' between the USA and the USSR, with the respective governments willing to pump vast resources into the contest.

It was an age of landmark achievements. In 1957, the Soviet Union launched *Sputnik 1*, the first man-made satellite, and in the same year sent a live animal (Laika the dog) into orbit for the first time. In 1961,

The Launch of Apollo 11 via the Saturn V Rocket

Yuri Gagarin became the first human in space, followed in 1963 by Valentina Tereshkova as the first woman in space. With the USSR seemingly in the ascendency, the USA struck back by landing the first man – Neil Armstrong – on the moon in 1969. As Armstrong famously said, it was one small step for a man but a giant leap for mankind.

Space exploration also poses ethical and philosophical questions. What rights do we have to other areas of space? And what sort of relations might we have with putative alien life? In 1960, Dwight Eisenhower asked this of the United Nations: 'The emergence of this new world poses a vital issue: will outer space be preserved for peaceful use and developed for the benefit of all mankind?'

While there are genuine concerns, astronaut Alan G. Poindexter (1961–2012) succinctly put the positive case for our reaching out into the cosmos:

I'm really hopeful about the future of space exploration and human spaceflight. Civilization as we know it has been defined by exploration. You know, we need to go off and find out what's around the next corner and what's just beyond what we already know. It's part of our being; it's part of our moral fibre to go off and explore.

THE MULTIVERSE

The multiverse is a hypothetical realm comprising not only our universe but an indeterminate number of other universes too. It is closely allied to the notion of parallel universes, a conceit of particular theoretical significance within the field of quantum mechanics (see page 80).

Credit for first expressing the idea of the multiverse is generally given to Erwin Schrödinger, who warned his audience at a lecture in 1952 that what he was about to postulate might 'seem lunatic'. The famous 'Schrödinger's Cat' thought experiment involved a hypothetical cat which was simultaneously both alive and dead (due to poison released – or not – by quantum activity), until its box was opened and one state or other was observed. At the quantum level, Schrödinger was illustrating the possibility of a multitude of different histories occurring not as alternatives, but happening simultaneously, though his thought experiment was intended to illustrate the absurdity of this concept.

Concepts of the multiverse have split scientists and philosophers ever since. Many dismiss the idea as essentially unscientific; others, though, are more sympathetic. Professor Brian Cox, for instance, has observed:

'That there's an infinite number of universes sounds more complicated than there being one. But actually, it's a simpler version of quantum mechanics. It's quantum mechanics without wave function collapse . . . the idea that by observing something you force a system to make a choice.'

The infinite 'you'

Why, it may be reasonably asked, is there a need to imagine a multiverse given that the universe seemingly contains all that there is? Part of the answer comes down to the question of history. A single universe allows only for the application of a single history. As you are where you are, doing what you're doing (reading this book), our single universe does not allow you to be somewhere else, doing something else at the same time. But what if there is a 'you' experiencing an alternative history that has led you down an entirely different path? Conceivably, the multiverse allows for a potentially infinite number of 'yous' living out an infinite number of histories.

While this may not seem to have particular relevance to us on a personal, day-to-day level, it has more immediate theoretical implications for the quantum physicist.

THE END OF THE WORLD

Just as humanity has long yearned to understand our roots and our place within the cosmos, so we have dwelled on the question of how (or even, if) it will all end. Many of the great religions predict an 'End times' – a climactic conclusion to our world, sometimes associated with notions of judgement and transformation. In more recent centuries, scientists have got in on the act too as they attempt to predict the ultimate course of the cosmos.

Historically, we have tended to envisage the 'End of Days' either in supernatural terms (for instance, heralding the return of one divine figure or another) or related to natural disasters. Such predictions stem either from supposition or claims of religious revelation. The scientist, meanwhile, faces one significant quandary – since there is necessarily no precedent for the end of the universe, there is no concrete evidence upon which to model predictions, though plenty have risen to the challenge.

How will it all end?

There is a clear demarcation between the destruction of our species and planet, on the one hand, and the end of the universe in its entirety, on the other. The risks to humanity and the Earth are plentiful, according to many within the scientific community. We may be wiped out by a pandemic, a super-volcano or giant tsunami, a magnetic pole shift, a general environmental collapse or the creation of super-destructive weapons. Stephen Hawking, among others, has highlighted the potential dangers of the unfettered development of artificial intelligence (see page 85), while others posit that the planet will succumb to an asteroid strike or a solar flare fired out by the Sun as its temperature inexorably increases.

But what of the universe as a whole? At the more 'science fiction' end of the scale, there have been predictions of intergalactic wars that could cause our collective demise. We also know that the universe is expanding and some scientists believe that if it remains on that course, ultimately everything will drift so far apart that the stars will die and the cosmos will begin to cool on its way to an everlasting 'heat death'. An alternative theory says that as the universe increases in size and the amount of dark matter within it grows, so growth will accelerate to the point where the fabric of the universe is ripped apart. Fortunately, though, a 'Big Rip' is unlikely to come to fruition for several billion years according to latest predictions.

PART TWO

MATHEMATICS

'If in other sciences we should arrive at certainty without doubt and truth without error, it behooves us to place the foundations of knowledge in mathematics.'

Roger Bacon

Mathematics – the science of number, quantity and space – provides us with the intellectual tools and language that make possible all other scientific investigation. As Bertrand Russell put it in his *Study of Mathematics* (1902): 'Mathematics takes us still further from what is human, into the region of absolute necessity, to which not only the world, but every possible world, must conform.' Given its abstract nature, mathematics provides a uniquely pure and exacting framework upon which to base the exploration of other ideas. Furthermore, many great minds have detected a quasi-mystical relationship between mathematical laws and the nature of the world. As that pioneer of quantum mechanics, Paul Dirac, wrote in *Scientific American* in 1963:

One could perhaps describe the situation by saying that God is a mathematician of a very high order, and He used very advanced mathematics in constructing the universe. Our feeble attempts at mathematics enable us to understand a bit of the universe, and as we proceed to develop higher and higher mathematics we can hope to understand the universe better.

NUMBERS

Current evidence suggests that mankind 'invented' numbers some 40,000-plus years ago. Even the most basic society needs some form of numeracy to operate – for instance, to keep track of the passage of days and nights, to record lunar cycles and to keep a tally of property. Yet, to imagine number in a world in which it does not conceptually exist ranks high among the great achievements of humanity; it may be regarded as one of those landmarks that helped secure our species' pre-eminence on the planet.

Anthropologists believe that counting began by early humans developed a system of hand-to-eye number communication (e.g. holding up two fingers to indicate the two sheep you own or want to trade) as a precursor to written number systems. But as any school-age child can tell you, your fingers will only get you so far when it comes to numeracy. Next came the tally stick – typically made of wood, bone or stone – on which could be engraved marks to denote amounts. So instead of holding up two fingers, the shepherd could record 'two sheep' (or 'twenty-seven sheep') on his tally stick. One such tally stick found in the Lemombo Mountains in southern Africa has been dated to around 43,000 years ago and its notches are putatively said to correspond to lunar phases – possibly as a means for women to track their menstrual cycles.

For a more formal system of written numbers, we must fast-forward to Iran in about 4,000 BCE. A new method, seemingly to assist trade, emerged using clay tablets that corresponded to different numbers of a given commodity. There was, for instance, a symbol engraved into a tablet to denote one ox, another for one sheep, another for ten goats and so on. These tablets were then baked into a sort of clay envelope (as a means of preserving the record) upon which were engraved symbols summarizing the contents within. Over the next millennium, various societies developed systems in which numerals were written in abstract form, separate to the thing it was representing.

The history of numeral systems took distinctly different routes in different parts of the world. The ancient Egyptians had a hiero-

Early Number Systems

glyph system distinct from the letter-based system used by the Romans or the numeral/letter-based system adopted in China. The numbers with which we are familiar today (Hindu–Arabic numerals) originated in India from around the 5th century CE, before finding their way to Europe via Arab mathematicians only in the 12th century.

ARITHMETIC

Having established number systems as a means of tallying, the next great mathematical leap forward was the development of arithmetic – a discipline concerned with the properties and manipulation of numbers. At the core of arithmetic are the four principal operations of addition, subtraction, multiplication and division.

Place-value systems

We can say with confidence that the basic arithmetic functions were in use by 2000 BCE in both Egypt and Babylonia. This was in large part thanks to the evolution of place-value systems – in other words, a system where the position of a digit determines its value. For instance, in our base-10 standard system, the number 125 denotes 1×100, 2×10 and 5×1. The Babylonians also operated a base-6 system that is reflected in the way we measure time (in hours of sixty minutes and minutes of sixty seconds) and in the 360 degrees in a circle. Place-value systems made arithmetic possible in a way that was unimaginable using, for instance, Roman numerals or Egyptian hieroglyphs.

Next it was the turn of the Greeks to move things along. To begin with, they used three different types of numerical notation for units, tens and hundreds. By the 2nd century BCE, however, Ptolemy had introduced the idea of 'zero' into his calculations – a philosophical leap of the imagination that required mathematicians to accept that 'nothing' may act as a 'something' within their hypothetical realm. However, the real breakthrough – adding zero into the place-value system to fill gaps (i.e. to represent 'no tens' in the number 501) – was the work of Indian scholars. By the 7th century, the Indian mathematician Brahmagupta gave a comprehensive explanation of how zero could be used within the decimal place-value system that we continue to use today. The basic arithmetic functions now being easy to execute, the full potential of arithmetic began to reveal itself.

The humble tally stick provides one of the first hints of arithmetic. Discovered in 1960 in what is now the Democratic Republic of the Congo, the Ishango bone is believed to be some 20,000 years old. Experts dispute exactly how it was used, but some have interpreted its groupings of numbers as indicative of an early form of arithmetic that extended far beyond merely keeping a tally. Nonetheless, exactly what was being calculated and how remains a subject of fierce dispute.

ALGEBRA

Algebra is the branch of mathematics where letters and other widely recognized symbols replace numbers in formulae and equations. In this way, algebra is able to establish general axioms (i.e. statements that are taken to be true). By then substituting the letters and symbols with numbers relevant to a particular problem, it becomes possible to use the axiom to solve specific sums. Whereas arithmetic is only possible where all the values are known, algebra is a way of solving problems in which some values may be unknown (such values being called variables).

Algebra works on the principle that both sides of an equation (i.e. the terms to the left and right of the '=' sign) are balanced. Take, for instance, perhaps the most famous equation in all of mathematics and science: Einstein's $E=mc^2$. Here, the 'E' denotes kinetic energy, the 'm' stands for mass and the 'c' for the speed of light in a vacuum. The speed of light is a known constant (that is to say, it remains the same whatever the numbers for 'E' and 'm' are), so it thus becomes possible to find out the value of 'E' if we know what 'm' is, or vice versa, by a simple process of 'balancing' the equation.

The Persian mathematician Omar Khayyam established himself as a pioneer of the discipline with the *Treatise on Demonstrations of Problems of Algebra* (*c.* 1070), translations of which were key to the dissemination

THE LITTLE BOOK OF BIG IDEAS

Ancient cultures and algebra

The ancient Babylonians are the first culture known to have used algebra, employing it to establish general arithmetical proofs, while the ancient Greeks developed a system of geometric algebra. Credit for first using the word *algebra* is believed to rest with the Persian mathematician Muhammad ibn Musa al-Khwarizmi – it being Arabic for 'the reuniting of broken parts'. His *Compendious Book on Calculation by Completion and Balancing*, written around 820 CE, did much to establish algebra as a mathematical discipline distinct from geometry and arithmetic.

of algebra in Europe. By the 17th century, several Europeans were themselves extending the discipline – among them François Viète (who helped lay the groundwork for modern algebra) and René Descartes, who was responsible for introducing much modern algebraic notation. Seki Kwa in Japan and Gottfried Leibniz also made important contributions, while the birth of abstract algebra followed in the late 19th century. While algebra may remain the bane of many a school pupil's day, its applications in the modern world are myriad – in fields as disparate as engineering, computing, medicine and financial services.

GEOMETRY

Geometry (which comes from the Greek for 'measurement of the Earth') is the branch of mathematics that seeks to address questions of shape, size and space, as well as the relationship between points, lines, curves and surfaces. Ancient humans had long conjured with problems of length, area and volume within the context of everyday life – how could one trade, for instance, olive oil without some concept of its volume? Or how could land be allocated among a tribe without a grasp of its area?

There is evidence that from around 2000 BCE there was a concerted effort among the Egyptians and Babylonians to apply formal mathematical ideas to solving what we now understand to be geometric problems. By the 7th century BCE Thales of Miletus was spearheading the Western tradition, using mathematical theorems to calculate, for instance, the distance of ships from the shore. But it would be a further four centuries or so before the Greek mathematician Euclid laid the foundations of the modern discipline of geometry. His landmark work, the thirteen-volume *Elements*, took all hitherto established geometric principles and assimilated them into a unified, coherent system. He adopted an axiomatic approach – he first established a small set of axioms and from those deduced a great many more propositions and theorems, which he then sought to prove empirically. In this way, he constructed a comprehensive system of logically deduced geometric knowledge. It set a benchmark of intellectual rigour for mathematicians of all branches for well over two thousand years.

Euclid's five basic axioms

When introducing his work on plane geometry, Euclid outlined five basic axioms (or postulates):

- A straight line may be drawn joining any two points.
- Any straight-line segment can be extended indefinitely in a straight line.
- With any straight-line segment, a circle can be drawn having the segment as its radius and one endpoint as its centre.
- All right angles are equal to one another.
- Where two lines intersect a third so that the sum of the inner angles on one side is less than two right angles, then the two lines inevitably must intersect each other on that side if extended far enough.

Euclid's logical reasoning of geometric truths, as noted by Einstein millennia later, was without precedent, giving human intellect the necessary confidence for its subsequent acheivements.

NON-EUCLIDIAN GEOMETRY

Euclidian geometry stood unchallenged until the 19th century, when the development of non-Euclidian geometries began. Non-Euclidian geometry may be thought of as any form of geometry different to that devised by Euclid. This development prompted a revolution in human knowledge – not least that Einstein's Theory of Relativity only works in non-Euclidian space.

For around 2,000 years, no one seriously challenged Euclid's theories. But his fifth postulate, concerning parallel lines, had long posed certain problems for some of the greatest mathematicians from the Western and Arabic traditions (Omar Khayyám, Nasir al-Din al-Tusi, and Giovanni Girolamo Saccheri to name a few) who attempted to formulate alternative theories, their work helping pave the way for the eventual discovery of non-Euclidian geometries.

The emergence of non-Euclidian geometry has allowed for innovations across a disparate array of mathematics and science disciplines, but it has also had philosophical significance. After millennia in which most mathematicians assumed Euclid had revealed a system of unassailable truth, his teachings were shown to be but one of many interpretations of space. While freeing Einstein to consider the cosmos in an entirely original way – and liberating generations of mathematicians, scientists and engineers to tackle problems with new tools – the full implications of the existence of non-Euclidian space remain to be discovered.

Hyperbolic and elliptic geometry

In the early 1830s, two mathematicians – the Russian Nikolai Lobachevsky and the Hungarian János Bolyai – published independent treatises on hyperbolic geometry, thus sharing credit for defining the first non-Euclidian geometry. Hyperbolic geometry (often known as Bolyai-Lobachevskian geometry) deals with 'curved' space and though it has much in common with Euclidian geometry, incorporates fundamental differences too. For instance, in hyperbolic geometry ultraparallels curve away from each other the further they get from the point of intersection with their shared perpendicular. It is within the realm of hyperbolic geometry that we may make sense of the General Theory of Relativity.

Then, in the mid-1850s, the German Bernhard Riemann introduced his theories of elliptic geometry, in which space is considered to be a sphere and lines as great circles. Again, Euclid's fifth postulate required rewriting, since in this system the parallel lines curve towards each other until finally intersecting. Hyperbolic and elliptic geometry remain the classical non-Euclidian geometries, but a significant number of other self-consistent non-Euclidian systems have subsequently been discovered. In other words, space does not exist in a single, standardized form as suggested by Euclid's geometry.

INFINITY

Infinity – the idea that something is without limit or bound – challenges the reach of all but a few minds. It is nonetheless of enormous value within the field of mathematics in solving both practical and theoretical problems.

Infinity has applications across many fields, though in none of them is it easy to grasp. Within the metaphysical field, it may, for example, relate to our understanding of the nature of an infinite god – one without end or beginning, whose love is limitless etc. In physics, meanwhile, we may conjure with the concept as we attempt to understand the nature of the cosmos. How big is the universe? If it has an end, where is it? And are there infinite stars in infinite galaxies? Will the cosmos go on for ever? What was there before the universe existed?

In maths, infinity is usually related to an unending sequence of numbers. In its most simple form, we may think of infinity in terms of an unimaginably large number to which we may always add one more. However, infinity is not always big – just endless. The ancient Greek philosopher Anaximander (c. 610–c. 546 BCE) is often credited with first coming up with the concept of infinity, although Zeno of Elea (c. 490 BCE–c. 430 BCE) was the first to use it in a mathematical context. Pythagoras, in his study of geometric shapes, famously discovered ratios that went on infinitely, but probably the most well-known example of an infinite number is pi (see page 47). Several of the great thinkers were highly sceptical of the idea of infinity. Aristotle accepted the notional concept (in terms of always being able to 'add one' when you count) but rejected the idea of a 'real' infinity, whether spatial, temporal or numerical.

Mind-boggling infinity

In the late 19th and early 20th centuries, the German mathematician Georg Cantor did much to formalize ideas of infinity. His work in set theory (based on the simple notion that numbers may be put into sets) revealed that there are multiple types of infinity and that some of them, mind-bogglingly, are larger than others. 'I see it, but I do not believe it,' he is said to have commented on his discovery. In the hundred and more years since his startling revelations, mathematicians continue to struggle to get to grips with the implications. Meanwhile, innovators in fields as disparate as mechanical engineering, software development and cosmology reap the practical benefits of the mind-bending idea of numbers without end.

The idea of infinity doggedly held on. In the 17th century, the notion of infinitely small numbers that are nonetheless greater than zero were pivotal to Isaac Newton and Gottfried Leibniz independently developing their systems of calculus (see page 48). Meanwhile, English mathematician John Wallis may claim the glory for introducing the common symbol for infinity – ∞ – back in 1657.

IRRATIONAL NUMBERS

An irrational number is a number that cannot be expressed as a ratio of integers – in other words, as a fraction. As such, an irrational number written as a decimal either does not end or has a segment. While that may seem all rather esoteric, it just so happens that irrational numbers regularly play crucial roles in mathematics and geometry. Probably the most famous of irrational numbers is pi (π).

The first proof of irrational numbers is thought to have been achieved by one of Pythagoras's followers around the 5th century BCE. It is said that while studying a pentagram, the unknown pupil discovered that there was no common unit of measurement between two sides, regardless of the smallness of the unit. By applying some simple algebra, he was able to prove that there must then exist a number that cannot be expressed as a ratio of two integers.

As other mathematicians uncovered further proofs, and the algebraic tradition failed to accommodate them, Greek mathematical culture took a decisive step towards privileging geometry over algebra – with significant repercussions for the development of Western mathematics. It was only thanks to breakthroughs in Islamic scholarship in the medieval period that it became possible to treat irrational numbers as algebraic objects.

The origins of pi

The origins of the idea of pi may be traced back some 4,000 years, when the Babylonians calculated the area of a circle by tripling the radius – thus attributing a value of 3 to pi. By the early part of the 2nd century BCE, there is evidence that the estimate had been honed to 3.125. By the third century BCE, Archimedes established it as between 3 1/7 and 3 10/71. Madhava of Sangamagrama (c. 1340–c. 1425) is credited with uncovering a more exact formula for π, using infinite series, while today we can calculate pi to several trillion places after the decimal point (beginning 3.14159) with computer assistance.

While that level of accuracy is not necessary for many of pi's practical applications, this most useful of irrational numbers is crucial to any scenario involving arcs and circles – the swing of a pendulum, the calibration of a speedometer, the arc of a free kick, the projection of an image on a cinema screen, for example. In the words of mathematician and computing innovator Antranig Basman: 'Pi is not just a collection of random digits. Pi is a journey; an experience; unless you try to see the natural poetry that exists in pi, you will find it very difficult to learn.'

CALCULUS

Calculus is the mathematical study of continuous change, and is split into two distinct but related fields – differential calculus and integral calculus. Differentiation allows us to find out how much something changes (e.g. the acceleration of a car), while integration allows us us to work out how far the car has travelled if we know its rate of acceleration.

Calculus makes it possible to take very complex problems and divide them into a series of much smaller sections, allowing us to reach an exact answer. This is useful when dealing with quantities that change in a non-linear way (from the speed of a rocket as it soars through space to the flow of electricity around a circuit). If you imagine a mathematics problem illustrated by curves on a graph, differential calculus concerns the slopes of the curves and integral calculus looks at those areas between and beneath the curves.

Elements of calculus were developed in antiquity by mathematicians from traditions as disparate as the Greek, Indian, Chinese, Japanese and Islamic. It was in Europe in the 17th century, that the Italian, Bonaventura Cavalieri (1598–1647), showed how volumes and areas may be computed as the total of the volumes and areas of infinitesimally small cross-sections. René Descartes, Pierre de Fermat, Blaise Pascal and John Wallis also made significant strides.

But who 'invented' it?

Credit for 'inventing' calculus became the subject of a ferocious dispute between Isaac Newton on one side and Gottfried Leibniz on the other. Leibniz introduced much of what became the standard theory and notation, while Newton was the first to apply calculus practically, to explain, for instance, planetary motion in his *Principia* (1687). Newton accused Leibniz of plagiarism, accusations that bedevilled the German until his death. Remarkably, the likely truth is that two great minds independently hit upon similar groundbreaking insights contemporaneously and divided by several countries. Both took what had hitherto been rather ragged and inconsistent ideas and theories, and synthesized them into a fully functioning system of mathematics.

Today, calculus has applications in an extraordinary number of fields – from physics and astronomy to mechanical and electrical engineering, and even in the social sciences.

PROBABILITY THEORY

Probability theory seeks to apply mathematical rules to the analysis of random events. It aims to model and predict likely outcomes under uncertain conditions. It also evaluates the likelihood of a particular hypothesis occurring on the basis of the available evidence and taking into consideration the impact of stochastic processes – that is to say, processes that may be analysed statistically but not predicted precisely.

Gambling on probability theory

In 16th-century Italy, the polymath and keen games-player, Gerolamo Cardano, first seriously attempted to use mathematics to predict the outcomes of games of chance. Then, in the following century, Pierre de Fermat and Blaise Pascal conducted a legendary correspondence on topics such as how best to divide a stake in a game of chance. Around the same time, Christiaan Huygens wrote the most comprehensive study of the subject thus far.

Take, say, a simple game of coin toss. Using a standard, unadulterated coin, it is obvious that there is a 50-50 chance of the coin landing on heads, and the same probability of tails. Furthermore, given no skulduggery, it is impossible to predict accurately what the result will be. However, by looking at a larger statistical sample, certain patterns can be traced. The tossing of a coin is therefore a stochastic process – unpredictable at the level of the individual instance but more predictable on a larger scale. The law of large numbers, for example, says that if an event with the same likelihood of separate outcomes (such as a coin-toss) is carried out enough times, the occurrence of each particular outcome will even out. So if you toss a coin once or twice, you cannot predict the likely ratio of heads-to-tails results. However, if you toss the coin a thousand times, you might reasonably expect close to 500 instances of tails, and 500 of heads.

The Swiss Jacob Bernoulli (1654–1705) and the French Pierre-Simon Laplace (1749–1827) put probability theory on a still sounder mathematical footing before the Russian Andrei Markov (1856–1922) ushered in the period of modern probability theory – not least through his elucidation of 'memorylessness', whereby future states may be predicted only on the evidence of the present state and not past events. His fellow countryman, Andrei Kolmogrov (1903–87), further built upon and extended Markov's insights over the course of the 20th century.

Probability theory has many obvious applications where there is gain to be made from accurate forecasting – from gaming and financial speculation to meteorology and insurance. But, arguably, probability theory's most profound influence is in a field undreamt of by Cardano and the other early pioneers: quantum mechanics, the study of the sub-atomic world that abounds in apparent unpredictability.

STATISTICS

The modern era of statistics – the collection and analysis of numerical data in order to make statistical inferences – dates back to the mid-17th century. One of its key features is to take a representative sample of information and draw out from it broader assumptions about the whole data set.

Historically, statistics is closely aligned with demographics – the study of data related to society (such as births and deaths over a set time period) to discern trends within the population at large. The Roman Empire, for example, conducted censuses to gain a statistical overview of their dominions in terms of population, geographical extent, wealth etc. One of the earliest cases of non-demographic statistics was documented around the 5th century BCE by Thucydides, who described how the Athenians counted bricks in a section of the wall of Platea in order to calculate its full height. Having done so, they obtained ladders of the requisite length to scale the wall and launch an attack.

By the 9th century CE the Arab polymath Al-Kindi was describing how to use frequency analysis of statistics in order to break codes, and by the 16th century the concepts of the mean and median (respectively, the average value and the numerically middle value in a statistical set) were in widespread use. By the 18th century, figures such as Thomas Bayes and Pierre-Simon Laplace were bringing new rigour to the discipline, while William Playfair encouraged the graphical representation of statistical information in forms such as the line chart and bar chart.

Then, at the turn of the 19th century, Francis Galton and Karl Pearson ushered in a new wave of developments that saw statistics take on many of the characteristics it possesses today. Galton, for example, finessed concepts such as standard deviation – a value expressing by how much the members of a group differ from the group's mean value. Pearson, meanwhile, strove to show how statistical analysis could be used to solve scientific problems. Furthermore, statistics now came to have greater social and political uses, whereas previously it had been a tool only for the mathematician and the scientist. For instance, Florence Nightingale heavily employed statistical analysis in her attempts to reform healthcare.

Big data

In the 21st century, the field of statistics continues to develop, not least in the arena of Big Data. Given the massive volumes of information collectable in our digital age (for instance, mobile phone records and receipts of sales transactions), statisticians are faced with the task of devising new ways to curate and process this data so as to be able to mine it for useful knowledge – in so doing, spawning an entirely new Big Data industry.

CHAOS THEORY

Chaos theory is that branch of mathematics that looks at how the behaviour of complex, dynamic systems are influenced by their initial conditions. It seeks to find underlying patterns in apparently chaotic systems.

The analogy of the butterfly effect is often invoked to explain how a small change in one discrete aspect of a system can significantly impact the system in a later state. The theory goes that an action as minor as a butterfly flapping its wings at a certain point in time and space precipitates the precise conditions for, say, a subsequent hurricane in a distant part of the world.

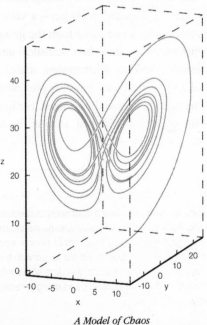

A Model of Chaos

Chaos theory is thus a concept with wide-ranging applications – anything unpredictable, such as the weather, stock markets and the human psyche, may all be interpreted under its terms. The mathematical modelling of transitions from order to turbulence includes key concepts such as feedback (think of a stock-market crash driven by the desire of people to sell their stocks at knockdown prices in order to escape the crashing market), loops, repetition and fractals (never-ending patterns).

Computers and chaos theory

The advent of the modern computer was instrumental in the development of chaos theory. One of its earliest pioneers was Edward Lorenz, who in 1961 discovered certain anomalies while running weather reports through a computer. He noticed that the weather predictions differed wildly on the basis of tiny variations in input (for example, by using numbers rounded to three decimal places rather than six). Such small differences in precision ought, experts believed, to have caused little variation in results, but Lorenz had stumbled on proof that their impact was much bigger. He came to summarize it thus: 'Chaos: when the present determines the future, but the approximate present does not approximately determine the future.'

Chaos in a mathematical sense turns up in the most unexpected places – in the trajectory of space rockets, the ocean currents, the flow of blood through our bodies and even in music and art. Chaos theory thus gives us some chance of better predicting the unpredictable, and so to impose order where disorder might otherwise reign.

PART THREE

SCIENCE

'What science cannot discover, mankind cannot know.'

Bertrand Russell

'Science' is such a wide-ranging concept that a precise definition is often elusive or unhelpful. In its broadest terms, though, it may be thought of as the area of intellectual endeavour that seeks systematic, rational explanations for what happens around us, from the microscopic to the cosmological level.

Carl Sagan, described it as 'more than a body of knowledge. It is a way of thinking . . . Science invites us to let the facts in, even when they don't conform to our preconceptions. It urges on us a fine balance between no-holds-barred openness to new ideas, however heretical, and the most rigorous sceptical scrutiny of everything – new ideas and established wisdom.'

THE PHYSICAL SCIENCES

Science can be broken down into myriad categories and sub-categories but to begin with it is useful to think of the natural sciences, as distinct from the 'formal sciences' of mathematics and logic, or the 'social sciences' (disciplines, such as geography, that seek to explain human and social behaviour). The natural sciences are often divided into the two major branches of the physical sciences and the life sciences.

The physical sciences are primarily concerned with the inorganic, inanimate world. Traditionally, they are considered to include astronomy, chemistry, physics and the Earth sciences, although there is overlap between the various branches. Astronomers, for instance, investigate celestial objects (stars and planets, asteroids and comets, galaxies and the universe in its entirety) distinct of the Earth, though not excluding the Earth as a unified entity. But in striving to understand the past, present and future of such objects, the astronomer constantly calls upon physics and chemistry for answers.

At a basic level, physics may be seen as focused on the nature and behaviour of individual atoms and sub-atomic matter, whereas chemistry looks at molecules (collections of atoms). Earth science, meanwhile, is concerned with the physical make-up of our planet and its atmosphere as a whole. Geology, oceanography and meteorology are, thus, all sub-sets of Earth science, and there are a great many more besides.

There is evidence of the development of scientific discipline among the ancient cultures of the Egyptians, Greeks and Mesopotamians, among others. As humans grew unsatisfied by mythical, mystical, animist and theological explanations for the natural phenomena they witnessed, a more rational, observation-based attempt to make sense of the world slowly evolved. In terms of the physical sciences as we understand them today – at least in terms of methodology – the modern age is general considered to have started around the 18th century and the time of the Enlightenment (see page 143).

THE LIFE SCIENCES

On the other side of the 'science coin' from the physical sciences are the life sciences – a multi-disciplinary area concerned with the study of living organisms, comprising microorganisms and all types of flora and fauna (including our own species). At the core of the life sciences is biology, under which may be found sub-fields ranging across medicine, botany, biochemistry, bioethics, ecology, genetics, neuroscience, physiology, zoology and a great many more besides.

Biology – which comes from the Greek for 'the study of life' – took on its modern form in the 18th century, with the German naturalist, botanist and physician, Gottfried Reinhold Treviranus, being among the first to define the scope of the discipline: 'the different forms and manifestations of life, the conditions and laws under which these phenomena occur, and the causes through which they have been effected.' Nonetheless, the study of the natural world had been prevalent in all the major ancient civilizations too. Indeed, some of the giants of ancient Greek thought (including Hippocrates and Aristotle) approached the subject with an academic, empirical rigour that bears comparison with modern science, while the study of medicine and anatomy was particularly strong among medieval Islamic scholars.

However, these earlier traditions are better thought of in terms of natural philosophy – in other words, wide-ranging ruminations based on observation, rather than a focused evidence-based search for general principles. That is not to belittle the work of the pre-moderns, but rather to acknowledge a fundamental difference in approach.

The microscope and cell theory

One of the driving forces in the evolution of modern biology was the development of technological equipment. For instance, improvements in the microscope (notably by the Dutchman Anton van Leeuwenhoek in the 17th century) made possible methods of investigation that opened up hitherto entirely unknown aspects of the world. The ability to examine the microscopic world made it possible, for example, to develop one of the key pillars of modern biology: cell theory. This posits that cells are the most basic building blocks of life, creating life through the process of cell division, providing fuel, storing DNA and even holding the key to those processes that ultimately snuff life out again.

Besides cell theory, major themes of modern biological study include energy transference (without which life cannot be sustained), evolution (the theory that all life shares a common origin and from which each life form has emerged and developed), genetics (genes being units of inheritance that ultimately determine both the form and function of living organisms) and homeostasis (how an organism regulates its internal environment to provide the stability necessary for ongoing life).

Life science impacts our lives every day – from the food we grow and the medicines we take, to the way we power our homes and how we keep animals in our zoos and safari parks.

TAXONOMY

Taxonomy: the process of methodically classifying into ordered categories – has been one of the fundamental pillars of scientific progress since antiquity. However, taxonomy – as with so much of science – took on a truly modern guise only in the last three centuries or so. Today, it is one of the basic tools for organizing human knowledge.

Taxonomic systems are in use all around us: the periodic table that categorizes the chemical elements and the Dewey decimal system long beloved of librarians are good examples. Search engines such as Google are also vast taxonomic systems, arranging and classifying data on an unimaginable scale.

Traditionally, though, taxonomy tends to be associated with the naming, describing and classifying of living organisms. Taxonomists helped provide the language upon which the life sciences operate. The discovery of a new species only attains meaning when contextualized within the wider taxonomy; the ecologist cannot hope to save a tree unless she can ascertain what species it is. Nor may a doctor treat a snakebite if he does not know what type of snake it is.

Some of the earliest evidence of taxonomy comes in Egyptian wall paintings dating to around 1500 BCE and depicting different types of medicinal plant – an enterprise only possible in a culture that envisaged flora existing as a set of species with certain defined characteristics. Aristotle in the 4th century BCE made one of the earliest-known concerted efforts at classification. His *History of Animals and Parts of Animals* identified some 500 distinct species of living creatures and introduced important classifications (for example, he divided the animal world into those with blood and those without, equivalent to modern classifications of vertebrates and invertebrates). He also looked at the number of legs possessed by each species, the nature of its reproduction (whether by giving birth or hatching eggs) and so on.

Aristotle's pupil, Theophrastus, undertook important work of his own, identifying several hundred plant types and leaving a legacy built upon by Pliny the Elder three centuries later. It would be another 1,500 years or so before the next major leaps forward, partly thanks to the development of more specialized optical equipment. The Italian Andrea Cesalpino (1519–1603) undertook the classification of almost two thousand plants, although it was a Swedish botanist, Carl Linnaeus (1707–78), who came to be known as the father of modern taxonomy. In a series of works, he revolutionized the field, bringing order to an academic discipline that had grown and evolved in a distinctly unsystematic way.

The Linnaean taxonomy

The Linnaean taxonomy (as his system came to be known) works on a hierarchical structure, covering three top-level 'kingdoms' (animals, minerals and plants). Each kingdom is then subdivided into phylum, then (in descending order) classes, orders, families, tribes, genera, species and variety.

He thus categorized a European human:

Rank	
Kingdom	*Animalia*
Phylum	*Chordata*
Class	*Mammalia*
Order	*Primates*
Family	*Hominidae*
Genus	*Homo*
Species	*Sapiens*
Variety	*Europaeus*

Linnaeus's system remains popular today, although with certain revisions. For example, as Darwin's theory of evolution established itself, many taxonomists looked to adapt the system to reflect the notion of common descent. More recently, the cladistic approach has gained ground, in which shared characteristics traceable to a most recent common ancestor are identified, thus bringing together those groups assumed to have a shared history. In the same way, virtually all modern taxonomic systems can themselves claim a common ancestor in Linnaeus.

THE SCIENTIFIC METHOD

Science as we understand it today is rooted in the 'scientific method' developed in the 17th century. At the heart of the scientific method is the idea that in the quest for knowledge, one must seek to prove or disprove a hypothesis by a process of systematic observation, measurement and experiment. The hypothesis, meanwhile, should not be created out of thin air but should be devised on the basis of previously acquired knowledge. A hypothesis provable by repeatable experimentation may be considered 'right' (at least, until such a time as it is able to be disproven), while one disproven by experimentation ought to be either set aside or else modified in light of knowledge acquired as a result of the experiment. The method, in other words, is essentially an empirical one – that is to say, we may only treat as true that which is verifiable by observation and experience.

So established is the method that it is difficult to imagine a time when scientists would think to diverge significantly from its approach. However, for long periods of human history, knowledge acquisition was associated with religion (divine revelation), superstition ('It is flooding because we have offended the gods') or rationalism. The rationalists were the great intellectual opponents of the empiricists, arguing that reason (i.e. the human capacity to analyse and form judgements logically) provides the foundation of certainty in knowledge, ahead of experience. In other words, the rationalist knows that 1+1=2 because it can be logically established within the mind, whereas the empiricist will need to provably test the hypothesis. This conflict has a long history. Aristotle, for instance, argued against his own teacher, Plato, that knowledge is derived from experience and observation. Yet the primacy of rationalism (along with superstition and theology) as a method of comprehending phenomena persisted through to the Enlightenment period in much of continental Europe.

Although Roger Bacon outlined a proto-scientific method in the 13th century in his description of a process of observation, hypothesis, testing and verification, it was not until the likes of Galileo and Copernicus were active in the 16th century that Bacon's theories were put into significant practical effect. It was another Bacon, Francis (1561–1626), who formally laid out what would become known as the scientific method in his 1620 work, *Novum Organum*. He espoused the idea that knowledge is acquired by accumulating empirical knowledge and then using it as the basis for inductive reasoning that can then lead to more generalized conclusions.

Look for the cracks

Bacon also warned that the scientist must be on guard against complacency, being always sceptical and avoiding the temptation to fool oneself. Even if all the available evidence suggests a certain path of thought, one must entertain the notion that there may be contrary evidence yet to be found. The true scientist, he suggested, ought not to be content with the evidence that supports his hypothesis, but should seek out that which might disprove it. Only under circumstances of such rigorous testing can we ever hope to arrive at true knowledge.

CAUSALITY

Underpinning most – though notably not all – scientific progress is the notion of causality. So hardwired into our psyches that it seems an indisputable reality, it is nonetheless a formidable intellectual assumption. Causality is what links a cause with an effect. Stick your finger into a fire and you will get burnt. Water your crops and they will grow. Turn on a switch and a light will come on.

In causality, the cause is considered always at least partially responsible for the effect, while the effect is dependent upon the cause. Furthermore, there is a defined temporal framework in which cause and effect must exist – the prior must always occur before the latter. In other words, we cannot retrospectively put our finger in the fire to explain why our finger is burnt.

Armed with the notion of causality, scientists are able to devise and then test hypotheses. By a process of repeatable experimentation combined with logical reasoning in regard to probability, it then becomes possible to reach a conclusion and formulate a general law. Imagine the first caveman to encounter fire. Perhaps a pile of twigs caught light under a baking sun. He approaches the fire and feels his skin tingle with the temperature. He removes his hand and then returns it to the vicinity of the flames. Again the skin tingles. Soon he realizes that it must be the fire causing the unpleasurable sensation. He knows that the feeling of burning was not merely a one-off chance occurrence but is clearly linked to getting close to the fire. In future he will know to approach fire with caution.

Thankfully, causality appears at least in part instinctive. When a newborn cries, for instance, it alerts its parents to its needs. The baby cannot *know* what its tears will do, but its survival instinct compels it to cry nonetheless.

The scientist, meanwhile, adapts causality in different ways. It allows him to draw a link between two occurrences but compels him to test whether the link is but an incidental one. When the water boiled, it was 100°C. It was also snowing outside and I was wearing a green jumper. The scientist must experiment and analyse to determine whether the effect (the water boiling) was a result of its being heated, or the weather outside, or his choice of pullover.

Causality also requires a philosophical acknowledgement that there is inherent order in the world. Incident A happens and Occurrence B follows naturally. Yet, whereas causality has propelled scientific discovery forward through most of human history, there are significant branches of modern scientific thought that in some respects undermine the very notion. Quantum mechanics, for instance, is predicated on the idea of random actions at the microscopic level. The quantum physicist necessarily utilizes a discourse not of certainty and causality but merely of probability.

FALSIFIABILITY

In 1934 the great Austrian philosopher of science, Karl Popper, devised the idea of falsifiability, thus redefining the parameters of science. A scientific theory need not be proven by experimentation and induction, he said, but must instead have the potential to be disproven by observation.

The origins of the concept of falsifiability go back a century and a half earlier, to David Hume, who highlighted what became known as the 'problem of induction'. The problem, he explained, was that science draws general conclusions from specific observations that may never be conclusively proven.

Black and white

A scientist observes a thousand swans and discovers they are all white. He therefore concludes that all swans are white, yet he cannot know this for certain unless he observes all swans, past, present and future. That, of course, is not possible, so how can we ever regard a theory as scientifically legitimate?

Popper outlined his response in the landmark work of 1934, *The Logic of Scientific Discovery*. Taking Hume's concerns, he reframed the question of scientific validity. Rather than a scientific theory needing to be observably verified beyond all doubt (impossible, as Hume showed), it instead needs merely to be capable of being disproven by observation. Therefore, for example, the scientist with the thousand white swans could legitimately theorize that all swans are white, because it reflected the observable data but also remained falsifiable (by, for instance, observation of a black swan). Once the scientist had evidence of the black swan, his theory could no longer be called scientific and would need revision (for instance, to 'most swans are white') – just as Newton's theory of universal gravitation was accepted as scientifically valid in its entirety until the Theory of Relativity demanded a revision. Meanwhile, other statements that cannot be disproven by observation (e.g. 'God exists') may not be treated as scientific.

There is, however, the potential for anomaly in Popper's theory of falsifiability. Technical innovations and advances in knowledge may render a theory falsifiable long after it was formulated. Thus, conceivably, a non-scientific theory may change into a scientific one over centuries or even millennia after being initially proposed.

THE ELEMENTS

As previously mentioned, chemistry is distinct from physics in its focus on matter at the molecular level. The taxonomy of the elements is the method that provides the underlying language of the field, describing the basic, indivisible building blocks of the known matter of the universe. It is a list that intermittently expands as new elements are discovered – and our understanding of the fabric of our world incrementally increases.

A chemical element defines types of atoms that all share the same quantity of protons in their atomic nuclei. Hydrogen, for example, is classified as element No. 1, since hydrogen atoms contain a single proton. Carbon, by contrast, has six protons, and oganesson, 118. At the time of writing, a total of 118 elements have been discovered, of which 94 occur naturally and the remainder are synthetic. Most elements have a number of isotopes too – that is to say, variants where the number of neutrons in each atom changes even as the number of protons stays constant.

Elements such as gold, silver and forms of carbon, including diamonds, are relatively abundant in form. However, most elements appear in compounds – groups of different elements in which the atoms are attached by chemical bonds. The most famous compound is water (H_2O, where each molecule is formed of two atoms of hydrogen combined with one of oxygen).

In antiquity matter was often thought to be composed of a combination of four basic elements – air, earth, fire and water. Although mining and early extractive methods such as smelting required a fairly advanced grasp of elemental difference (for instance, between gold and copper), achieving an effective system of categorization has been a drawn-out (and ongoing) process.

Today, for instance, elements may be divided between conductive metals, non-conductive non-metals and semi-conductive metalloids. Alternatively, they may be categorized by their state (solid, liquid or gas) at a particular temperature and pressure, or according to whether they occur naturally or are the synthetic result of man-made nuclear reactions.

The periodic table

Undoubtedly the most famous mode of cataloguing is the periodic table, the creation of Russian chemist Dmitri Mendeleev and first published in 1869.

Containing sixty-six elements at that stage, the table arranges the elements into rows (periods) by increasing atomic number, while the columns group elements that share particular physical and chemical properties. Mendeleev also proved highly effective at predicting the nature of several then unknown elements. While virtually all of the known naturally occurring elements had been identified by 1900, the most recent additions (four of them) were added only in 2015. The table continues to be tweaked and expanded as new knowledge is acquired. Kosuke Morita, who led a Japanese team credited with finding one of the newest ones (element 113), immediately looked to the future, explaining that he now planned to 'look to the uncharted territory of element 119 and beyond'.

While the elements make up all of the universe's 'ordinary matter', it is thought that some 95 per cent of the universe comprises unobserved 'dark matter' and 'dark energy' (see page 30) consisting of something other than the chemical elements we list in the periodic table.

GRAVITY AND NEWTONIAN MOTION

Isaac Newton (1642–1727) was a polymath who made vital contributions across an array of scientific disciplines. However, it was his formulation of the laws of motion and the theory of gravity that established him at the very forefront of the pantheon of history's greatest scientists.

Among Newton's multitude of achievements, he played an important role in the development of telescopic lenses, infinitesimal calculus and even alchemy, to name but a few. But his *magnum opus* was *Philosophiæ Naturalis Principia Mathematica* (*Mathematical Principles of Natural Philosophy*), published in 1687.

Newton's three laws of motion

In his *Philosophiæ Naturalis Principia Mathematica* Newton elucidated his three laws of motion, so becoming the first to account comprehensively for the movement of objects through space using theoretical mathematics:

The law of inertia: 'An object at rest will remain at rest unless acted on by an unbalanced force. An object in motion continues in motion with the same speed and in the same direction unless acted upon by an unbalanced force.'

The second law says that acceleration is produced when a force acts on a mass. The larger the mass, the larger the force required to accelerate it.

The third law says that 'for every action, there is an equal but opposite reaction'.

In the same work, Newton also detailed his theory of universal gravitation – the notion that all things are attracted to all other things in space by means of an invisible force. It is famously said that the idea

Newton Under the Tree

of a universal force of attraction came to him as he sat under a tree and an apple fell on his head. Inspired, he was prompted to ask why the apple should always take that course and not for instance fly off upwards or sideways. Whatever the theory's origins, it was instrumental to his laying the foundations of classical mechanics. Not only did he provide mathematical proof of the veracity of the heliocentric model (see page 24); he essentially explained for the first time why things move as they do – on Earth and in the heavens.

Newton made good use of the planetary observations of Joseph Kepler in formulating his theories. Nonetheless, most would concede that Newton was a giant in his own right, revealing more about the workings of the universe than anyone before him.

Newton's ideas went unchallenged for three centuries. Einstein himself acknowledged the unique position Newton holds in the history of human understanding, writing in 1952: 'Newton's discoveries have passed into the stock of accepted knowledge.'

ELECTRICITY

Of course, no one had the idea of creating electricity, since it is a form of energy that simply exists. Yet it took great minds making incremental jumps forward over a period of millennia to harness this energy that so revolutionized humanity's existence – providing us with the means to keep the world lit and our houses warm, to power our communications and the vehicles that carry us about the place, and to produce the goods and services that we consume.

Electricity is perhaps best conceptualized as a store of energy that may flow from one place to another. It is made up of atoms in which electrons outnumber protons, thus producing an electrical charge. When gathered in a single place, it is known as static (i.e. non-moving) electricity, and when flowing around a circuit (any closed loop, whether artificially created or naturally occurring) it is called current electricity. To get an idea of the vast potentials of energy involved, consider a bolt of lightning – a naturally occurring instance of current electricity caused by a build-up of too much static electricity – and the damage it can cause as it leaps from sky to Earth.

That which propels electrons round a circuit is known as an electromotive force or, in more common parlance, voltage. The clouds storing the excess energy that prompts a lightning bolt are a natural form of voltage, while batteries and power points are examples of artificial ones. The greater the voltage, the greater the current and, correspondingly, the more power is unleashed. The 6th-century-BCE sage, Thales of Miletus (see page 122), is often credited with discovering static electricity – supposedly by rubbing animal fur on amber, although the historical credentials for this story are unclear. However, the journey from recognizing the existence of static electricity to harvesting the energy of current electricity was long and arduous.

In the middle period of the 18th century, Benjamin Franklin – an American Founding Father and remarkable polymath – was the first to elucidate how matter could be negatively or positively charged. He also carried out a series of trailblazing experiments, not least flying kites in thunderstorms to prove the electric nature of lightning.

Meanwhile, in around 1799 the Italian scientist Alessandro Volta invented the Voltaic pile, generally considered the world's first battery.

The golden age of electricity

The first half of the 19th century was a golden age of discovery in regard to electricity. The Danish physicist, Hans Christian Oersted (1777–1851), established the relationship between electricity and magnetism, while André-Marie Ampère undertook his own groundbreaking work on electromagnetism over in France. In the same period in Germany, Georg Ohm developed the concept of electric resistance, while scientist Michael Faraday built primitive electric motors and generators in England, and the Scottish physicist James Joule provided evidence that electricity is a form of energy. Come the 1860s, and another Scotsman, James Clerk Maxwell, gave the most thorough explication yet of the theory of electromagnetism – work so fundamental that it would influence the ideas of Einstein, among others.

As the 20th century approached, practical applications came thick and fast. Around 1878, for instance, the American inventor Thomas Edison and his British rival, Joseph Swan, independently invented incandescent filament light bulbs. By the 1890s, understanding of electricity had increased to such an extent that not only was it being commercially supplied but there was a War of Currents between the 'direct current' pioneered by Thomas Edison in America and the 'alternating current' of his one-time employee, Nikola Tesla. While Edison won the early battles, Tesla won the war and the modern age of electricity supply was upon us, putting the previously unthinkable – instant street lighting, labour-saving home appliances, super-fast personal computers, clean electric trains and cars – within our grasp.

EVOLUTION

Evolution describes the process by which different kinds of living organism are thought to have developed from earlier life forms over the passage of history. It is evolution, for example, that places modern humans in a complex lineage of species that connects us back to ancient apelike ancestors who walked the planet millions of years ago. Indeed, theoretically all extant species are traceable back to common biological ancestors.

Our understanding of how evolution happens is a work in progress and there are many conflicting opinions – both between evolutionists themselves and between evolutionists and those entirely opposed to the notion, such as believers in the literal truth of the Christian creation story. Underpinning all evolutionary theories is the notion that sometime after the Earth came into existence (about 4.5 billion years ago), life began with the emergence of basic self-replicating forms (e.g. simple molecular structures that could copy themselves in the manner of DNA). Over a process of millions of years, these life forms gradually grew more complex.

Those best equipped – or born with genes best suited – to adapt to a given set of circumstances (such as distinct climactic conditions, natural environments and food sources) survive and more effectively reproduce as a result of 'natural selection'. Meanwhile, those creatures with characteristics ill-suited to their environment are more likely to die off and their genes less likely to be passed to a future generation. It is this lengthy process, so the theory goes, that causes some species to die out and others to thrive.

The giant intellectual figure in the development of the theory of evolution is the English naturalist, Charles Darwin (1809–82), who wrote his masterpiece, *On the Origin of Species*, in 1859. (Although it should be noted that his contemporary, Alfred Russel Wallace, arrived at similar conclusions around the same time as Darwin.) After travelling for several years to observe flora and fauna in disparate environments, Darwin came to realize that there is competition between and within species for vital limited resources, such as food, water and shelter. Those that win this competition are the ones who live to reproduce and so pass on their genes – a process commonly heralded as 'the survival of the fittest'. In his own words:

> *Owing to this struggle for life, any variation, however slight and from whatever cause proceeding, if it be in any degree profitable to an individual of any species, in its infinitely complex relations to other organic beings and to external nature, will tend to the preservation of that individual, and will generally be inherited by its offspring.*

The Evolution of Humankind

The evolution of the giraffe

Darwin's ideas were not without precedent. Several ancient philosophers had posited the notion that species emerge not fully formed but one from another. Meanwhile, in the early 19th century the French scientist Jean-Baptiste Lamarck had argued for a process of acquired characteristics. He suggested that any characteristic not used in a species eventually dies out, while those that are used become stronger and more established. For Lamarck, then, the giraffe developed a long neck to be able to feed better, and passed the characteristic on. For Darwin, by contrast, giraffes with long necks prospered because they were best suited to access high-level food. It is a subtle but significant difference in interpretation.

Darwin's theory was supported by evidence, including fossil finds. While the fossil record is far from complete, clear patterns of evolutionary development may be traced. Furthermore, research into the genetic inheritance of plants conducted by Gregor Mendel during Darwin's own lifetime further corroborated his thesis, and today, few serious scientists dare dispute the evolutionary nature of life.

THERMODYNAMICS

The laws of thermodynamics govern how and why energy is transferred, and its relationship to heat and temperature. Energy is best understood as that which makes it possible for a system to do work, and it is stored in different types of materials. It is by changing the state of materials, then harnessing the energy that is released, that we can direct energy towards specific tasks (rather than it merely escaping, usually in the form of heat). Thermodynamics is thus vital to understanding how to make energy work for us.

The academic discipline of thermodynamics is strongly associated with the development of steam engines during the period of the Industrial Revolution. In 1824 a Frenchman, Sadi Carnot – known as the 'father of thermodynamics' – published *Reflections on the Motive Power of Fire*, in which he explored the links between energy, efficiency, heat and power. His work was built upon over the next few decades by the likes of the German Rudolf Clausius and the Scotsmen William Rankine and William Thomson (Lord Kelvin). By the 1850s, they had reached consensus on the first two of the four laws of thermodynamics that we have today. The third law was developed by the German chemist Walther Nernst over several years up to 1912, while Ralph Fowler and Edward Guggenheim are credited with devising the fourth law (actually known as the 'zeroth law') in the 1930s.

The laws of thermodynamics

- Zeroth law: When two systems are in thermal equilibrium with a third system, they are also in thermal equilibrium with each other.

- First law: Energy can neither be created nor destroyed, but rather changes form. In a thermodynamic cycle, additional heat equals additional work done.

- Second law: The entropy (often characterized as the degree of 'randomness' in a system) of an isolated (i.e. closed) system increases over time.

- Third law: As the temperature gets towards absolute zero, a system's entropy approaches a constant minimum.

While that may all sound a little bewildering in isolation, these laws have become established as basic principles of physics, explaining how different systems will respond to changes in their environment. From the engines in our vehicles, to our refrigerators and central heating systems, to the operation of power plants and the development of renewable energies, thermodynamics has myriad practical applications.

RELATIVITY

When we talk about 'the theory of relativity', we are actually referring to the ideas contained within two distinct papers, written eleven years apart, by the German physicist Albert Einstein. Taken together, the papers turned upside-down our previous assumptions about physics and cosmology, and brought about a genuine scientific revolution, the full implications of which are still being explored today.

The first paper appeared in 1905 and outlined Einstein's 'Special Theory of Relativity', which emerged from a thought experiment he conducted when he was just sixteen. A thought experiment is an experiment carried out solely in the mind – usually because the physical evidence to prove or disprove the hypothesis is unavailable or too difficult to obtain. In Einstein's case, he imagined riding alongside a light beam and came to the conclusion that if he could keep up with it, the beam would appear to be stationary – in just the same way as if you were sat in a railway carriage, staring at another train going in exactly the same direction and at the same speed as you. Yet he knew that such a phenomenon ran contrary to established scientific theories, so he carried out another thought experiment.

This time he imagined a moving train struck by lightning at both its ends at precisely the same moment. Einstein wondered how the event might seem to a stationary observer on an embankment and to someone aboard the train. The person on the embankment, in line with the middle of the train as the lightning strikes, sees the two bolts simultaneously. However, the person on the train is travelling in the direction of the bolt that hits the front of the train, so sees that one momentarily before the other bolt. In other words, the exact same event appears to happen at different times to different observers.

The Special Theory

Drawing on his knowledge of the work of, for example, James Clerk Maxwell, Henri Poincaré and Heinrich Lorentz, Einstein reached the somewhat esoteric conclusions that the laws of physics are the same for all observers moving at constant velocity relative to each other, and that the speed of light in a vacuum is constant. So, what is it that makes the Special Theory so important? It's because, for centuries, the world had accepted Isaac Newton's proofs that space and time were absolutes, and Einstein was showing that they were not. In Einstein's own words, the Special Theory of Relativity 'employs a modification of the theory of space and time'.

Einstein wanted to establish rules that were general and universal, and the Special Theory frustrated him because it applied to only very specific conditions (where motion is at a constant velocity and in a straight line). So he conducted yet another thought experiment – this time about a man floating freely in an enclosed box as it freefalls through space. If the man in the box takes off his watch, that too floats freely beside him. It feels to the man as if he is inside a box sitting still in a non-gravitational field, even though gravity is pulling the box towards the Earth. Equally, if the box was speeding up through space far from the pull of gravity, the subject inside would be pushed to the floor just as if he *were* being pulled by gravity. Traditionally, gravity and acceleration were regarded as different phenomena, though both related to mass. Einstein now realized that gravitational mass and inertial mass are equivalent – an idea that he called the Equivalence Principle.

Thinking about the freefalling box again, he also concluded that if you pierced a hole in one of its sides, a beam of light would hit the opposite wall at a higher point than it entered, its trajectory having been bent by gravity. In other words, light under the influence of gravity does not always – as had been assumed until then – travel in straight lines. Now he could extend the Special Theory to relate it to any sort of motion, whatever the acceleration and direction.

The General Theory

The General Theory showed how gravity warps both time and space, and also provided the field equations to explain how gravity acts on matter and how matter generates gravity by curving space-time. To picture this last concept, think of a basketball bouncing on a trampoline. The fabric of the trampoline bends as the ball travels across it and comes to rest. Add a second ball and it rolls until coming to rest next to the first ball. This is not because the first ball exerts some mysterious force on the second, but simply because the trampoline fabric has been warped by Ball One.

Among its many contributions to science, the General Theory opened the way to our greater understanding of phenomena including black holes, wormholes and the Big Bang. In the words of physicist Max Born, the theory counts as 'the greatest feat of humans thinking about nature – the most amazing combination of philosophical penetration, physical intuition and mathematical skill'.

NUCLEAR FISSION

Fission is the term used to describe splitting the nucleus of an atom – a process capable of producing vast quantities of energy. Splitting the atom has had enormous implications for mankind, both paving

**the way for the development of nuclear reactors producing enormous
volumes of useful energy, and ushering in the age of the atom bomb.**

A major breakthrough came in 1932 when James Chadwick discovered
the existence of the neutron. This led to further important research by
Enrico Fermi in Italy, before Otto Hahn and his assistant Fritz Strassmann
conducted a series of experiments in Germany in which they bombarded
uranium with electrons. Hahn suggested that the uranium had been
changed into barium, but correspondents including Lise Meitner and Otto
Frisch doubted that conclusion. Instead, Meitner said, the nucleus of the
uranium had been rended roughly in two. The age of nuclear fission (as
Frisch termed it) was upon us.

That this was a game-changing discovery was quickly understood by
the scientific community. Several years earlier, the Hungarian physicist
Leó Szilárd had suggested that the splitting of heavy elements (i.e.
those with an atomic number higher than 92, such as uranium) could

Splitting the atom

Ernest Rutherford, a New Zealand-born physicist who spent much of his
life working in London, was instrumental in splitting the atom. As Chair
of Physics at the University of Manchester from 1907, he assembled a
stellar team around him featuring such eminent names as Lawrence
Bragg (Nobel Prize-winner in 1915), Hans Geiger (inventor of the radiation
counter), the philosopher Ludwig Wittgenstein and the quantum pioneer
Niels Bohr.

Rutherford established that the mass of an atom resides in its nucleus,
which itself is surrounded by orbiting electrons. Where once the atom
was regarded as the most basic building block of life, Rutherford proved
that it might theoretically be divided. In 1917, he conducted the first
artificially induced nuclear reactions using nitrogen atoms. Moreover,
a host of other heavyweight intellects – among them Bohr, Henri
Becquerel, Marie and Pierre Curie, Ernest Walton and John Cockcroft –
developed and extended his ideas.

be used to spark a nuclear chain-reaction capable of massive energy release. Based in the USA in 1939, Szilárd (having co-opted Einstein to the cause) warned the White House of the dangers if this technology got into German hands. By 1942 the American government had authorized the top-secret Manhattan Project under the guidance of J. Robert Oppenheimer, culminating in the creation of the atom bomb – two of which were dropped on the Japanese cities of Hiroshima and Nagasaki in 1945, killing hundreds of thousands at a stroke.

Einstein was among those who could never greet the splitting of the atom with anything other than concern. 'The unleashed power of the atom', he wrote in 1946, 'has changed everything save our modes of thinking and we thus drift toward unparalleled catastrophe.'

QUANTUM MECHANICS

Quantum mechanics is the branch of science that aims to explain how matter and energy behave at the atomic and sub-atomic levels. A constantly evolving discipline since it became established in the early 20th century, quantum mechanics describes sub-atomic phenomena that often seem incompatible with the assumptions of classical, large-scale physics. As the Dane Niels Bohr, one of the founding fathers of quantum science, once said:

Those who are not shocked when they first come across quantum theory cannot possibly have understood it.

German physicist Max Planck is regarded as the originator of quantum physics. Around 1900 he suggested that light, traditionally regarded as being emitted in waves, is emitted in discrete packets of energy, which he termed quanta. In 1905 Albert Einstein confirmed this thesis – light exists as both wave and particle and cannot be said to be one or the other. It was a conclusion that flew in the face of scientific orthodoxy, but come the 1920s, French physicist Louis-Victor de Broglie realized the same could be said of matter. Wave–particle duality, as it is known, was just the first of quantum mechanics' many mysterious features to, as it were, come to light.

In the first couple of decades of the 20th century, Niels Bohr constructed a new model of the structure of atoms using quantum principles. Erwin Schrödinger, meanwhile, worked on establishing the fundamental mathematical equations that underpinned the emerging field. He was pivotal, along with Max Born, in developing the key quantum idea of uncertainty – not least in his famous thought experiment, with the striking conclusion that a cat in a locked box may be concurrently alive and dead (though his intention was to illustrate how absurd this is). Using so-called wave functions, it is possible to indicate the probability of specific particles being at a particular place at a given moment – as encapsulated in Werner Heisenberg's uncertainty principle.

Despite this randomness and indeterminacy, quantum physics has proven itself unrivalled at predicting the nature and behaviour of atomic and sub-atomic systems under different circumstances. Such is its complexity that there are a number of competing interpretations of quantum mechanics – most famously the Copenhagen interpretation (devised in the 1920s and spearheaded by Bohr and Heisenberg) that says that the act of measuring a system will force it to produce certain results.

Quantum mechanics has given rise to such revolutionary theoretical frameworks as string theory (in which the point-like particles of particle physics are superseded by one-dimensional strings) in a bid to explain the secrets of the cosmos – not to mention driving the technological revolution.

Few areas of science are more intimidating to the layman than quantum mechanics, yet in its shadowy corners potentially lie the answers to our biggest questions. Writing in 1982, Richard Feynman – the Nobel Prize-winning quantum theorist – explained his own uncertainty principle:

We have always had a great deal of difficulty understanding the world view that quantum mechanics represents... You know how it always is, every new idea, it takes a generation or two until it becomes obvious that there's no real problem. I cannot define the real problem, therefore I suspect there's no real problem, but I'm not sure there's no real problem.

CONTINENTAL DRIFT

Our understanding of the changing geography of our planet was greatly expanded by Alfred Wegener (1880–1930), who introduced his the-ory of continental drift in the early 20th century.

A German meteorologist, Wegener was fascinated by the way that the coastlines of Africa and South America seem like they should lock together. It occurred to him that perhaps the continents had once been joined as a supercontinent (which he would eventually come to call Pangea), before slowly breaking up and drifting apart. For evidence of his thesis, he turned to the fossil record to show how the same types of ancient fossils were present in both South America and Africa. He also cited mountain ranges and rock formations on the respective continents that seemed to match one another. Prior to Wegener, it was thought that mountains formed as a result of the planet cooling and contracting, creating 'wrinkles' in the Earth's crust. Wegener instead suggested they resulted from collisions between drifting continents.

However, there was little appetite for his theory, and his suggestion that the continents powered across the oceans at a significant pace but without any obvious driving force lacked plausibility. Nonetheless, Wegener managed at least to sow seeds into some of the more fertile minds then working in geoscience. One such was the British geologist, Arthur Holmes, who kept Wegener's ideas alive in the 1930s and 40s when few others did. Then, in the 1950s, magnetic readings revealed that the ocean floors were moving apart by a few centimetres every year. Scientists now began to develop the theory of tectonic plates – huge slab-like structures in the Earth's crust and mantle that broadly fit together but which slowly move over long timeframes, creating mountains and volcanoes, as well as causing earthquakes. Crucially, movement of the tectonic plates over millions of years would account for the drift of the continents. Decades after his death, Wegener's theory was at last recognized as scientifically valid.

CYBERSPACE

Cyberspace is the hypothetical environment in which communications between computer networks take place. With the rise of the Internet, a significant proportion of human interaction – commercial, social and political – now takes place within its realm.

The term 'cyberspace' was coined by the cyberpunk author William Gibson in his 1984 novel, *Neuromancer*. It entered into popular usage in the 1990s as the Internet came into more widespread use. The Internet, however, had been around since 1969, when an academic research network called ARPANET was created for the military Advanced Research Projects Agency. Yet its genesis was relatively slow and for the next two decades its use was largely restricted to a small number of academics. Then, in 1989, a Briton, Tim Berners-Lee, invented what became known as the World Wide Web. Using hypertext (a software language permitting extensive cross-referencing of materials), he devised a way to link together documents across different networks, and created a browser to facilitate viewing files. Crucially, he allowed his innovations to enter the public sphere for free. The Internet underwent rapid development and before long, anyone with an Internet connection could share information and ideas with other users across the world. By 1995, Internet users still only accounted for about 1 per cent of the world's population but by 2016 the figure was about 40 per cent – some three billion people. The cyberspace revolution has been so profound that it has been likened to the Industrial Revolution in its impact.

Free for all

One of the defining features of cyberspace is that – unlike physical spaces – no one owns or controls it. This, inevitably, has its plus and minus points. On the upside, it promotes freedom of ideas and expression on an unprecedented level. Indeed, the Internet has been cited as key in coordinating mass social action, as exemplified by the social networking aspects of Barack Obama's presidential election campaigns and even the Arab Spring uprisings of 2011. However, there is a darker side, where the 'Wild West' nature of the Internet allows for malevolent activities, from the sale of illicit drugs to the commissioning of international terrorism. All attempts to regulate a set of shared rules and standards – commonly known as cyber-ethics – have inevitably lagged behind the exponential growth in user numbers. Cyberspace, then, remains an only partially charted land but also an extraordinary reflection of humanity.

'[N]o one could have imagined the effects the Internet would have: entire relationships flourish, friendships prosper . . . there's a vast new intimacy and accidental poetry, not to mention the weirdest porn. The entire human experience seems to unveil itself like the surface of a new planet.'

J. G. Ballard.

ARTIFICIAL INTELLIGENCE

Artificial intelligence (also known as AI) refers to 'intelligence' exhibited by machines or software, as well as the industry that aims to develop these 'intelligent' machines. Underlying AI is the idea that machines can be 'taught' to adapt their behaviour to specific circumstances, thus achieving effective outcomes.

The idea of intelligent inanimate objects has long fascinated humans – a fact attested by the attempts of the ancient Egyptians to build automatons (nor were they the only culture of antiquity to try). In cultural terms, AI has cast a long shadow too – Mary Shelley's *Frankenstein*, for example, may be seen as forewarning of the dangers of creating 'artificial' intelligent life, while movies like *Terminator* and *I, Robot* reflect our contemporary concerns.

Man versus machine

The modern concept of AI was arguably born at a conference at Dartmouth College, New Hampshire, in 1956, where the term was first used. One of the attendees that day, cognitive scientist Marvin Minsky, had high hopes. 'Within a generation,' he would predict, 'the problem of creating "artificial intelligence" will substantially be solved.' While that may have been over-optimistic, there have been high-profile successes in AI development over the years. In 1997, for instance, a computer (IBM's Deep Blue) became the first machine to beat a chess champion, defeating Russian grandmaster Garry Kasparov. The computer had been trained to 'think through' the implications of each move better than even Kasparov could manage.

Yet there are deep moral and social implications to consider. What happens when machines are routinely more intelligent than us? What if they decide they should be in charge? Or what if their malice grows with their intelligence. In 2015, Stephen Hawking said:

The real risk with AI isn't malice but competence. A super-intelligent AI will be extremely good at accomplishing its goals, and if those goals aren't aligned with ours, we're in trouble.

Another area of concern is the potential development of 'autonomous weapons' (sometimes known as 'killer robots') that could theoretically select and engage targets without any human involvement. War might conceivably be conducted by machines alone, erasing lines of human responsibility and removing opportunity for human mediation. Others fear that the robots will ultimately displace human workers on a mass scale – why employ a fallible and demanding human when a robot will do the job uncomplainingly for you? And what if a robot gets so smart that it decides simply to ignore, or even get rid of, its human overlords? Hawking's suggested solution is to focus less on creating pure, undirected artificial intelligence in favour of what he calls 'beneficial intelligence' – machines that will only ever seek to serve our interests.

TIME TRAVEL

Time travel – the idea that one can either travel backwards in time or else forwards at a greater than normal rate – stands at the very edge of scientific possibility. For most of history, the idea has been the preserve of storytellers. However, some have suggested that Einstein's reconceptualization of the universe moved us, tantalizingly, a step closer to time-travelling reality. Debate continues to rage within the

scientific community as to whether or not it is even theoretically possible.

Whereas time travel once seemed the preserve of fiction, its putative theoretical viability opens up new vistas of scientific exploration. In his 1985 novel, *Contact*, Carl Sagan helped popularize the notion of time travel via wormholes – hypothetical tunnels linking different points in spacetime. To travel down one, the theory goes, and you could take a shortcut to a different moment in history. However, it is thought

The fact and fiction of time travel

The idea of time travel as a literary device has a long heritage. For example, the ancient Indian *Mahabharata* plays with the concept, as do texts of the Western canon, like Washington Irving's *Rip Van Winkle* (1819), while H.G. Wells is often credited as the first writer to bring the idea of machine-based time travel into mainstream consciousness, with his 1895 novel, *The Time Machine*.

Then came Einstein's General Theory of Relativity in 1915, with its description of time travelling at different speeds in different parts of the universe – the result of heavy objects (like planets) acting as a drag on time. A black hole serves as a similar drag and it has been suggested that were it possible to send a crew into orbit around a black hole, they might experience time at half the rate as those left back on Earth.

Another theoretical means of time travel relies on the law of the speed of light. Given that the laws of physics do not allow anything to exceed the speed of light (about 186,000 miles per second), as an object approaches that speed, time starts to go slower to ensure it remains within the speed limit. Thus, if a spaceship was travelling at, say, 99.9999 per cent of the speed of light and someone on board that ship was running at sufficient velocity that they might surpass the speed of light, time on board will effectively put them into slow motion. In other words, if you can travel fast enough, you could experience an earth year in perhaps just a few hours.

wormholes exist only at the sub-atomic level in what is known as the quantum foam, so to access one you'd need be no taller than a billion-trillion-trillionths of a centimetre. Nonetheless, if – as some scientists believe – future technology provides us with the tools to enlarge a wormhole sufficiently to allow a human through, just maybe we could zip around spacetime at will.

Yet what might happen if we could? The enterprise seems burdened with potential paradoxes – the classic of which is the Grandfather Paradox. What would happen, it asks, if you travelled back in time and killed your own grandfather in his youth? Your mother could not then be born, who in turn could not give you life. So how could you be alive to go back in time in the first place? It is a mind-boggling conundrum, all solutions to which are resolutely unverifiable.

PART FOUR

MEDICINE AND PSYCHOLOGY

'Wherever the art of medicine is loved, there is also a love of humanity.'

Hippocrates

Medicine – the practice of diagnosing, preventing and treating disease – has existed for thousands of years, although its nature has changed markedly over that period. Where once we looked at illness as the judgement of the gods, or a manifestation of the natural cycles of the world, we now look to science to free us from its shackles. Moreover, it not only offers a reflection of humanity's increasing pool of knowledge and skills, but speaks of more fundamental changes in our conception of ourselves. The revered medical historian Fielding Hudson Garrison once observed:

The history of medicine is ... the history of humanity itself, with its ups and downs, its brave aspirations after truth and finality, its pathetic failures. The subject may be treated variously as a pageant, an array of books, a procession of characters, a succession of theories, an exposition of human ineptitudes, or as the very bone and marrow of cultural history.

THE IDEA OF MEDICINE

Whereas ancient civilizations had a tendency to seek supernatural explanations for medical conditions, modern medicine looks for answers in science and nature. The Greek physician Hippocrates (c. 460–370 BCE) is perhaps the key figure in establishing many of what are now the central tenets of modern medical practice and theory.

The first identifiable physician in history is Imhotep, who worked in Egypt in the third millennium BCE. In this period, much medical practice was ritualistic and spiritual in nature. Remedies often took the form of plants, animal parts or minerals perceived as having magical restorative properties. It wasn't until Hippocrates that there was a fundamental change in approach – one that established medicine as a profession rooted in rationalism.

Hippocrates looked for natural causes of disease, rather than relying on mystical explanations. Ill health, he suggested, was caused by an individual's diet, habits and environment, rather than by affronting the gods. In particular, he held with the idea that disease was caused by an imbalance of the body's four humours (bodily fluids): blood, yellow bile, black bile and phlegm. Rather than aiming for precise diagnoses (see next entry) and targeted medication, he sought instead to follow more generalized and passive schemes of treatment aimed at rebalancing the humours. He recommended that patients combine exercise with rest, keep themselves clean and regulate their intake of food and drink. He also introduced the idea of illnesses being either acute or chronic, as well as pioneering the concepts of endemic and epidemic conditions.

In terms of professionalizing medicine, he insisted that the physician should be kind, calm, honest and serious – not to mention well presented. Other innovations included taking patients' medical histories, making clinical observations (for instance, recording the pulse, noting areas of pain and checking on the bodily functions) and keeping clear records that might be shared with other professionals.

The Hippocratic Oath

Hippocrates' most celebrated contribution to medicine was the Hippocratic Oath, a pledge that still forms the basis of many modern-day medical oaths and laws. Among its most important clauses is that which is often summarized as 'to do no harm':

I will use treatment to help the sick according to my ability and judgement, but never with a view to injury and wrong-doing. Neither will I administer a poison to anybody when asked to do so, nor will I suggest such a course . . . Into whatsoever houses I enter, I will enter to help the sick, and I will abstain from all intentional wrong-doing and harm, especially from abusing the bodies of man or woman, bound or free. And whatsoever I shall see or hear in the course of my profession, as well as outside my profession in my intercourse with men, if it be what should not be published abroad, I will never divulge, holding such things to be holy secrets.

DIAGNOSIS

Diagnosis – the process of determining from what disease or ailment a patient is suffering by analysis of their symptoms and signs – is an integral component of modern medical care. It allows for the medical practitioner to establish a course of treatment on the basis of rational knowledge. As the renowned physician Martin H. Fischer observed: 'Diagnosis is not the end, but the beginning of practice.'

The modern doctor looks to a number of indicators when attempting to make a diagnosis. These include reported symptoms by a patient, along with the patient's medical history. There may then be tests to discern any changes from the normal within the patient, whether in terms of anatomy (e.g. a rash) a change in blood-sugar levels, functioning or mental state. It is often the case that a diagnostician will be confronted with a number of possible candidate diseases or conditions, which by a process of elimination they will attempt to rank in terms of likelihood. This is known as differential diagnosis.

The evolution of diagnosis

Over the course of history, diagnosis has taken many forms: divination was employed in some ancient cultures, while astrology remained a tool in European medicine well into the medieval age. However, methods more in line with current thinking were in practice at least as far back as the 11th century BCE, when the Babylonian Esagil-kin-apli wrote a diagnostic handbook based on the rational consideration of physical indicators.

Hippocrates was another early innovator, not least in his use of urine as an indicator of disease. Nonetheless, he was less interested in diagnosis than prognosis – that is to say, predicting the likely outcome of a patient's overall medical situation. Having established a prognosis – as discussed in the previous entry – he would then formulate a holistic programme of treatment, often centred upon imbalances in the humours.

Right up until the 19th century, there was tension between those who regarded the physician's role as to provide a general prognosis and those who thought he should offer a specific diagnosis. However, diagnosis is now commonly accepted as the precursor to establishing the most effective, targeted treatments. The job of diagnosis has also greatly benefited from technical innovations – from stethoscopes and X-rays to ultrasounds and genetic testing – granting the modern doctor the tools to diagnose with a hitherto unimaginable level of accuracy.

HUMAN DISSECTION

Anatomy is the branch of medicine concerned with the bodily structure of humans – both external and internal. Anatomical studies have been crucial to understanding how the body works and how to put things right when they go wrong. Yet cultural and religious sensitivities over much of human history ruled out human dissection as a means of increasing our anatomical knowledge. Only during the Renaissance did the idea of study through dissection receive widespread acceptance.

Anatomical knowledge among the ancient civilizations was severely limited, stemming primarily from the dissection of animals and, for example in Egypt, from the incidental study of human bodies as they were prepared for their putative afterlives. Around the 3rd century BCE Herophilus pioneered the idea of human dissection for medical research, usually using the bodies of condemned criminals. His career overlapped with that of Erasistratus, who made revolutionary new studies of the structure of the human brain.

Students Dissecting a Cadaver, c. *1900*

In the 2nd century BC, the Greek physician Galen significantly extended the pool of knowledge. Arguably Galen's greatest contribution was to establish that the body and its functions are the result of design, and not mere chance. Through the Middle Ages, there was interest within both the Christian and Islamic worlds in learning more about the nature of the body, and by extension humanity's place within the natural and spiritual order. Nonetheless, reluctance to 'desecrate' human bodies by dissecting them continued, so its practice was rare, with most physicians instead relying on the works of Galen.

It was not until the Renaissance in Europe that there was a marked shift in attitudes. Of particular importance was the publication in 1543 of Andreas Vesalius's *De humani corporis fabrica* (*On the Fabric of the*

Human Body), replete with illustrations based on observations from dissections. Vesalius, a professor at Padua, is regarded as the founding father of modern anatomy and gave the practice a new level of academic respectability – a status reinforced by the extraordinary collection of anatomical drawings made by Leonardo da Vinci (1452–1519).

Technical innovations such as improvements in the microscope propelled the discipline along still further and by the 19th century, human dissection was a required part of a medical student's training across much of the world.

PATHOLOGY

Pathology is the study of the causes, processes and effects of disease. In practical terms, pathology is often studied by the examination of bodily tissues within the laboratory setting. It comprises four principal subjects of enquiry – the cause of an illness (its aetiology), how it develops (pathogenesis), how cell structure is changed, and how the disease manifests itself.

The great pioneer of pathology was a German, Rudolf Virchow (1821–1902), who ushered in the era of 'microscopic pathology' by focusing on disease studied at the cellular level (histopathology). As *Rubin's Pathology*, a standard textbook on the subject, tells us: 'In the 19th century, Rudolf Virchow, often referred to as the father of modern pathology, proposed that injury to the smallest living unit of the body, the cell, is the basis of all disease. To this day, clinical and experimental pathology remain rooted in this concept.'

Virchow inspired a new generation, among them his student Julius Cohnheim, whose innovations included the freezing of materials prior to examination, and Friedrich von Recklinghausen (1833–1910), who published major studies on, for example, thrombosis, embolism and infarction. The 20th century was a period marked by a rapid succession of new discoveries. The work of Karl Landsteiner (1868–1943), for instance, laid the groundwork for modern blood typing. Meanwhile, technological advances – in, for example, microscopy and image processing – have ensured that pathology today is perhaps developing more quickly than ever before.

The primitive post-mortem

Although figures such as Hippocrates and Galen made efforts to understand the basic pathology of disease, the Arabian physician Avenzoar (1091–1161) is believed to have been the first to carry out a post-mortem dissection to establish the cause of a specific ailment (specifically, identifying a parasite as the cause of scabies). This was in stark contrast to the more usual reason for dissection: to gain a better understanding of the functions of the un-diseased body.

An Italian, Antonio Benivieni (1443–1502), then developed the idea of the autopsy as a means to establish an individual's cause of death. In 1761, another Italian, Giovanni Morgagni, published *De Sedibus et Causis Morborum per Anatomem Indagatis* (*On the Seats and Causes of Disease*), detailing his findings from some 600 autopsies, so cementing the relationship between illness and anatomical examination. Marie François Xavier Bichat (1771–1802), an army surgeon, then took the opportunity to examine bodies freshly retrieved from the guillotines of the French Revolution, so vastly expanding our understanding of the pathology of several diseases. Another Frenchman, Gabriel Andral, built upon and extended Bichat's work, publishing his two-volume *Précis d' Anatomie Pathologique* in 1828.

SURGERY

Surgery is the branch of medicine in which injuries or disorders of the body are treated by manipulation or removal of the relevant body part – typically using surgical instruments and via an incision made into the body.

The archaeological record suggests primitive methods of surgery – including the amputation of limbs and the stitching-up and cauterizing of wounds (including an ingenious ancient South American method that involved using insects to eat around the rotten edges of a wound before 'stapling' it with the insects' twisted-off heads) – have been practised for thousands of years. Trepanning, in which a hole is drilled into the skull, usually with a view to relieving pressure on the brain, is another particularly gruesome procedure with a long history. By the 18th century BCE, the Babylonians had even produced a system of precise payments for successful surgeries – along with punishments for less effective surgeons, including the removal of their hands.

For millennia, practical restrictions meant that surgery had amounted to little more than amputations and the removal of external growths, but later in the 18th century a much wider range of treatments became available. In 1884, for instance, an English surgeon, Rickman Godlee, became the first to remove a brain tumour, while the following year witnessed the first successful heart surgery (conducted by a Norwegian, Axel Cappelen). The horrors of the First World War demanded new innovations and developments, and it was in this period that viable blood transfusions were pioneered, along with restorative plastic surgery. The 20th century would be filled with other landmarks – for example, the first gender reassignment operation and the first hip replacement. The processes of transplanting healthy organs to replace diseased ones also developed at a pace from the 19th century. After the first modern skin graft in 1823, the first cornea transplant followed in 1905, with the first kidney transplant in 1950, the first heart and liver transplants both occurring in 1967, the first hand transplant in 1998 and the first face transplants in the 2000s.

Furthermore, in recent years, with the development of microsurgery (using microscopes and miniaturized instruments) and keyhole surgery (which is minimally invasive thanks to the use of technologies including fibre optics), surgery has become a field in which ever more is possible as the risks involved decline.

The lowly surgeon

The 6th-century-BCE Indian physician Sushruta and the Greek Galen (129–c. 210 BCE) are among the first named surgical pioneers, each displaying a volume of knowledge and expertise unrivalled in their respective eras. Nonetheless, as of the medieval period, surgeons enjoyed a distinctly lower status than physicians. While doctors required a university education, so-called barber-surgeons were largely unregulated and might or might not be highly skilled. They used crude tools for everything from the setting of broken bones to the removal of limbs. All the while, three great impediments remained to the development of surgery: basic inabilities to control bleeding, infection and pain.

Despite the notable efforts of figures including Al-Zahrawi (936–1013) in the Arab world, the Italian Rogerius (author of *Practica Chirurgiae – The Practice of Surgery* – published around 1180), and the 16th-century Andreas Vesalius working out of Padua (see entry on Human Dissection), it was not until the 18th century that surgery started to get on to a firmer setting. It became more professional thanks to figures like the Scottish surgeon and anatomist John Hunter (1728–93), who not only demanded rigour in practice but personally collected some 14,000 anatomical specimens for study. Surgery also became a discipline studied in university, bringing an end to the era of the semi-skilled surgeon-barber.

THE CIRCULATORY SYSTEM

The circulatory – or cardiovascular – system is the means by which blood travels around the body, delivering oxygen and nutrients to the body's cells and disposing of waste products. Credit for providing its first comprehensive description falls to the physician William Harvey, who published *Exercitatio Anatomica de Motu Cordis et Sanguinis in Animalibus* (*An Anatomical Exercise on the Motion of the Heart and Blood in Living Beings*) in 1628. His was a discovery that not only revolutionized medicine but also had philosophical repercussions, as it overturned millennia of scientific orthodoxy and invited humans to see themselves in a different light.

What good is the heart?

Since antiquity, there had been theories as to the purpose of the heart, with the Ebers Papyrus (originating in 16th-century-BCE Egypt) even outlining a circulatory system in which it was thought the heart pumped air around the body via the arteries. About a thousand years later, the Indian physician Sushruta speculated that vital fluids were driven around the body, though exactly how remained unclear. Over the ensuing centuries, others identified the valves of the heart and distinguished between arteries and veins, so that by the 2nd century CE Galen was able to describe how blood vessels carry blood. Another thousand years on and Ibn al-Nafis made strides towards a better understanding of pulmonary circulation, whereby deoxygenated blood is taken from the heart to the lungs and returned oxygenated.

In the early 17th century William Harvey was a student of Hieronymus Fabricius, who had made his own contribution to the field by describing the valves of the veins (despite being unaware of their precise function).

By an exhaustive process of experimentation, Harvey was able to construct a complete picture of the circulatory system. Whereas it had been widely believed that the heart heated the blood, he recognized that its primary role was to keep up a constant transport of blood by pumping it. He also fully mapped out the venous and arterial systems, recognizing that the arteries carry blood from the heart while the veins (complete with the stepladder valves described by Fabricius) bring it back, and capillaries (tiny blood vessels) serve as the means of getting oxygenated blood from the arteries to the tissues and then deoxygenated blood back into the veins.

Medically, the implications were vast. It became possible, for example, to undertake far more ambitious forms of surgery and medicines could be administered far more effectively with a better grasp of how they are communicated around the body. Moreover, humans were able to conceive of their bodies as awesome machines, correspondingly impacting the way we perceive our place in nature. Yet for all this, it took many years for the conservative medical establishment fully to recognize the extent of Harvey's achievement. The significance of his legacy is expressed in Richard Bergland's *The Fabric of Mind* (1985): 'Few would have predicted that the discovery of the circulation of the blood would have changed the way philosophers view the world, theologians conceive of God, or astronomers look at the stars, yet all of that happened.'

ANAESTHESIA

Anaesthesia is that area of medicine concerned with inducing temporary loss of sensation or awareness in a patient – either through general anaesthetic (which causes loss of consciousness) or local anaesthetic (which causes loss of sensation in an isolated part of the body only). The development of anaesthetics revolutionized the field of surgery, allowing for procedures all but impossible on a patient who was not desensitized.

Chloroform and cocaine

In 1846 James Young Simpson, a Scottish obstetrician, showed that chloroform (which had been invented in 1831) could be used to put people to sleep, and he promptly began employing it with the expectant mothers under his care. By 1853, it was sufficiently established that Dr John Snow felt confident enough to treat Queen Victoria with chloroform during the birth of Prince Leopold. Meanwhile, another Englishman, Benjamin Ward Richardson, built upon Simpson's suggestion that a local anaesthetic might be even more beneficial than a general one and pioneered the use of ether spray to numb specific regions of the body. Then, in the 1880s, the Austrian ophthalmologist Karl Koller promoted cocaine as a local anaesthetic, although by the mid-20th century lidocaine was the preferred local anaesthetic for most medics. By then, spinal and epidural anaesthesia had also been developed, blocking the transmission of pain by injections directly into the spinal cord.

Before the 18th century, anaesthesia was usually crude in the extreme. The first recorded use of it was by the Chinese physician Hua Tuo (140–208), who dosed up his patients with herbal solutions prior to operating on them. In antiquity, ethanol was another trusted means of knocking out a patient, along with a quick blow to the head and compression of the carotid artery – all highly risky measures with the potential to cause unforeseen side effects and even death.

There was markedly little progress in the story until the late 18th century. In England in 1784, James Moore used nerve compression to desensitize a patient prior to an amputation, although this appears to have been a one-off. Of greater import was the publication in 1799 of chemist and inventor Humphrey Davy's *Researches, Chemical and Philosophical: Chiefly Concerning Nitrous Oxide*, in which the author suggested the use of laughing gas during surgical procedures. Although there was scarcely any practical adoption of this idea, it sowed the seeds of an idea. Michael Faraday investigated the anaesthetic properties of ether, while a general practitioner called Henry Hill Hickman argued the case for carbon dioxide inhalation to create a state of suspended animation.

In America, the gauntlet was taken up by a dentist, Horace Wells. Struck by the effects of nitrous oxide he had seen demonstrated in a travelling show, he attempted to use it on a volunteer prior to a tooth extraction. It had limited success (the patient screamed out in pain though could remember little of the experience afterwards) so one of Wells's students, William Morton, decided to find a more efficient anaesthetic agent. He plumped for ether vapour, which he successfully demonstrated at Massachusetts General Hospital in 1846 – an event that ushered in the modern age of anaesthesia.

The field of anaesthesia continues to evolve as more efficient and less dangerous drugs are developed and improved for use in ever more complex operations.

GERM THEORY

Germ theory states that most infectious diseases are caused by microorganisms within the body. While the importance of sanitation in preventing the spread of disease is considered basic common sense today, germ theory only established itself around the mid-19th century.

The ancient Greeks had recognized that disease could be spread from person to person, but they were unsure how. The prevailing theory was that disease was caused by miasma – in other words, diseased air. In 1546, an Italian, Girolamo Fracastoro, described a prototype germ theory, but few medical professionals gave it serious consideration and although microorganisms were seen under the microscope for the first time in the 17th century, no clear link was made between them and disease. Then, in the 1840s, a Hungarian physician called Ignaz Semmelweis began to investigate the high death rates from puerperal fever on the maternity wards of a clinic where he worked.

The originator of antisepsis

When one of his medical colleagues died after a cut on his finger became infected during the dissection of a cadaver, Semmelweis came to a shattering conclusion. A large number of his obstetric staff were in the habit of studying dead bodies before going on their maternity rounds. Unaware of the danger posed by germs, they did not bother to wash their hands in between. These medical staff were inadvertent angels of death for the young women preparing to give birth. Semmelweis instituted a regime of cleaning with a chloride of lime wash. Its effect was immediate, with the death rate falling from 11.4 per cent to 1.2 per cent in a year. Soon the hygiene regime was extended to all members of staff and to objects as well. Semmelweis is thus the originator of antisepsis – the prevention of infection by arresting the growth and spread of germs. Yet Semmelweis would receive little credit for his life-saving leap of the imagination before his death in 1865.

Another early proponent of germ theory was English physician John Snow, whose many achievements included identifying a public water pump as the source of an outbreak of cholera in London in 1854. Meanwhile, in 1864 Louis Pasteur (1822–95) introduced pasteurization to the world – a process that kills the germs which cause food and drink to go off by heating them. A couple of years later, surgeon Joseph Lister published a landmark paper in which he detailed how carbolic acid could be used to kill germs and prevent infection of wounds.

Then, in the 1880s, German physician and pioneering microbiologist Robert Koch developed his 'four postulates' for establishing the relationship between specific organisms and diseases. He identified the bacterial causes of cholera, septicaemia and tuberculosis. In the same period, French microbiologist Charles Chamberland proved the existence of viruses (as distinct from bacteria) and Scottish doctor Patrick Manson investigated the role of vectors (for instance, mosquitoes and tsetse flies) in the spread of certain diseases. Thus armed with germ theory we became empowered to fight (and prevent) diseases in new, efficient ways.

IMMUNOLOGY

Immunology is the branch of medicine concerned with immunity – the ability of the body to resist specific illnesses and diseases. While there has been some understanding of natural immunity since antiquity, its modern phase began in the 18th century, firstly in China and then spreading to Europe.

In 1798, an English country doctor called Edward Jenner realized that milkmaids who had previously been infected with cowpox escaped infection by the more serious smallpox. He thus developed the idea of inoculating patients with cowpox to ward off smallpox. After successfully testing out his hypothesis on unwitting local lad, James Phipps, Jenner's idea of vaccination gradually spread, despite fierce opposition from parts of the medical firmament. His method proved far safer than that of variolation, so it is Jenner who is widely considered the father of modern immunology.

As scientists in the 19th century got a grip on germ theory (see previous entry), the field developed at a pace. In particular, Louis Pasteur discovered that chickens infected with a weakened strain of cholera were protected from reinfection. In other words, he realized that introducing a regulated amount of a pathogen (i.e. a disease) into the body can promote the production of what we now know are antibodies to fight off something worse. He was subsequently able to develop vaccines for both rabies and swine erysipelas.

Around the turn of the 20th century, German physician and scientist Paul Ehrlich hypothesized that specific antigens might create particular antibodies, although it was another thirty years or so before his ideas were clinically proven. Then, in the 1940s, research began in earnest into the role of specific cells within the human body's wider system of disease defence. Much of the work of this period supported the speculative theories of Russian zoologist Élie Metchnikoff, who back in the 1880s had suggested that cells which he called *phagocytes* (from the Greek for 'devouring cells') were crucial in fighting infection. In more recent years, meanwhile, it has been developments in the field of genetics that have opened up the most promising new frontiers in immunology.

What doesn't kill you makes you stronger

In Greece in the 5th century BCE, Thucydides described how some people survived the plague that was then ravaging Athens, but while there was some understanding that these individuals had developed immunity, exactly how remained a mystery. Little progress was made until the Middle Ages, when a process known as variolation was developed in China. Healthy subjects were exposed to material from the lesions of sufferers from smallpox (then endemic in the country) – most commonly by taking the scab of a pustule, grinding it into a powder and putting it up the nose. Although the treatment was not without risk, it proved remarkably effective in bringing about immunity. By the 18th century the technique had been adopted by the Ottomans, travelled across Europe, and thence been adopted in the Americas.

PHARMACOLOGY

Pharmacology is that part of medicine specifically concerned with how drugs (i.e. chemicals both naturally occurring and manufactured) affect the body's biochemical functioning. Those chemicals that can be used for medicinal purposes – that is to say, to diagnose, treat or prevent disease – are therefore called pharmaceuticals. The ideas behind modern, scientific pharmacology only emerged in a meaningful way in the 19th century.

Humankind's attempts to cure illness by the application of natural plant-based substances have a prehistoric heritage, while the first documented use of medicinal drugs is contained in the Egyptian Kahun

Papyri, dating to around 1800 BCE. Among the treatments detailed in these documents was the taking of honey to fight infection. Then, from about 1500 BCE, the Babylonians are known to have produced pills and creams for medical use.

The medieval age saw the publication of several important overviews of medicinal knowledge – notably the 9th-century Arabic tome *De Gradibus*, in which Al-Kindi strove to quantify the strength of various drugs, and Avicenna's 11th-century epic *The Canon of Medicine*. Nonetheless, pharmacology was very basic – opium and quinine were among the most effective drugs available but the widespread use of metal-based compounds was often actively injurious to the patient. Nor would things improve much until the early decades of the 1800s, when figures such as French physiologists François Magendie and Claude Bernard pioneered the scientific study of the physiological effects of specific drugs through a process of experimentation and observation. They built upon the legacy of William Withering (1741–99), who had identified digitalis as the active ingredient in a folkloric herbal remedy for dropsy. Then, in 1847, the German Rudolf Buchheim became the university professor of pharmacology at Dorpat (in what is now Estonia), bringing an unprecedented level of scientific rigour to the study of drugs and their effects. He is credited with changing pharmacology from an essentially descriptive discipline to an experimental one.

Come the 20th century, and pharmacology was firmly established not only as an academic discipline but as a major new industry and pharmaceutical laboratories became the focus of medical practice.

PSYCHIATRY AND THE UNCONSCIOUS

Psychiatry is the medical discipline concerned with the diagnosis and treatment of mental disorders – that is to say, serious abnormalities reflected in behaviour, cognition, mood or perception. Whereas psychologists look at the human mind and its workings in general, psychiatrists seek to address specific dysfunctions. As the American humourist Shannon Fife put it: 'Psychiatry is the art of teaching people how to stand on their own feet while reclining on couches.'

In ancient times, mental disorders were commonly seen either as evidence of supernatural displeasure or as manifestations of moral degeneration or physiological problems (the latter being a view shared by Hippocrates and Democritus among the ancient Greeks). In the 11th century, Avicenna, that leading light of the Islamic golden age, identified broad categories of emotional disorder (among them anger, anxiety, depression and obsession) and even suggested the possibility of reordering a patient's disordered thinking patterns.

Nonetheless, for the next eight hundred years or so, those with serious psychiatric illnesses were contained rather than treated – often in asylums where terrible conditions typically prevailed. Only in the 18th century was there a concerted move towards more compassionate care of the mentally ill, and even then it remained a case of managing, not curing, sufferers.

The term *psychiatry* – the word derives from the Greek for 'physician of the mind' – was used for the first time in 1808 in a paper by a German, Johann Christian Reil. As the discipline gained greater academic prestige, the trend was to seek physiological causes of serious mental conditions such as mania, psychosis and depression. The associated field of neurology, meanwhile, sought to explain more minor cases of neuroses by reference to physical dysfunctions within the nervous system. Then, around the turn of the 20th century, an Austrian, Sigmund Freud, arrived on the

The ego and the id

In his 1923 paper, 'The Ego and the Id', Freud significantly revised his 1900 model as he introduced the idea of:

- the *ego* – the seat of our conscious perception and intellectual functioning;

- the *id* – that which strives for the immediate satisfaction of pleasure and, correspondingly, avoidance of pain;

- the *super-ego* – the self-critical, moralizing part of ourselves (our conscience, if you like), which reflects the standards of wider society.

scene. In a series of landmark works, most famously *The Interpretation of Dreams* (1900), Freud established the unconscious – that part of the mind inaccessible to the conscious (i.e. aware) part but which nonetheless is taken to affect behaviour and emotions – as a subject of serious scientific study. In doing so, he virtually single-handedly created psychoanalysis as a method of treating mental disorder. As Freud himself once wrote: 'The poets and philosophers before me discovered the unconscious; what I discovered was the scientific method by which the unconscious can be studied.'

In *The Interpretation of Dreams*, Freud described the mind as split into three distinct hypothetical areas – the conscious (the part of the mind comprising those things of which we are aware); the preconscious (consisting of those ideas and memories that are latent most of the time but which may easily become conscious); and the unconscious (those desires, impulses and wishes normally inaccessible to the conscious mind). He suggested that much like an iceberg, only a small proportion of the mind – the conscious – is visible above the water line, while the rest is hidden beneath. Moreover, the conscious and unconscious constantly battle each other, while the preconscious attempts to mediate between the two.

Psychoanalysis became the dominant mode of treatment in psychiatry for much of the first half of the 20th century, but in the second half it lost ground to the rival school of biological psychiatry. The development of an array of apparently highly effective antipsychotic drugs and antidepressants saw a move towards pharmacological treatments at the expense of psychotherapy (which by its nature struggles to provide empirical proof of its success). The widespread use since the 1970s of neuroimaging – scans that provide detailed images of the neurological system – has further bolstered the cause of biological psychiatry, so that today psychiatry remains firmly split between the two approaches. Others, meanwhile, remain sceptical of psychiatry in its totality, arguing that we remain far from a true, broad-ranging understanding of how the human mind works. In the words of G. K. Chesterton, writing for the *Observer* in 1934: 'It seems a pity that psychology has destroyed all our knowledge of human nature.'

The unconscious desire

Freud argued that the unconscious is primarily driven by the libido (i.e. sexual desires and instincts). As we grow older, his theory went, we repress our unconscious thoughts because they run contrary to the interests of the conscious mind and are incompatible with social norms. However, the unconscious continues to manifest itself in a number of ways – for example, in our dreams, in slips of the tongue (Freudian slips), jokes and also in nervous conditions.

It is the interrelationship between these aspects of the mind, Freud said, that induces in us feelings such as anxiety, guilt and inadequacy, which we strive to deal with by employing strategies including denial, displacement and repression. It is by mining the unconscious, he believed, that we may discover and address the causes of our anxieties and neuroses – a process that we know today as psychoanalysis.

BEHAVIOURISM

Behaviourism is the theory that human and animal behaviour is conditioned – that is to say, learned from the environment. This contrasts with the idea that behaviour is fundamentally innate or inherited. Behaviourists say that we are born with a *tabula rasa* (a 'blank slate' mind) and it is environmental conditioning that moulds our behaviour and ways of thinking. By altering patterns of destructive behaviour, the theory goes, it thus becomes possible to address psychological disorders.

The behaviourist movement is generally considered to have begun in 1913 when the American psychologist John Watson published an influential paper entitled 'Psychology as the Behaviourist Views It'. Among his many startling ideas was the notion that animals and humans essentially behave in the same way and so research may be carried out as effectively on animals as on humans. By measuring observable behaviour only, he suggested, the behaviourist may more accurately assess the effectiveness of a particular mode of treatment.

A major influence on Watson's theories was the Russian physiologist, Ivan Pavlov, who at the end of the 19th century had documented the famous case of his dogs. While carrying out experimentations into the role of saliva in a dog's digestive processes, he noted that his dogs would salivate not only at the appearance of meat but also at the mere sound of a bell they had been conditioned to associate with the appearance of meat (even when the meat itself was absent). The dogs had been conditioned to respond to an entirely neutral stimulus.

Watson's brand of behaviourism became known as methodological behaviourism, while B. F. Skinner (1904–90) evolved the alternative school of radical behaviourism. Although he agreed with Watson's central tenet that the psychologist should look to predict and control behaviour,

The Little Albert experiment

Intent on proving that a similar response to that of Pavlov's dogs could be induced in humans, Watson and his graduate student, Rosalie Rayner, undertook a notorious experiment, the results of which were reported in 1920. In what became known as the 'Little Albert' experiment, the scientists conditioned a nine-month-old child to develop a fear of a white rat (and assorted other furry creatures that initially induced no sign of fear in the boy) by striking a steel bar with a hammer behind him as he played with the animals. The boy's fear of the loud noise conditioned him into a corresponding fear of the rat, which was merely another neutral stimulus.

Skinner believed that we are born with some innate behaviours too. He also considered that the internal thought processes of an individual might be explained in the analysis of behaviour, if not used as an explanation of the behaviour itself. Behaviourism has proved an enduring if controversial idea, and continues to find practical applications today. Perhaps the most famous is cognitive behavioural therapy, in which negative patterns of thought are challenged in order to alter unwanted behavioural patterns or treat mood disorders such as depression and anxiety.

DNA

DNA – deoxyribonucleic acid – is a molecule that carries genetic information within living organisms. It effectively instructs cells within an organism as to what they should do. For example, the human body comprises some 210 variant types of cells – such as blood cells and brain cells – each of which 'reads' the genetic code within DNA to determine their development and purpose.

When nuclein became DNA

Interest in genetics began seriously with the work of the Czech friar Gregor Mendel in the mid-19th century. He spent years experimenting on pea plants, exploring the inheritance of particular traits such as height and colour. He established that certain traits are *recessive* and others *dominant*, which we now know to be the result of genetic factors. However, it was Swiss physician Friedrich Miescher, in 1869, who first isolated DNA, although he called it *nuclein*. And it was not until the 1920s that its role in passing on genetic information started to be understood, thanks principally to the work of Nikolai Koltsov, Frederick Griffith, Phoebus Levene and, later, Oswald Avery.

In 1952 Alfred Hershey and Martha Chase conclusively proved the role of DNA in heredity. Around the same time, Rosalind Franklin, Raymond Gosling, James Watson, Francis Crick and Maurice Wilkins combined to confirm its distinctive spiral-like double-helix structure. DNA is made up of four chemical bases (adenine, guanine, cytosine and thymine), which pair up and join with a sugar molecule and a phosphate molecule to form nucleotide, which in turn are arranged in two long strands that forge the double helix.

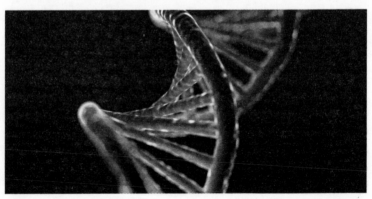

DNA

Humans share about 99.9 per cent of DNA in common, and indeed even the variation between different species is relatively low (we have about 98 per cent in common with chimpanzees and even 36 per cent with a fruit fly). Yet understanding DNA and exploring genetic variation has opened up myriad new avenues of investigation.

There have been plenty of landmarks in genetic research in the years since. In 1985 Sir Alec Jeffreys invented genetic fingerprinting, which was first used to gain a criminal conviction three years later. The first laboratory-modified plant was produced in 1983, with the first genetically modified food going on commercial sale in 1994. Then, in 2003, the international collaborative effort to map the human genome (the Human Genome Project) was declared complete after thirteen years and the sequencing of all three billion base pairs in the human genome. Nonetheless, much work remains to be done in the field as a whole and it is reasonable to assume that the practical impacts of our increased understanding of DNA and genetic inheritance are only just beginning to be felt (see the entry on Cloning, below). The American physician and writer Lewis Thomas has described DNA as 'the greatest single achievement of nature to date' while Richard Dawkins once noted:

'DNA neither cares nor knows. DNA just is. And we dance to its music.'

CLONING

Cloning describes the process of producing genetically identical copies of a biological entity. The genetic copy is thus called a clone. A relatively new field of scientific endeavour, cloning offers up an array of potential benefits but also poses a correspondingly high number of ethical questions, especially concerning the potential for human cloning.

Artificial cloning

Artificial cloning – as opposed to naturally occurring processes of cloning as displayed, for instance, by some plants and single-celled organisms, as well as in identical twins – is typically divided into three main branches:

- Gene cloning, which reproduces specific genes or segments of DNA.

- Reproductive cloning, which produces animals that are perfect copies of their antecedents.

- Therapeutic cloning, which creates embryonic stem cells, usually with the aim of producing living tissues that can replace diseased or injured tissues.

Gene research is generally considered the least controversial strand, typically involving isolating and inserting a specific gene into a third-party carrier (a vector) – for instance, bacteria or viruses – where it is then encouraged to grow. The resulting cloned genes can then be used for research and experimentation.

Reproductive cloning, by contrast, creates a whole new, distinct life form by removing mature, somatic cells (cells from the body such as skin cells) from the animal to be cloned, extracting DNA from it and inserting it into an egg cell that has had its nucleus (in which its own DNA resides) removed. After an initial period of development in the laboratory, the egg is then implanted into an adult female who will birth the clone. For now, there has been no proven instance of successful human cloning.

Animal cloning has both potential medical and agricultural implications. For example, animals may be genetically modified to produce particular proteins for use in medical treatments, or may be used in medical experimentation (freeing researchers of having to process the impact of countless 'variables' inherent in non-cloned subjects). Agriculturally, it becomes possible to breed animals with, for example, high milk yields or particularly good meat – although as yet the costs ensure that cloned animal products in the local supermarket remain some way off.

In therapeutic cloning, an embryo is cloned for the single intention of harvesting stem cells – a simple cell that may develop into any one of various kinds of other cells – for the purpose of medical experimentation and, in theory, the production of replacement tissues. Whereas reproductive cloning raises ethical questions by creating entities that exactly physiologically mimic a naturally occurring life – with attendant implications for issues of identity, autonomy, dignity, and social and religious custom – therapeutic cloning challenges us because it demands the destruction of embryos in their earliest stages of development. Not to mention the potential dangers of passing on 'faulty' or unfavourable genes through the generations.

Such moral quandaries remain essentially unanswered despite rapid technological progress and the needle of our collective moral compass continues to spin in uncertain directions.

EUTHANASIA

Euthanasia – the act of painlessly assisting the death, or else enabling the death by withholding treatment, of a patient suffering from an incurable condition – is one of the most emotive and controversial ideas in medicine. To its supporters, euthanasia is a synonym for 'mercy killing', while others claim it breaches a basic tenet of the Hippocratic Oath – 'to do no harm'.

The 'good death'

In truth, euthanasia has been practised throughout history and the word *euthanasia* is derived from the Greek for 'good death'. In ancient India, there is evidence that some incurable patients were drowned in the sacred River Ganges, while in ancient Israel incense was used to hasten death. Plato even wrote: 'Mentally and physically ill persons should be left to death; they do not have the right to live.' However, Hippocrates responded with his assertion that physicians should 'not administer poison to anyone when asked to do so, nor suggest such a course.' Many societies have actively legislated against the practice, even as they might turn a blind eye to it under certain circumstances.

In *Utopia* (1516), Thomas More gave an apparent defence of euthanasia, writing : 'if a disease is not only distressing but also agonising without cessation, then the priests and public officials exhort this man . . . to free himself from this bitter life . . . or else to permit others to free him . . .' Francis Bacon (1561–1621) then wrote that doctors 'ought to acquire the skill and bestow the attention whereby the dying may pass more easily and quietly out of life.' Yet since he also identified one of the chief duties of a physician as prolonging life, he is often understood to have been prefiguring modern ideas of palliative care (i.e. care of the terminally ill) rather than active euthanasia.

Come the 19th century, and in 1870 an English schoolteacher, Samuel Williams, wrote a landmark essay outlining the case for active euthanasia by medical professionals, and in the 1890s Friedrich Nietzsche added his thoughts:

> *To die proudly when it is no longer possible to live proudly. Death freely chosen, death at the right time, brightly and cheerfully accomplished amid children and witnesses: then a real farewell is still possible, as the one who is taking leave is still there; also a*

real estimate of what one has wished, drawing the sum of one's
life – all in opposition to the wretched and revolting comedy that
Christianity has made of the hour of death.

In 1920, things took a darker turn when two German professors, Alfred Hoche and Karl Binding, published *Permitting the Destruction of Worthless Animals*, in which they argued for the killing of those with lives deemed 'devoid of value' and considered a taint on the gene pool. It would become a founding text for Third Reich advocates of mass involuntary euthanasia, which ultimately resulted in the murders and sterilizations of countless patients condemned as 'useless and unrehabilitative'. Nonetheless, the international movement for voluntary euthanasia continued to gain momentum and in 1942 the Swiss authorities permitted assisted suicide. To qualify, a patient must be rationally capable of choosing to die and must be able to take the final act – typically, drinking a lethal dose of barbiturates – unaided and in the presence of a nurse or physician and two other people.

Today, voluntary euthanasia is legal in Belgium, Canada, Colombia, Luxembourg and the Netherlands, while assisted suicide is allowed in Switzerland and certain US states as well. Indeed, Switzerland is now the favoured destination for many people from around the world who want an assisted death, giving rise to the phenomenon of 'suicide tourism'.

TRANSHUMAN MEDICINE

Transhumanism (sometimes known as posthumanism) is at the cutting edge of medicine. It speculatively investigates how technology may be used to create people who exhibit, in the words of Swedish philosopher Nick Bostrum, 'a general central capacity greatly exceeding the maximum attainable by any current human being.'

It is an area that raises myriad serious ethical questions. For example, what are the implications of using methods of genetic manipulation to maintain high levels of physical and cognitive functioning far beyond what we now consider normal lifespans? Such manipulation raises the prospect that future generations may be able to pre-design their children, heralding an age of engineered humans that once seemed merely the product of science fiction. Or what of developing cooling processes so that individuals may be kept alive even as their heart ceases to work, existing in a state of suspended animation for hitherto impossible periods of time? On the one hand, this might allow a surgeon longer to complete complicated heart surgery, while on the other hand it could see humans kept in 'deep freeze' to be brought back to life at a much later date.

Transhumanist thinking is often traced back to the work in the 1920s of J. B. S. Haldane, a British-born geneticist and evolutionary biologist. He was convinced that the great scientific developments that he predicted would extend life and improve our mental and physical capacities were destined to be greeted initially with horror by the population at large. However, it was British evolutionary biologist Julian Huxley who, in the 1950s, introduced the term 'transhumanism' to the wider world. 'Up till now,' he wrote,

> *human life has generally been, as Hobbes described it, 'nasty, brutish and short'; the great majority of human beings (if they have not already died young) have been afflicted with misery . . . we can justifiably hold the belief that . . . The human species can, if it wishes, transcend itself – not just sporadically, an individual here in one way, an individual there in another way, but in its entirety, as humanity.*

Huxley's ideas have been championed in recent years by thinkers including Britain's Max More, the German metahumanist Stefan Lorenz

Sorgner, Sweden's Nick Bostrom and British philosopher David Pearce. The latter two co-founded the World Transhumanist Association (later renamed as Humanity+) in 1998 and subsequently defined transhumanism thus: 'The intellectual and cultural movement that affirms the possibility and desirability of fundamentally improving the human condition through applied reason, especially by developing and making widely available technologies to eliminate aging and to greatly enhance human intellectual, phys-ical, and psychological capacities.'

While that might sound highly desirable (the science writer Ronald Bailey has called transhumanism the 'movement that epitomizes the most daring, courageous, imaginative and idealistic aspirations of humanity'), others harbour grave doubts. Among them is political philosopher Francis Fukuyama, who in 2004 nominated transhumanism as one of the 'world's most dangerous ideas'. 'If we start transforming ourselves into something superior,' he said, 'what rights will these enhanced creatures claim, and what rights will they possess when compared to those left behind?'

PART FIVE

PHILOSOPHY

'Philosophy, being nothing but the study of wisdom and truth . . .'

George Berkeley

The word *philosophy* derives from the ancient Greek for 'love of wisdom' and describes humanity's eternal quest to uncover knowledge – about ourselves and the world around us. It is an extraordinarily broad-ranging discipline, encompassing everything from the nature of reality and knowledge to how we ought to behave and what sort of government works best. Nonetheless, William James felt able to reduce it to fairly simple terms, describing it as 'our more or less dumb sense of what life honestly and deeply means. It is only partly got from books; it is our individual way of just seeing and feeling the total push and pressure of the cosmos . . .' Even as philosophy fails to answer all of our questions, we grow by knowing that which we do know and recognizing that which we don't. In the words of Ludwig Wittgenstein: 'Philosophy is like trying to open a safe with a combination lock: each little adjustment of the dials seems to achieve nothing, only when everything is in place does the door open.'

PRE-SOCRATIC PHILOSOPHY

The Pre-Socratic Greek philosophers – literally, those who pre-date Socrates – embraced a disparate range of thought and are mostly known to us only through the recollections of later philosophers. Nonetheless, they were key figures in establishing the discipline of philosophy by seeking rational explanations for how and why the world is as it is, rather than relying on religious or mythological narratives.

Thales of Miletus (c. 624–546 BCE) is often cited as being the first philosopher because he sought naturalistic explanations for the phenomena he witnessed. Where events in the natural world were considered the result of supernatural forces, he instead sought to understand them through a process of observation and reasoning. His most significant contribution was connected to the theory of monism: the idea that the universe is made from a single basic material. Seeking this 'source of all things' (or *arche*), he concluded that the fundamental building block of the cosmos must be variously capable of change and motion as well as able to support life. Water, he came to believe, was the mysterious 'source of all things'. While we know this to be incorrect, it nonetheless stands as the first known attempt to decipher the world through reason and not revelation.

Thales's influence was formidable. His pupil, Anaximander, continued his proto-scientific legacy (along with his friend Anaximenes) and also taught Pythagoras, another of the great Pre-Socratics who (see page 46) sought order in mathematics. Heraclitus, meanwhile, developed his theory of the *Logos* – an objective, universal cosmic law – and

Atomism

Other notable figures in the Pre-Socratic tradition included Anaxagoras, Empedocles, Gorgias, Parmenides of Elea, Protagoras, Zeno of Elea, and Democritus, who formulated the theory of atomism. It is through the actions of the atoms and changes in the void that all phenomena – from thoughts and ideas to natural disasters – may be explained. While many of their ideas may seem naïve and overly simplistic now, they were responsible for making vast strides forward in the history of human thought. By seeking answers that fitted with the available evidence and eschewing explanations reliant on supernatural causes, they paved the wave for the golden age of ancient philosophy that began with the emergence of Socrates.

contended, in opposition to most of his contemporaries who believed in a fundamentally unchanging cosmos, that the universe was in perpetual flux.

THE SOCRATIC METHOD

Unlike the Pre-Socratic philosophers, Socrates (470–399 BCE) focused less on explaining the nature of the cosmos and more on investigating morality and ethics (see page 131). His ideas helped establish ancient Athens as the cradle of Western civilization and his influence on the development of human thinking is incalculable. In particular, his method of intellectual investigation changed the path of philosophical thought.

Virtually single-handedly, Socrates shifted the axis of philosophy, so that it was no longer dominated by an abstract 'looking out' at the cosmos. Instead, its gaze was redirected towards the nature and conduct of individuals and society as a whole. Confronting such fundamental questions as what constitutes good and evil and what is justice, he shone a light into dark corners. Suddenly, philosophy was the stuff of public debate, with the conduct of individuals placed under unprecedented scrutiny. It was, as may be imagined, a sometimes uncomfortable environment in which to be operating.

Alas, none of Socrates' personal writings remain, so our knowledge of him derives solely from the accounts of others (most notably those of his student, Plato, who depicted his master in imaginary conversations in works such as *Republic*). From these, we may draw certain conclusions about Socrates's various philosophical positions. We know, for example, that he considered self-knowledge to be vital to the health of the soul. He called knowledge 'the most valuable of possessions', since it guides the individual to live a virtuous life, which he considered the ultimate goal of existence.

The dialectic method

Arguably Socrates' greatest contribution to philosophy was his development of what we now call the Socratic (or dialectic) method – a revolutionary form of inductive argument. Socrates compared his role in the birthing of ideas to his mother's profession of midwifery. The dialectic approach demands that a topic, idea or argument is subjected to probing questioning, during which the precise terms of reference of any given philosophical position are tested to breaking point. Should an idea fall down, it must either be discarded or else reviewed and revised. Via this process of robust cross-examination, those involved in the dialectic use the answers reached to further their base of knowledge. If this sounds like it has much in common with the Scientific Method (see page 61), it does.

Socrates was a master of the method. When the oracle at Delphi famously proclaimed him as the wisest person alive, he set about disproving the assertion by entering into debate with other prominent 'wise people' to show himself less wise than them. However, time after time he exposed their philosophies as flawed. Furthermore, he asserted his own wisdom by recognizing its limits. As Plato quotes him in *Apology*: 'What I do not know, I do not think I know.'

SCEPTICISM

Scepticism in philosophical terms says that we cannot have complete certainty in human knowledge and so should refrain from claiming to make statements of truth. In more general terms, scepticism has become synonymous with a questioning attitude and a refusal to accept that which is presented to us as fact.

The Greek philosopher Pyrrho of Elis (360–270 BCE) is often identified as the original sceptic. Struggling to distinguish the 'truth' from the many versions proffered by disparate philosophical schools, he came to his inner peace by accepting that this was because none of them had logically proven their version as correct. Pyrrho thus became associated with the rejection of received wisdom and dogma, but his position was not merely negative. The Sceptic school that he founded remained committed to searching for truth that could be justified on a rational basis.

Pyrrho followed in a tradition arguably founded by Socrates, whose method of intellectual enquiry demanded the questioning of those who claimed knowledge.

The five major grounds for doubt

In the 1st century CE, Agrippa the Sceptic established the five major grounds for doubt:

- Dissent – uncertainty as shown by differences of opinion.

- Progress *ad infinitum* – proofs rooted in statements themselves in need of proof, and so on and on.

- Relation – an apparent proof may change as its relations change or it is viewed from a different perspective.

- Assumption – a statement of truth based on unsupported assumptions.

- Circularity – a statement of truth involving circular reasoning, so that the proof is dependent on the original statement.

By the 17th and 18th centuries, many of the Enlightenment's leading figures – for example, France's René Descartes and Blaise Pascal, England's Francis Bacon and Scotland's David Hume – started off from a position of scepticism. Indeed, the single best-known statement of the age, Descartes' assertion that 'I think, therefore I am', is an implicit rejection of all other knowledge. In fact, the French literary critic Antoine Léonard Thomas famously revised Descartes' words to 'I doubt, therefore I think, therefore I am.' Scepticism is today regarded as a necessary and admirable attribute for anyone undertaking serious intellectual investigation.

MATERIALISM

Materialist philosophy is predicated on the idea that only matter truly exists and that all phenomena result from the interactions of matter. To the materialist, concepts such as the soul and consciousness thus have no role in defining reality. As such, materialism is a monist philosophy (believing that everything is comprised of matter alone) and stands in contrast to idealism (see next entry).

Although he post-dated the earliest materialist traditions (which existed in India from around the 6th century BCE, and in Greece where it was variously propounded by, among others, Thales, Democritus and Epicurus), the great Roman thinker Lucretius wrote the first widely known treatise on materialism around 50 BCE. In *De rerum natura* (*On the Nature of Things*), he explicated the idea of atomism (see page 123).

For a great many centuries, the idea of materialism fell out of favour across much of the world, with the rise of the Abrahamic religions fuelling belief that there exists an immaterial world separate from the material one. However, the onset of the Enlightenment revived interest in the concept. René Descartes famously investigated the mind–body problem (see entry on Rationalism), with his resulting philosophy of Cartesian dualism arguing that the mind and the body are two different entities. This was in opposition to the ideas of Thomas Hobbes, who had suggested all human experience derives from mechanical processes within the material body.

While Cartesian dualism allowed for the existence of a soul (and thus could be accommodated within the traditions of Christian teaching), another Frenchman, Baron d'Holbach (1723–89), took a radical atheistic, materialist line, claiming that everything that happens is the result of matter and its motion. In his masterpiece, *The System of Nature* (1770), he wrote:

*Man's life is a line that nature commands him to describe upon
the surface of the earth, without his ever being able to swerve from
it, even for an instant . . . he is unceasingly modified by causes,
whether visible or concealed, over which he has no control, which
necessarily regulate his mode of existence, give the hue to his way
of thinking, and determine his manner of acting. He is good or
bad, happy or miserable, wise or foolish, reasonable or irrational,
without his will being for any thing in these various states.*

The German physician Ludwig Büchner (1824–99), meanwhile, wrote
Kraft und Stoff: Empirisch-naturphilosophische Studien (*Force and Matter:
Empiricophilosophical Studies*) in which he argued the materialist case from
a purely scientific perspective. Indeed, the broad scientific developments
of the 19th and 20th centuries – such as evolution, neuroscience and
atomic theory – generally bolstered the materialist position, while the
role of the spirit and theology gradually lost leverage among much of the
scientific community.

IDEALISM

**Idealism is the philosophical position that says reality only exists
within the context of ideas and thoughts. In other words, reality is a
mental entity, not a physical one, and there is no reality external to
consciousness and thought. Idealism contrasts with materialism (see
page 127) and realism (which says that reality exists independently of
our capacity to conceptualize it).**

Plato was the first major figure of idealism. He argued that the 'real'
world consists of idealized Forms separate from our own material
world. It is sometimes said that he was not a true idealist because
he acknowledged a material world of sorts, or else he is labelled a

Immaterialist idealism

In the 17th century, René Descartes toed an idealist line of sorts by concluding that we cannot be sure of the existence of anything other than our own selves, whose existence is evidenced by the very act of thinking (see Rationalism on page 149). Then, in the 18th century, the Irish philosopher and bishop, George Berkeley, devised the theory of 'immaterialist idealism' or 'subjective idealism' – perhaps the most complete doctrine of idealism hitherto described. Rejecting the existence of material substance, he insisted that an object only exists to the extent that it perceives or is perceived – existence, in other words, is reliant upon conceptualization. However, he allowed for the existence of apparently unperceived objects by accepting God's perception as universal and eternal. So, for example, a tree may fall down in the middle of a forest even if there is no human to see or hear it because God observes it.

realist (since his Forms exist to some extent independently of being conceptualized). However, others insist he is a pure idealist because his basic contention is that 'true reality' exists only in the realm of thought. He theorized that prior to our earthly existence, we inhabit a world of Forms and bring the memory of these ideal Forms into our earthly souls. Thus, for instance, we recognize that a dog is a dog because we are born imbued with the concept of the ideal dog in our minds. Whether sheepdog, greyhound or bull terrier, we recognize each as variants of the ideal dog. And as for dog, so for anything else you can think of: cars, flowers, colours, biscuits – even concepts such as justice and virtue. Our material realm, Plato said, consists only of 'shadows' of the ideal forms of 'true reality'.

German idealism

In the 17th century, Immanuel Kant spearheaded the influential school of German Idealism. He considered philosophy had so far failed in one of its chief goals: to determine once and for all whether there is an external world entirely distinct from ourselves. In his *Critique of Pure Reason*, he said that the mind is a blank slate, on to which we inscribe knowledge acquired by observation of the external world. Then, he suggested, the mind is pre-arranged to allow us to organize, structure and make sense of experiences. As our mind moulds our perceptions of reality, we may only know things as they seem to us (what he called *phenomena*) but cannot grasp a 'thing-in-itself' (something as it is in its true nature external to our minds – what he called *nuomena*). He went on to describe how the human mind is pre-programmed with concepts such as space and time, causality and substance, to assist us in experiencing life in a meaningful way. Kant thus believed that we should be content with the reality of our perceptions, and give up on the vain goal of comprehending an external reality beyond the reach of our intellectual faculties. By accepting our limitations, he said, our minds may be set free – a philosophy sometimes described as transcendental idealism.

Another important strand of idealism was the so-called absolute idealism championed by G. W. F. Hegel in Enlightenment-era Germany. His sometimes-elusive philosophy teaches that there exists an all-inclusive unity, comprising all events, phenomena and ideas, in what he characterized as the Absolute Spirit (a sort of universal mind and soul) that is revealed to us through the process of history. It is an ideology that influenced, among others, Karl Marx and Friedrich Nietzsche. Indeed, idealism in its various guises has informed the thinking of many of the world's foremost philosophers and forces us to confront the deepest questions of what we are and what we mean by reality and the 'real world'.

ETHICS

Ethics is a major branch of thought concerned with what is good and bad, what is right and wrong, and what constitutes a life well lived. Ethics demands we explore what we ought and ought not to think and do, outside the realm of formal legislation. As Immanuel Kant put it: 'In law a man is guilty when he violates the rights of others. In ethics he is guilty if he only thinks of doing so.'

The ethical triangle

Though it is often used interchangeably with 'morality', ethics is arguably the more broad-ranging concept. It can be useful to think of it as comprising three distinct areas:

- Normative ethics: what is right and wrong, good and bad? What criteria do we use to reach a decision?

- Applied ethics: looking at specific, often complex, ethical problems. For instance, war, abortion, animal rights, and crime and punishment.

- Meta-ethics: what is ethical judgement? How do we evolve and discourse on ethical principles?

While there are general 'ethical truths' to which most of us adhere – for example, that it is wrong to kill another person for personal gain – the full ethical profile of any two individuals is likely to differ starkly, having been formed by a multitude of influences, including religious belief, philosophical contemplation and cultural traditions. That is why, for instance, some of us are vegans and others joyous carnivores, why some of us will do whatever we can to reduce our tax bills while others unquestioningly pay them, why some of us believe a freed convict has paid his dues while others wish the key had been thrown away, and why one man's terrorist is another's freedom fighter.

Socrates is often considered the founding father of the Western tradition of ethical philosophy. His basic contention was that the wise, self-aware individual will be naturally driven to behave in a good and right way, as that is the means by which happiness is achieved. Contrastingly, he believed, 'wrong' behaviour directly stems from ignorance. 'There is only one good, knowledge,' he claimed, 'and one evil, ignorance.'

Modern ethics continues to accommodate a range of contrasting positions. One may, for instance, take a consequentialist approach, whereby the morality of an action is judged upon its result. Alternatively, deontology suggests we should focus not on outcomes but on the inherent rightness of an action, often considered in relation to our duties and obligations. Virtue ethics, on the other hand, looks more at the all-round character of a person and their adoption of virtuous activity over a lifetime, rather than at specific actions in isolation. Indeed, Aristotle may be said to have favoured a virtue ethics approach. We must then consider whether or not there are objective moral values or in fact all moral decisions are subjective.

As well as having profound implications for our personal conduct, the philosophy of ethics moulds how our society operates, in areas as disparate as medicine, law, business and the media.

DETERMINISM AND FATALISM

Determinism is a philosophical viewpoint that stands in opposition to the idea of free will. It holds that everything happens as the result of a chain of prior events through a system of cause and effect (see Causality on page 63). It is closely related to the idea of fatalism, which says that humans are best served by accepting that they have no influence over what happens now or in the future. Nonetheless, some determinist positions allow for limited human agency. In contrast, the doctrine of free will suggests that we, as rational agents, have the freedom to pick specific courses of action that materially determine what will happen in due course.

Religion and science have been variously cited as providing evidence of the deterministic nature of the world. Theological concepts such as predestination and cosmic cycles of reincarnation have been interpreted as eliminating independence of human action. Meanwhile, others have interpreted many of the big scientific ideas – from the atomism of Democritus to the laws of Newtonian movement and, more recently, the Big Bang theory – as evidence of the futility of thinking that our personal decisions can meaningfully alter what happens within the 'big picture'. A number of classical philosophers, including Aristotle, explored determinism/fatalism in variants of the 'Idle Argument'. In the 3rd century CE Origen termed it thus:

If it is fated that you will recover from this illness, then, regardless of whether or not you consult a doctor you will recover. But if it is fated that you won't recover, then, regardless of whether or not you consult a doctor you won't recover. But either it is fated that you will recover from this illness or it is fated that you won't recover. Therefore it is futile to consult a doctor.

Free will and freedom

Certainly, the notion of free will has been key to the development of many of the social structures upon which our lives and societies are built. René Descartes described the human will as 'by its nature so free that it can never be constrained'.

There would be no democracy without free will, nor any reason to take care of our health, to work hard or to save money. Indeed, without it, there can be no justification for doing anything. In the words of Stephen Hawking:

> *I have noticed that even people who claim everything is predetermined and that we can do nothing to change it, look before they cross the road . . . One cannot base one's conduct on the idea that everything is determined, because one does not know what has been determined. Instead, one has to adopt the effective theory that one has free will and that one is responsible for one's actions.*

ARISTOTELIANISM

Aristotelianism is the school of philosophy based on the wideranging teachings of Aristotle (384–322 BCE). He is credited as the first to lay down a complete system of philosophical thought embracing, for instance, ethics, politics, logic, science, aesthetics, metaphysics (concerned with the nature of reality) and epistemology (which looks at the nature of knowledge).

Aristotle was a pupil of Plato and though he respected and was identified with his master, Aristotle was not afraid to disagree with him. In doing so, he created a philosophical overview that is widely considered to have more relevance to the everyday than the often-abstract ideas of his teacher.

Significantly, he contradicted Plato's theory of Forms (see Idealism, above). Aristotle argued that instead of knowledge stemming from our innate recognition of the ideal forms of things, observation leads us to knowledge (which he conceived of in terms of universal truths). For instance, we do not comprehend a dog because it is an imperfect version of the idealized dog form, but because the dog possesses an essential 'dogginess', which our senses and the accumulated evidence of our experience allow us to recognize. Unlike Plato, he thought that all things are characterized by the unity of matter (that which is observable and measurable) and form (that which cannot be observed, such as know-ledge, virtue and the soul), which together create an 'essence'. His belief in the value of observation and experience marks him out as an early advocate of scientific thought.

Teleology and the golden mean

In terms of metaphysics and epistemology, the Platonic idea of teleology considers that all things and phenomena have an intrinsic purpose by which they may be judged. A 'good' eye, therefore, is one that sees well, a 'good' boat one that sails well and a 'good' rosebush one that blooms. Aristotle strongly argued that virtue is not something which may be acquired through study but is achieved by doing virtuous things. To this end, he championed the idea of the 'golden mean' – moral behaviour that lies in the middle between the extremes of excess and deficiency. For instance, courage is the golden mean between cowardice and rashness, and modesty the golden mean between shamelessness and bashfulness.

Aristotle made many further contributions to the development of human thought and along with Socrates and Plato, he is regarded as one of the three giants of ancient thought. His influence has extended through the ages too. Centuries after Aristotle's death, Thomas Aquinas spent much of his life attempting to reconcile Christian teachings with Aristotelian thought, and many of Aristotle's ideas have permeated into modern science and politics too.

CONFUCIANISM

Often characterized as the epitome of 'Eastern wisdom', Confucianism revolutionized Chinese civilization by promoting a code of conduct demanding correct behaviour in both the public and private spheres.

Born in the Lu state of China in 551 BCE, Confucius grew up in a period of upheaval between the relative calm of China's so-called Spring and Autumn Period and the more troubled Warring States Period. Hailing from a family of moderate wealth and prestige, he became a civil servant in the Lu court, where he honed his skills as a diplomat and developed a model of secure, moral, centralized government. However, after getting caught up in dynastic disputes, he went into voluntary exile and so saw few of his ideas come to fruition in his own lifetime. It was, instead, later generations who took his teachings to heart.

In his desire for just and fair governance, Confucius emphasized the links between personal conduct and the wider social good. He confronted Chinese tradition by disputing that power and virtue are divinely bestowed on an elite. Rather, he saw humanity as an agent of divine will, charged with carving out moral order. Virtue, he said, is not given but cultivated. He argued that everybody, regardless of their social station, could behave with virtue and benevolence and thus have a role to play in developing the social structure. He furthermore said that judgement and wisdom are more important than unthinking obedience to rules, and that those with power ought to set a moral example. By doing right, Confucius argued, we shall be treated rightly in return, and thus society becomes intrinsically fairer. In the words of his Golden Rule: 'Do not do to others what you would not have done to yourself.'

Most fundamental of all to Confucianism is the concept of sincerity, of which he said it is 'the end and beginning of things; without sincerity there would be nothing.' *The Doctrine of the Mean*, a key text of Confucianism probably written by his grandson, put it like this:

Sincerity is the way of Heaven. The attainment of sincerity is the way of men. He who possesses sincerity is he who, without an effort, hits what is right, and apprehends, without the exercise of thought; he is the sage who naturally and easily embodies the right way. He who attains to sincerity is he who chooses what is good, and firmly holds it fast.

LOGIC

Logic is the study of the principles of reasoning and the formal validity of argument. A logical argument is one in which a conclusion is drawn from premises (accepted or assumed propositions), so that to accept the premises but deny the conclusion is inconsistent and without merit. A logical argument, however, need not necessarily result in a 'correct' conclusion, merely an internally consistent one.

Aristotle is generally credited with creating the first formal logic system when he devised a method of deductive reasoning known as a syllogism. Within this scheme, a conclusion is inferred from two accepted premises – a major premise (the predicate of the conclusion) and a minor premise (the subject of the conclusion). For instance: all fish

A	B	A and B	A or B	Not A
False	False	False	False	True
False	True	False	True	True
True	False	False	True	False
True	True	True	True	False

The Boolean Table

have gills. A salmon has gills. Therefore, a salmon must be a fish. This is an example of deductive logic, but the conclusion is not always factually correct. Consider the following: All birds have wings. An aeroplane has wings. An aeroplane is a bird. It is, nonetheless, a logically valid argument within the basic terms of the syllogism.

Aristotle's groundbreaking work in logic analysis, along with that of the Stoic school of philosophy, laid the foundations of logic through to the 19th century. Nonetheless, there were some notable developments in between. For instance, modal logic was developed with a view to incorporating propositions of contingency, necessity and possibility into a logic framework, while Avicenna constructed a rival system of logic in the medieval Islamic world. A number of Christian scholars, meanwhile, attempted to reconcile scriptural teachings with logical argument. Yet Aristotle remained the unrivalled giant of logic until the 19th century when an Englishman, George Boole, introduced the idea of symbolic logic – a system using symbols to replace certain terms and propositions within a logical argument. Its near-relation, mathematical logic, followed fast behind. It is mathematical logic that underpins computer science and the technological revolution of the late 20th and early 21st centuries – evidence that logic is not merely an abstract intellectual plaything but a system of thought with deep practical applications.

HEDONISM

Hedonism – from the Greek for *pleasure* or *delight* – is the appealing ideology that the highest and correct aim of human existence is the pursuit of pleasure and the satisfaction of our desires. It is often lumped together with Epicureanism (see next entry), although they are profoundly different in outlook despite some overlap. Hedonism is considered a highly individualistic philosophy.

At the heart of hedonist philosophy is the notion that pleasure is the 'good' of life and pain the 'bad'. Therefore, it is not merely pleasant but a duty and a psychological imperative to seek the maximum overall level of pleasure (in effect, our net pleasure minus net pain). The Cyrenaics – followers of the teaching of Aristippus of Cyrene in 4th-century-BCE Greece – probably constituted the earliest Hedonist school. Partly in response to Socratic teachings (Aristippius was a pupil of Socrates), the Cyrenaics held that pleasure is an outcome of moral action. Moreover, Aristippus said that the pleasures of the flesh are superior to those of the mind, and that immediate gratification should not be denied with a view to longer-term gain.

Hedonism, happiness and sin

Hedonism largely fell out of favour with the rise of Christian teachings and their emphasis on charity and the avoidance of sin. However, Humanist thinkers (see page 142) like Desiderius Erasmus and Sir Thomas More created space for the notion that the pursuance of pleasure conforms to God's wish for humans to be happy. Hedonism also fed into other, more modern schools of philosophical thought – among them utilitarianism (see page 153), libertarianism and aestheticism (see page 255). Meanwhile, most modern forms of hedonism – such as that espoused by the Hedonist International group – link the pursuit of pleasure with ideas of equality and self-determination.

While hedonism has often historically been condemned as selfish and immoral, Oscar Wilde gave it this spirited defence in *The Picture of Dorian Gray*, published in 1890:

> *...it appeared to Dorian Gray that the true nature of the senses had never been understood, and that they had remained savage and animal merely because the world had sought to starve them into submission or to kill them by pain, instead of aiming at making them elements of a new spirituality ...*

EPICUREANISM

Epicureanism – based on the teachings of the Greek philosopher Epicurus (341–270 BCE) – holds that happiness and peace of mind result from the attainment of pleasure and the avoidance of pain and fear. Epicurus took peace of mind as the ultimate indicator of a life lived virtuously, and drew a direct correlation between pleasure

and good on the one hand, and pain and evil on the other. Epicurus did not advocate the unyielding pursuit of pleasures of the senses. Rather, he recommended seeking pleasure through knowledge, temperance, self-sufficiency and friendship. Not for Epicurus a life of unadulterated sensual thrill-seeking, but something more akin to a Buddhist-like search for tranquillity.

He set up a school in Athens, the Garden, to help disseminate his ideas, at the gate of which hung a sign reading 'Stranger, here you will do well to tarry; here our highest good is pleasure.' Nonetheless, those who joined the commune were expected to follow an ascetic lifestyle. Moreover, followers were urged to free themselves of the fear of death, with Epicurus teaching that happiness is most easily found in an existence of quiet seclusion. He also contended that pleasure is maximized when it is achieved without doing harm to others: 'He who has peace of mind disturbs neither himself nor another.'

Shortly before his death, Epicurus wrote that it was 'a happy day to me, which is also the last day of my life.' Not believing in an afterlife but instead holding the atomist view that the body merely dissolves away, death held no threat of physical, conscious sensation for him, nor fear of what might come next. It was but the final step along the road of pleasure seeking – a journey he summed up thus: *'Non fui, fui, non sum, non curo'* – I was not; I was; I am not; I do not care. Care or not, his ideas nonetheless endured – the US Declaration of Independence, for example, echoed his sentiments in its advocating the 'pursuit of happiness' as a basic human right.

HUMANISM

Humanism is a broad philosophical standpoint that credits humanity with possessing the potential to address its problems through the compassionate application of reason, without recourse to any supernatural entity. Most strands of humanism believe that progress (see page 145) is attainable without outside agency and that humans are capable of making sound moral judgements free from the strictures of religious doctrine. Politically, humanism tends to emphasize individual rights and personal responsibilities.

'Humanism is a progressive philosophy of life that, without supernaturalism, affirms our ability and responsibility to lead ethical lives of personal fulfilment that aspire to the greater good of humanity.'

The Humanist Manifesto III

Renaissance humanism

Desiderius Erasmus (1466–1536) was a beacon of Renaissance humanism, which was intrinsically linked to the rediscovery of ancient writings (the very word is derived from an Italian term for a teacher or student of classical texts). Erasmus's masterpiece was *In Praise of Folly* (1511), which he dedicated to another leading figure of the movement, the Englishman Thomas More. Erasmus ferociously critiqued Roman Catholic dogma (although he remained committed to the faith, instead arguing for a return to the original sources of Christian teaching) and called for a simpler way of life as the route to personal happiness. Erasmus's belief that the individual in possession of free will may mould his own destiny marked him out as the prototype modern humanist, regardless of his maintenance of religious faith.

Elements of humanism can be traced to such ancient Eastern traditions as Confucianism and Buddhism. In the West, meanwhile, the edict inscribed at the Temple of Apollo at Delphi to 'Know thyself' is considered an early Western manifestation of humanist thought. A host of classical Greco-Roman thinkers, from Thales onwards, encouraged humanistic explorations of the world. However, the end of the Roman Empire and the rise of Christianity effectively curtailed humanist expression until the Renaissance period.

It was only with the onset of the Enlightenment and a decline in religious adherence that humanism became synonymous with atheism. Moreover, it was only from the 19th century that humanists began to organize into recognized groups – the British Humanist Association was founded in 1896, its American counterpart not until 1941, and then the International Humanist and Ethical Union in 1952.

THE ENLIGHTENMENT

The Enlightenment (also known as the Age of Reason) refers to a distinct period in the history of European thought that roughly correlates to the late 17th and 18th centuries. It incorporated a wealth of ideas that fundamentally reformed science, religion, politics and economics. The specific ideas of many of its leading figures are looked at in more detail elsewhere in this book – among them John Locke, David Hume and Edmund Burke, Voltaire and Jean-Jacques Rousseau, George Berkeley and Adam Smith, Isaac Newton and Immanuel Kant. Nonetheless, the Enlightenment as a whole is worthy of appraisal for the way in which it unified thinkers from disparate traditions in a commitment to principles such as reason, democracy and the rights of the individual.

The Enlightenment is so important because it marked the beginning of the modern age of thought – spreading first from Europe's traditional centres of learning across the continent as a whole and then to the world at large. Intellectually, it signified a decisive move away from superstition, and saw science supersede religion as the primary source of accepted knowledge-acquisition. In the words of Locke: 'To love truth for truth's sake is the principal part of human perfection in this world, and the seed-plot of all other virtues.' Politically, it signposted the way towards democracy and away from models of oppressive government and their attendant arbitrary application of the law. Immanuel Kant contended:

> *Enlightenment is man's release from his self-incurred tutelage. Tutelage is man's inability to make use of his understanding without direction from another.* Sapere aude! *'Have courage to use your own reason!'* – *that is the motto of enlightenment.*

The early Enlightenment was bookmarked by the appearance of such revolutionary works as Newton's *Principia* and John Locke's *Essay Concerning Human Understanding*, but it soon took on differing characteristics in different places. There were, for example, distinct 'Enlightenments' associated with England, France, Germany, Scotland, Switzerland and America.

The Enlightenment's bible

In France in the third quarter of the 18th century, Denis Diderot was instrumental in publishing the *Encyclopédie*, which may be regarded as the Enlightenment's bible. It brought together writings from many of the age's foremost minds in a bid to create a comprehensive compendium of all human knowledge. It was also key to fomenting the conditions in which the seeds of the French Revolution could bloom – an event Pankaj Mishra has said 'actualised the Enlightenment's greatest intellectual breakthrough: detaching the political from the theocratic.' Although the Age of Reason was drawing to a close, many of the foundations had been laid for the political, scientific and philosophical movements that have shaped the centuries since.

PROGRESS

In philosophical terms, the concept of progress is concerned with how advances in, for example, knowledge, technology, and social and economic organization can drive ongoing improvement in the quality of life. Since the Enlightenment period, much of our collective thought has been informed by the idea that progress will come from the application of reason in addressing problems.

Yet it was not always thus. Many cultures believed (and some continue to do so) that the fate of our species is divinely ordained and cannot be fundamentally changed by our actions – although there were always some dissenting voices. It was not until the Enlightenment that 'progress' started to become a widely accepted element of philosophical and intellectual discourse. In an increasingly secularized age, humanity came to be seen as having its fate in its own hands.

The great tenets of the Enlightenment – scientific reason, the rights of the individual, liberalism, democracy – were held up as beacons, lighting the path to a better world. As the French statesman Turgot wrote in 1750: 'the whole mass of humankind, alternating between calm and agitation, good and bad, marches constantly, though slowly, toward greater perfection'.

Such ideas were integral to the American Founding Fathers and the leaders of the French Revolution. Both insisted that 'the people' could (and should) actively determine their own fate. The 'pursuit of happiness' as an 'inalienable right' is perhaps the most famous expression of the idea of progress in history. Into the 19th century, the theory of evolution (see page 72) seemed to bolster the idea that progress is a natural state of existence, while Herbert Spencer developed the concept of social Darwinism – the now largely discredited theory that certain social groups are subject to the same laws of natural selection as species of plants and animals.

The weakling's doctrine of optimism

Some significant voices remeined doubtful that progress was inevitable, or even desirable. Thomas Malthus (see page 225) argued that progress brought with it the conditions that would lead to eventual regression, so that progress is merely a cyclical phenomenon. Nietzsche (see page 154), on the other hand, derided the idea of progress as among the 'weakling's doctrines of optimism' that stood in the way of the emergence of the Übermensch. Immanuel Kant (1724–1804), alternatively, suggested that progress was only inevitable within the context of the broad sweep of history, being a painful and slow business only moderately influenced by such Enlightenment values as reason and knowledge-acquisition.

The idea of progress has proved a potent concept. From the French Revolution to the establishment of the United States, through the revolutionary politics of Karl Marx (see page 169), the development of liberal economics, the great advances in modern medicine, the technological revolution, right up to the promises of modern politicians to make everything better, it is evident in virtually every significant area of modern life. As the professor of political and social ethics, Felix Adler, put it in 1913:

The condition of all progress is experience. We go wrong a thousand times before we find the right path. We struggle, and grope, and hurt ourselves until we learn the use of things, and this is true of things spiritual as well as of material things. Pain is unavoidable, but it acquires a new and higher meaning when we perceive that it is the price humanity must pay for an invaluable good.

OPTIMISM AND PESSIMISM

Pessimism in philosophical terms is the acceptance that the world is flawed. By extension, pessimists reject what they regard as faith-based expressions of optimism, such as religion and progress – beliefs which, the pessimist says, are likely to result in disappointment. Optimists, meanwhile, hold that the world is either as good as it can be or else is set on a path towards that end. To this extent, most philosophers must be regarded as at least partly optimistic, since the very act of philosophizing suggests a hope that one might make things better.

The best of all possible worlds

We can look to works such as Plato's *Republic* and Thomas More's *Utopia* as examples of optimistic philosophy in their desire for social perfection. However, Gottfried Wilhelm Leibniz is the classic model of the optimist philosopher, largely thanks to his assertion in *Theodicy* (1710) that we have the 'best of all possible worlds'. That was not to say that he believed the world was perfect, but merely that it is as good as God could have created and thus any alternative would be worse.

Leibniz found himself bearing the brunt of Voltaire's mockery in his satirical masterpiece, *Candide, ou l'Optimisme* (1759). 'Optimism,' asked one of the characters in *Candide*, 'what is that?' 'Alas!' replied Candide, 'it is the obstinacy of maintaining that everything is best when it is worst.' Voltaire was thus the first public figure to be labelled a pessimist, a tag he struggled to shrug off thanks to other works such as his *Poéme Sur le Désastre de Lisbonne* reflecting on the relationship between Man and God, which he wrote in the aftermath of the devastating Lisbon earthquake of 1755. Jean-Jacques Rousseau helped establish France as the capital of Enlightenment pessimism through his assertion that the establishment of 'civil society' had brought down 'crimes, wars, and murders . . . horrors and misfortunes' upon mankind. Man, he argued, had been better off left in his 'natural state'. Nonetheless, Rousseau's great faith in the redeeming powers of human nature marks him out as an optimist in other respects.

Elements of pessimism also underpinned aspects of existentialism (see page 159) and absurdism (see page 161), marking out the battle between philosophical pessimism and optimism as still unresolved. In his 1973 novel, *Time Enough for Love*, Robert A. Heinlein reflected on it thus: 'Don't ever become a pessimist . . . a pessimist is correct oftener than an optimist, but an optimist has more fun, and neither can stop the march of events.'

The aimlessness of life

The archetypal pessimist philosopher is doubtless Arthur Schopenhauer (1788–1860), who believed that humans are subject to an unthinking, aimless universal will. Blending elements of Eastern and Western philosophy, he maintained that the will of the individual and the will of the cosmos are one and the same – responsible for all experience but eternal, indivisible and directionless. So while we may hope our lives have a point, he argued, we are ultimately driven by an aimless force. Moreover, even as the will compels us to strive to achieve our goals, we are destined for disappointment since we either achieve them (granting us only brief satisfaction and denying ourselves motivation to go on) or we fail and experience dissatisfaction. Schopenhauer argued that acceptance of our lot would provide us with the space to live lives compassionately and without unnecessary angst – echoing the 'non-existence' recommended by Buddhism.

RATIONALISM

Rationalism is the philosophical outlook that reason – the power of the mind to think logically and to weigh up ideas – is the basis of true knowledge rather than supernatural force, emotional response or observation (see entry on Empiricism). While rationalism classically allows that some knowledge may be known intuitively, it is generally assumed that a rational idea is the evident result of a series of logical steps.

The concept of rationalism is evident in the teachings of Plato, notably his argument that we inherently carry 'true' ideas within our minds (see Idealism) and that these provide us with the pathway to knowledge. While many rationalist philosophers came to accept that empirical observation is a practical means of unlocking knowledge, Plato contended that we come pre-programmed with knowledge and famously illustrated his philosophy with the 'Allegory of the Cave', in which he described a group of people chained up in a cave for the entirety of their lives. They face a blank wall, their necks manacled so that they may not avert their gaze. A fire burns behind them while marionette players on a raised platform cast shadows onto the cave wall. Thus the shadows come to represent reality to the prisoners, just as we use observation of our 'shadow world' as the basis of our knowledge rather than seeking it exclusively through reason.

The Allegory of the Cave

Descartes and the wax argument

In the 17th century, René Descartes established himself as the most famous rationalist of the modern age. Among his many ideas, he set about showing how almost all apparent knowledge may be doubted, even if that doubt seems to run contrary to perceived reality. We may be being deceived by our senses, for instance, or else 'reality' may in fact be illusory, or God may be seeking to mislead us, or maybe there is no God and we are surrounded by cosmic 'untruths'. He expounded his 'Wax Argument' to make his point. Take a piece of wax, he said, and your senses reveal its particular characteristics – shape, size, smell, texture, etc. However, melt the wax with a flame and it changes fundamentally. No longer is it the same shape or size, and it smells and feels different. Yet for all that, we comprehend that it is the same piece of wax, rendering our senses untrustworthy. Only logical reason is dependable: 'And so something that I thought I was seeing with my eyes is in fact grasped solely by the faculty of judgement which is in my mind.'

Descartes came to the conclusion that there is but one statement of which we can be rationally sure: 'I think, therefore I am.' As he explained in *Discourse on the Method*:

And as I observed that this truth, I think, therefore I am, was so certain and of such evidence that no ground of doubt, however extravagant, could be alleged by the Sceptics capable of shaking it, I concluded that I might, without scruple, accept it as the first principle of the philosophy of which I was in search.

Descartes' ideas were highly influential and were embraced, and adapted, by many of the greatest Enlightenment thinkers – among them Baruch Spinoza, Gottfried Leibniz, Voltaire, Jean-Jacques Rousseau, Baron de Montesquieu and Immanuel Kant (who commented that 'There is nothing higher than reason'). While much modern thought (especially scientific thought) demands at least some form of empirical evidence, the human ability to rationally process and logically evaluate information is still understood as a defining feature that sets us apart from the beasts.

EMPIRICISM

Empiricism says that all knowledge is derived from sensory experience. Rejecting the idea that we come into the world imbued with innate ideas, empiricists say that we formulate ideas by assessing the evidence of our experience, especially sensory experience (i.e. that which we see, hear and feel). By applying inductive reasoning (that is to say, drawing general conclusions from specific experiences), we arrive at knowledge. Empiricism is thus the basis of modern science, since it demands that all hypotheses be proven (or be capable of being disproved) by observation.

Empiricism has its roots in antiquity, when Aristotle argued for the importance of observation in order to understand the world around us (see Aristotelianism). His notion of the *tabula rasa* was taken up by the Stoics, among others. In the medieval period, Avicenna developed the concept, arguing that it is from 'empirical familiarity with objects in this world' that 'one abstracts universal concepts'. Francis Bacon (1561–1626) then used empirical evidence as the basis of inductive reasoning within a scientific context to birth the modern scientific method (see page 61).

Into the age of Enlightenment, and European philosophy was for a time divided between the rationalists dominant in continental Europe and the empiricists who thrived in Britain – most notably George Berkeley, David Hume and John Locke. Locke made a fairly moderate argument that most knowledge derives from experience but some (such as the existence of God) may be arrived at rationally. He rejected the existence of innate ideas on the basis that no single idea applies universally across all humans. Hume, however, took a harder line, arguing that all knowledge is acquired from experience, even our capacity to reason. Moreover, since we cannot be sure that what has happened in the past will happen again, drawing conclusions from past experience is without merit. Because we saw the moon last night, for instance, does not mean it will necessarily be there tonight. This led him to the conclusion that there are no natural laws, only theories we choose to believe based on custom and instinct. All that we can truly believe, then, is that which our sensory experience shows us to be.

Putting all one's eggs in the empiricist basket

Berkeley devised an alternative, even more extreme form of empiricism (in part inspired by his fear that Hume's conclusions threatened religious faith) that saw him argue against the very existence of matter. Things only exist, he suggested, to the extent that they are perceived (see his idea of 'immaterialist idealism' in Idealism on page 129) – an idea that was further developed by phenomenalist philosophers (including John Stuart Mill) in the 19th century. Into the 20th century, logical empiricists attempted to synthesize the ideas of British empiricism with the mathematical logic of, for example, Bertrand Russell and Ludwig Wittgenstein. Today, empiricism and science are often taken as one and the same thing. Yet no lesser figure than Einstein warned against putting all one's eggs in the empiricist basket:

I say that true knowledge is to be had only through a philosophy of deduction. For it is intuition that improves the world, not just following a trodden path of thought. Intuition makes us look at unrelated facts and then think about them until they can all be brought under one law. To look for related facts means holding onto what one has instead of searching for new facts. Intuition is the father of new knowledge, while empiricism is nothing but an accumulation of old knowledge.

UTILITARIANISM

Utilitarianism is the philosophy famously elucidated in the writings of the English lawyer Jeremy Bentham in the late 18th century. In his *Principles of Morals and Legislation* (completed in 1780 and published in 1789), he laid out the central tenet of utilitarianism: an action may be considered good if it promotes 'the greatest happiness for the greatest number.'

Utilitarianism emerged as a counterpoint to the ideas expressed in the US Declaration of Independence of 1776. Indeed, the Declaration prompted Bentham to write a blistering critique, entitled *Answer to the Declaration of the American Congress*, in which he dismissed the very idea of those 'natural' and 'inalienable' individual rights enshrined in the Declaration – including the pursuit of happiness 'wherever a man thinks he can see it, and by whatever means he thinks he can attain it.'

Rather than the pursuit of individual happiness, utilitarianism is based on the idea that every decision is either more or less efficient than any other in terms of 'utility' (that is to say, the most efficient generation of happiness and pleasure, which in turn is related to the absence of pain). According to Bentham, an action that conforms to the positive principles of utility is, therefore, a 'good' action and ought to be undertaken. Alternatively, an action that increases pain and unhappiness should be rejected. As he put it: 'Nature has placed mankind under the governance of . . . pain and pleasure. It is for them alone to point out what we ought to do, as well as to determine what we shall do.' Logically, an action that brings happiness to a single individual is less good than an action that brings happiness to many.

It was Bentham's hope that the adoption of utilitarianism would bring about simpler and fairer government, where the good of the many is always prioritized, so cutting back the risk of injustice and personal grievance.

He also believed that privileging the greater number over the few would bring about more social equality. Moreover, since he considered all sources of pleasure to be of equal value (from attending the opera to drinking a cup of tea to doing charitable works), he believed neither gender, nor social status, nor ability would act as a bar to accessing happiness.

Bentham's ideas were taken up and adapted in the early 19th century by John Stuart Mill. While Mill concurred with the idea of 'the greatest happiness for the greatest number', he argued for a qualitative distinction between 'higher pleasures' (e.g. intellectual and moral pursuits) and 'lower pleasures' (e.g. sensual pleasure). The 'lower pleasures', Mill said, were often more greatly enjoyed only because people had limited experience of the 'higher pleasures'. Furthermore, he suggested, those who aspire to the higher pleasures ultimately bring greater benefit to society – by most valuing the higher pleasures, he believed, we would move closer still to a society that truly achieves 'the greatest amount of happiness altogether.'

THE *ÜBERMENSCH* (SUPERMAN)

Friedrich Nietzsche (1844–1900) was one of the most important philosophers of his age, whose impact continues to be felt through to the modern day. In such celebrated works as *Thus Spoke Zarathustra* and *Beyond Good and Evil*, he introduced a raft of philosophical ideas, among the most important of which are the putative 'death of God' and the rise of the Übermensch.

Nietzsche was deeply affected by reading Arthur Schopenhauer's *The World of Will and Representation* as a young man. However, while Schopenhauer urged humanity to accept the futility of pursuing happiness (see entry on Optimism and Pessimism on page 147), Nietzsche was determined to carve out a new philosophical path that allowed for a life of fulfilment. In *Thus Spoke Zarathustra* (first published between 1883 and 1885), he told the story of Zarathustra (the Persian prophet Zoroaster) entering the wilderness and coming out a decade later to disseminate the wisdom he had gained. Nietzsche has Zarathustra proclaim the death of God – a reflection of Nietzsche's own disaffection with religion in general and Christianity especially, which he considered a damaging mythology holding back humankind. In broader philosophical terms, the death of God also represented the overthrow of traditional morality. For Nietzsche, established notions of good and evil served to shackle people into lives of duty and unhappiness in the hope of a better life after death. The death of God, he suggested, frees us to live in and for the present, free of the constraints of conventional morality and liberated to find happiness in everyday life.

The will to power

Nietzsche feared the void left by the loss of religious faith would be filled by a sense of nihilism. Therefore, he raised the idea of the *Übermensch* as a successor to God. Man, Nietzsche contended, is the bridge between the beasts and the *Übermensch*, a figure who encapsulates the attributes of independence and self-mastery, creativity and originality, and purity of conscience. Rejecting traditional notions of what drives human behaviour – such as the survival instinct and the sex instinct – Nietzsche believed the *Übermensch* is driven by what he called the 'will to power', a desire to master both the self and the external world. Governed by his own moral code and standards, the *Übermensch* thus embraces life in its totality, free from guilt and unhappiness.

In order for Man to prepare the way for the *Übermensch*, Nietzsche recommended a three-stage plan of action: firstly, the renunciation of comfort and the imposition of self-discipline; secondly, the assertion of personal independence; thirdly, the discovery of new innocence and creativity.

The *Übermensch* doctrine has had widespread appeal in the years since, from secularists and existentialists to, most controversially, the

Nazis under Hitler (who misconstrued Nietzsche's ideas to develop their notion of a 'superior' race of man). Today, Nietzsche has been largely rescued from the grip of the Far Right and he remains one of the most alluring figures of philosophy.

PRAGMATISM

Philosophical pragmatism argues that the meaning and truth of ideas are reflected in their practical consequences. In other words, if an idea does not work, it cannot be deemed to be true. It is an ideology born out of the discussions of a group of influential thinkers at Harvard University in the late 19th century. Its suggestion that truth is not fixed but is dependent upon effect has significantly influenced intellectual development in the last century and a half.

Charles Sanders Peirce (1839–1914) and William James (1842–1910) – both Harvard alumni – are usually credited as the originators of philosophical pragmatism. One crucial idea is that the meaning of a concept is derived from the subject that the idea relates to. In Peirce's own words: 'Consider the practical effects of the objects of your conception. Then, your conception of those effects is the whole of your conception of the object.' Thought, then, becomes less a means to describe a permanent reality than a tool to help us choose how to act in our best interests.

A subtext of Peirce's thesis was that many traditional ways of attributing meaning are pointless. To illustrate the point, he proposed the idea that diamonds are soft until they are touched – a suggestion that cannot be disproven, he said, but one also that does not impact on the effectiveness of the diamond once it has been touched and rendered hard. We customarily assume a diamond is hard in all states, he contended, not because we know it to be so but because it allows us to most easily think of the diamond in a useful way – just as we once accepted the world as flat until it was proven more useful to think of it as round.

James, however, took a significantly different line in his classic work of 1907, *Pragmatism*. Where Peirce had employed pragmatism as a way to consider the nature of knowledge, James adapted it to look at truth. His most significant contribution was to say that an idea may be considered true if considering it to be so reaps practical benefits. In other words, the extent to which an idea is true depends on whether or not it does what is required of it.

Making truth

Because our actions directly determine truth, James said, we have a responsibility to 'act as if what you do makes a difference.' He used the parable of a starving man lost in the woods. The man eventually discovers a path that leads out of the woods to salvation, but in order for it to provide salvation, he must believe that it will do so and thus follow it. If, however, he despairs that it is merely a dead-end, he will ignore it and so remain lost. The truth that the path offers a way out is therefore dependent on his belief that it does. In an age of individualism and declining religious faith, the notion that we have the power to 'make truth' has proved at once attractive and onerous.

MERITOCRACY

Meritocracy is a form of social organization in which power is held by those selected on the basis of merit – in other words, because an individual's abilities and talents make them best suited to a specific role. Traditionally, 'merit' has been measured by performance, typically in examinations.

Meritocratic systems have existed for many thousands of years. Confucius (see page 136), for example, was an early advocate of standardized examinations to select the most able people for public office (rather than selection by inheritance or patronage, as had hitherto been the more regular route to progression). While 'merit' has tended to be synonymous with intellectual ability and educational attainment, it may also encompass physical prowess and even mental attitude (such as an appetite for work). Nonetheless, in most meritocracies, education has served as the principal means of social advancement.

Plato was another to advocate the meritocratic system, when in *Republic* he argued for rule by philosopher kings so that power rests with those wisest enough to know how to use it. Aristotle, meanwhile, had this to say: 'The wise man must not be ordered but must order, and he must not obey another, but the less wise must obey him.' Nonetheless, Western meritocracy did not really get going until the 17th century when the British East India Company adopted its principles to appoint employees to its operations in India. After a long gestation period, meritocracy had at last crossed from East to West, so that by the 19th century John Stuart Mill was even arguing the case for giving greater voting rights to the more educated voter.

The rise of the meritocracy

It was not until 1958 that the term *meritocracy* came into popular usage when Michael Young published his essay, 'The Rise of the Meritocracy'. It was intended as a satire, depicting a dystopian United Kingdom of the future in which the education system perpetuated a privileged class of the intelligent and meretricious at the expense of an underclass of 'lower merit'. What Young had meant as a critique of the tripartite British education system of the time actually resulted in 'meritocracy' being widely adopted (not least by the political class) to denote earned entitlement.

EXISTENTIALISM

Existentialism highlights the individualist nature of existence, asserting that each person creates the meaning of their life in the absence of an overarching guiding force. According to the existentialists, we are fated to carve out our own destinies as we strive to make rational choices in an essentially irrational cosmos. To that extent, we are able to exert freedom of choice, and it is by choosing to embrace our existence that we can escape the underlying 'nothingness' of the universe. Existence, existentialism holds, precedes essence, meaning that we may 'write' the meanings of our lives.

'If man, as the existentialist sees him, is indefinable, it is because at first he is nothing. Only afterwards will he be something, and he himself will have made what he will be.'

Jean-Paul Sartre

Although he would not have recognized himself as such, Danish philosopher and theologian Søren Kierkegaard (1813–55) is often cited as the original existentialist. In works such as *Either/Or, Fear and Trembling, The Concept of Anxiety* and *The Sickness Unto Death*, he repeatedly explored the theme that humans have complete freedom of choice to determine the nature of their existence, which in turn invokes anxiety. In *The Concept of Anxiety*, for example, he likened the individual faced with choice to someone staring into an abyss, at once fearful of falling and also battling the compulsion to jump; anxiety is a common thread through existentialist thought, and Kierkegaard acknowledged its double-edged nature: 'Whoever has learned to be anxious in the right way has learned the ultimate . . . Anxiety is freedom's possibility . . .'

Being and Nothingness

In 1943, Sartre published the single greatest work of existentialist thought, *Being and Nothingness*. He intended it as a study of the consciousness of being and in it he revisited two concepts he had introduced in his earlier novel, *Nausea* – *pour-soi* (being-for-itself, denoting conscious awareness of the self) and *en-soi* (being-in-itself, denoting the non-human world that has its own essence but lacks consciousness and self-awareness).

Sartre's central tenet was that what humans can see is all that there is. He regarded humanity as defined by the absence of a preordained essence, and drew a comparison between the complete but incapable-of-change *en-soi* and the self-aware but incomplete *pour-soi*. Sartre argued that humans are left to create their beings from nothing, defining themselves by what they do – unlike, for example, a pebble on a beach that simply is what it is. He also echoed Nietzsche's dismissal of the notion of a Godhead figure who supernaturally imposes meaning on reality.

By acknowledging ourselves as *pour-soi*, he said, we are forced to confront our own essential nothingness but, as a result, gain the freedom to create ourselves. Thus Sartre treads a line between nihilism (human existence as a nothingness) and liberation of the consciousness that places the individual at the centre of everything. As he observed: 'Life has no meaning *a priori* . . . It is up to you to give it a meaning, and value is nothing but the meaning that you choose.'

Friedrich Nietzsche (1844–1900) is another who is regarded as having prefigured certain existentialist principles, both in his rejection of God and in his description of the self-liberating 'Superman' (Übermensch; see page 154). Yet for most people, existentialism is most famously encapsulated by two of the giants of 20th-century French philosophy, Simone de Beauvoir (see page 204) and Jean-Paul Sartre, her long-time partner.

ABSURDISM

Absurdism, most closely associated with the writings of Albert Camus, argues that we should accept the fundamental irrationality and meaningless of the world. Whereas existentialism – with which there are clear parallels – urges that the individual creates his own meaningful existence, absurdism suggests life may only be truly enjoyed once we cease searching for order and purpose.

Camus, born in Algeria in 1913, was a political activist who fought with the French resistance against the German occupying forces during the Second World War. A witness to regular atrocities in this period, his sense of the futility of life seems to have reached a peak around this time. In 1942 he wrote an essay, *The Myth of Sisyphus*, and a novel, *The Stranger* (also translated as *The Outsider*), that became the founding texts of absurdism.

Familiar from his days as a student in Algiers with the ideas of both existentialism and phenomenology (the study of consciousness

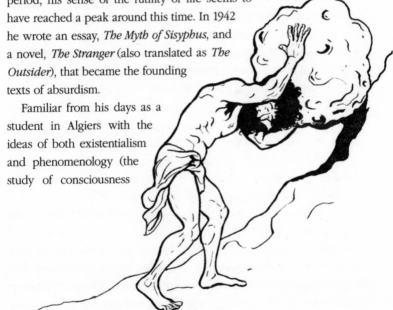

Sisyphus

and personal experience, as championed by Edmund Husserl), Camus evolved his own take on the inherent pointlessness of existence.

In *The Myth of Sisyphus*, he depicted the Greek mythical figure of Sisyphus as the classic absurdist hero. Sisyphus, the story goes, had a particularly cruel punishment imposed on him by the gods – he was compelled to roll a boulder up a mountain, only to watch it roll back down again before beginning the process again in a cycle of eternal futility. It was only by undertaking the task without harbouring any hope of success, Camus said, that Sisyphus stood any chance of happiness. So too humans, who Camus suggested was faced with three choices – to believe in a divine presence who gives meaning to existence, to conclude that life is indeed meaningless and so not worth living, or to accept the absurdity of life and carry on regardless.

His own answer was to accept futility as a means of liberating the individual to live a full, passionate life as one sees fit. It was a philosophy he further expounded in what is widely regarded as his masterpiece, *The Stranger*, the tale of an emotionally vacant and amoral figure called Meursault, whose behaviour takes unexpected turns as he seeks to live a life of total honesty. The pivotal event in the story is his decision to kill a man for no apparent reason – a crime for which he subsequently goes on trial.

With Meursault convicted and sentenced to death, the latter stages of the book focus on his awaiting his ultimate fate. Rather than contest his sentence, he decides to accept it in the knowledge that the same fate – death – awaits him sooner or later anyway. Thus freed from the burdensome hope of extending his lifespan, he is able to seek out pleasure in the time left to him.

Absurdism thus presents a powerful vision of the world, at once dark and optimistic, that has found significant resonance in a society that has increasingly moved away from those traditional religious narratives which previously gave meaning to life. As the Nobel Prize committee put it, when awarding Camus the prize for literature in 1957, Camus – and by extension, absurdism – 'with clear-sighted earnestness illuminates the problems of the human conscience in our times.'

PART SIX

POLITICS

'Man is by nature a political animal.'

Aristotle

Politics is the study of how power is distributed and exercised, and how different groups interrelate, within a society. Though politics has been practised and evolving since humans first came together into communities. Groucho Marx called politics the 'art of looking for trouble, finding it everywhere, diagnosing it incorrectly and applying the wrong remedies.' J. K. Galbraith described it as 'the art of choosing between the disastrous and the unpalatable.' Nonetheless, our collective aspiration to create happy and prosperous societies demands that we participate in political discourse and weigh up competing ideas.

THE RULE OF LAW

Pivotal to our sense of what a modern, democratic society should be is the rule of law – the idea that all members of a society (including its lawmakers) should be governed by the same laws and should not be subject to arbitrary decision-making by any agency of power. In return, citizens are expected to respect and comply with that which is legally decreed, even when they disagree with it. By extension, the law and its instruments of arbitration (most obviously, the courts) should be accessible to 'ordinary' people.

Law is freedom

Plato may stake a claim to be the first great thinker on questions regarding the rule of law. Prior to him, many societies had operated on the principle that a ruler might wield power without being subject to the same laws as those over whom they had sovereignty. Plato thus argued for a system of rule by those best equipped to rule – a concept encapsulated in the notion of the 'philosopher kings'. He also expressed a belief that the law should be 'the master of the government and the government is its slave, then the situation is full of promise and men enjoy all the blessings that the gods shower on a state.'

His pupil, Aristotle, later observed: 'It is more proper that law should govern than any of the citizens: on the same principle, if it is advantageous to place power in some particular individuals, they should be appointed only as the guardians and the servants of the laws.' Cicero, the great Roman statesman of the 1st century BCE, reiterated Aristotle's thoughts: 'We are all servants of the laws in order that we may be free.'

One of the landmarks in cementing the rule of law came in 1215 when a posse of English barons compelled King John to sign the Magna Carta, enshrining certain legal rights in perpetuity in return for granting the sovereign tax-raising powers. Then, at the end of the 17th century, the English philosopher John Locke contributed his own influential thoughts on the subject in his *Second Treatise of Government* (1690), arguing:

> *Freedom of people under government is to be under no restraint apart from standing rules to live by that are common to everyone in the society and made by the law-making power established in it. Persons have a right or liberty to (1) follow their own will in all things that the law has not prohibited and (2) not be subject to the inconstant, uncertain, unknown, and arbitrary wills of others.*

This may be said to signal the modern era of government by the rule of law.

In the mid-18th century the French Baron de Montesquieu published *The Spirit of the Laws*, in which he argued for the separation of powers between the executive, legislative and judicial authorities so that the judiciary may be able to execute the law without fear or favour. The ideas of both Locke and Montesquieu were highly influential on those who subsequently established the United States.

The British jurist Albert Venn Dicey was another high-profile advocate of the rule of law, proclaiming in the 19th century that 'no man is above the law [and] every man, whatever be his rank or condition, is subject to the ordinary law of the realm and amenable to the jurisdiction of the ordinary tribunals.' Today the rule of law is an accepted pillar of modern, liberal democracy – although its practical implementation remains a challenge in nations throughout the world.

PROPERTY

Property – the ownership of goods and land, and the rules and customs surrounding their ownership – has been a source of intense debate down through the ages. Questions as to whether individuals have natural rights to property, or whether it is best left in common ownership, have occupied minds for millennia, along with considerations of what a property-owner is beholden to do with that which they own.

Ever since humanity grouped together to serve its common interests, property has been at the heart of our interrelationships. In *Republic*, Plato called for a society based on collective ownership as the best means of pursuing collective interests. He regarded private property as a threat to social cohesion, arguing that 'when some grieve exceedingly and others rejoice at the same happenings', division is sure to follow. Aristotle, meanwhile, took a diametrically opposed view when suggesting that private property inspired personal virtues including discretion and prudence.

Thomas Aquinas (1225–74) developed Aristotle's idea by arguing that the poor have a positive right to expect those with property to provide succour. Thomas Hobbes (1588–1679) then altered the terms of the debate by suggesting that property is essentially a social construct – one into which all members of a society buy – designed to provide a stable environment in which the individual may be left 'in the peaceable enjoyment of what he may acquire by his fortune and industry.' By contrast, John Locke did not see property as subject to a system of universal consent, instead arguing that unclaimed resources may be unilaterally appropriated if an individual can make positive use of them.

Known as the 'First Occupancy Theory', Locke justifies the action of appropriation since no one else is directly dispossessed. This was an idea of particular power in the age of imperial expansion, during which the interests of colonizers often came up sharply against the property rights of indigenous populations.

Property and social health

The great economist Adam Smith, meanwhile, regarded private property as pivotal to the generation of wealth and the operation of the free market, which he believed offered the best hope of the efficient allocation of resources. Nonetheless, he recognized the potential for inequality inherent in private property. 'Wherever there is great property, there is great inequality,' he wrote. 'Civil government, so far as it is instituted for the security of property, is in reality instituted for the defence of the rich against the poor, or of those who have some property against those who have none at all.' Then, in the 19th century, Karl Marx – in part influenced by the somewhat abstract and esoteric theories of property propounded by Kant and Hegel – entirely rejected the idea that private property is compatible with the wider social good. Instead he favoured a system of collective ownership – a principle that was a bedrock of his socialist philosophy.

The issue of property and fair resource allocation remains among the overriding concerns of governments to this day. Most uphold the status of private property in law, yet our understanding of what constitutes property and how it should be utilized remains as fluid now as it ever was.

SOVEREIGNTY

Sovereignty refers to the supreme authority within a specified territory – typically, a nation-state. The concept embodies the right of a governing body to exert its authority over the polity without third-party interference. To fulfil the modern notion of sovereignty, there must be a distinct territory and population under the governance of an authority whose power is recognized both domestically and internationally.

The idea of sovereignty has long existed. The Roman Empire, for instance, recognized the sovereignty of its emperor, just as the ancient

Sovereignty and war

The idea of sovereignty continues to wield influence in contemporary political discourse. It has, for instance, been regularly cited as a reason to go to war – as when Britain declared war on Germany in 1939 in response to German violation of Polish sovereignty. More recently still, the European Union – established in a bid to maintain peace between Europe's sovereign states ('As long as there are sovereign nations possessing great power, war is inevitable,' Einstein once said) – has found itself seriously challenged by critics who accuse it of persistently undermining the sovereignty of its member states.

Egyptians accepted the sovereignty of generations of pharaohs. However, it has been argued that the idea of sovereignty waned in the Middle Ages, when the power of monarchs was constrained by the aristocratic classes. The modern conception of sovereignty is thus widely considered to have arisen with the emergence of modern nation-states from the 17th century onwards.

In the face of widespread civil and religious discord across much of Europe, the French jurist and political theorist Jean Bodin (1530–96) looked to a strong ruler because of a lack of faith in the ability of the populace to govern themselves. 'In a democracy,' he wrote, 'sovereignty is vested in a majority; and a majority is not only, at best, an ignorant, foolish and emotional mob, but shifts continually and alters from year to year.'

His ideas were echoed in Thomas Hobbes's *Leviathan*, published in 1651 (see The Social Contract on page 171), two years after the execution of Charles I in the English Civil War. Hobbes's ideal was a 'sovereign power' able to compel the people to 'act in the common good'. By contrast, Jean-Jacques Rousseau in France contended that sovereignty lies with the people – what he termed 'the general will' – while back in England, John Locke was making a similar case. Indeed, the concept found expression in France's post-Revolution constitution of 1791: 'Sovereignty is one, indivisible, unalienable and imprescriptible; it belongs to the Nation; no group can attribute sovereignty to itself nor can an individual arrogate it to himself.' Similar sentiments were shared by the authors of the American Declaration of Independence, formulated fifteen years earlier.

THE SOCIAL CONTRACT

The Social Contract refers to the hypothetical agreement struck between members of a society as to how they should be organized and governed. It seeks to explain how a ruler derives power from the ruled, an area most famously explored in the 17th century by, once more, Thomas Hobbes and John Locke in Britain and Jean-Jacques Rousseau in France. Their ideas have continued to inform our understanding of statehood – and the rights and responsibilities of the governing and the governed – ever since.

Plato was among the first to give consideration to the concept of a social contract, explaining that citizens give their implicit approval to be governed by remaining within a society. Hobbes began the wave of Enlightenment writings on the subject with *Leviathan* – his response to the bloodshed and discord caused by the English Civil War of the previous decade. He contended that government is necessary to elevate Man above his dismal 'state of nature' which he described thus:

In such condition, there is no place for industry; because the fruit thereof is uncertain: and consequently no culture of the earth; no navigation, nor use of the commodities that may be imported by sea; no commodious building; no instruments of moving, and removing, such things as require much force; no knowledge of the face of the earth; no account of time; no arts; no letters; no society;

and which is worst of all, continual fear, and danger of violent death; and the life of man, solitary, poor, nasty, brutish, and short.

Locke, in his *Two Treatises of Government* (1689), took a different line describing the 'state of nature' in these terms:

It is evident that all human beings – as creatures belonging to the same species and rank and born indiscriminately with all the same natural advantages and faculties – are equal amongst themselves. They have no relationship of subordination or subjection unless God (the lord and master of them all) had clearly set one person above another and conferred on him an undoubted right to dominion and sovereignty.

The people and power

Nonetheless, in common with Hobbes, Locke regarded the state of nature as unstable and perilous, claiming that people agree to come together in a society 'for the mutual preservation of their lives, liberties and estates, which I call by the general name, property.' Rather than the absolutist ruler of Locke's vision, Hobbes instead opted for government 'by the consent of the majority, giving it either by themselves, or their representatives chosen by them.' Crucially, he argued that should a government overstep its remit, the citizenry have the right to overthrow it – key liberal ideals that were evident in both the French Revolution and the American colonies' demands for independence.

Rousseau's great contribution to the subject was 1762's *Of the Social Contract, or Principles of Political Right*. He had a much more optimistic view of 'Man in his primitive state' as a morally uncorrupted figure 'at an equal distance from the stupidity of brutes and the fatal enlightenment of civil man.' Civil society, by contrast, he regarded as deleterious, enslaving Man though he is born free. Rousseau thus suggested a society in which the entire citizenry participates to create laws in accordance with the common will. So radical were his ideas that Rousseau was compelled to spend several years in effective voluntary exile away from France.

In the 19th century, Pierre-Joseph Proudhon argued for a utopian form of anarchism in which there is a social contract directly between citizens, whereby all agree to refrain from attempts at governing anyone but themselves. More recently, John Rawls in *A Theory of Justice* (1971) speculates as to what form of social organization would be favoured by subjects hypothetically rendered unaware of their own personal circumstances (e.g. gender, age, race and wealth). He suggested most would agree on two fundamental principles of governance: (a) the right to political liberty, and (b) that social and economic inequalities should be such that they are to the greatest benefit of the least well-off and should also guarantee equality of opportunity.

IMPERIALISM

Imperialism is the policy of expanding the influence and power of a nation-state beyond its borders. This is typically achieved by a process of colonization – taking political and economic control of a foreign country or territory, usually through use of military force preceding occupation. However, there are also 'softer' forms of imperialism. The USA, for instance, has been accused of practising cultural and economic imperialism, achieving dominant positions in foreign territories by astute manipulation of its wealth (as represented, for instance, by large companies) and cultural reach (epitomized by Hollywood and the music industry).

The good, the bad and the ugly

Imperialism has a long and not always noble history. Any consideration of world history abounds in tales of empire and few areas have been untouched. We may look to the empires that dominated life in ancient China, India and Japan, or the vast dominions of the Egyptians, Greeks and Romans, the Assyrians, Persians and Mongols, the Byzantines and Ottomans, and the Incas and Aztecs in South America. Not to mention the plethora of empires that stretched across Sub-Saharan Africa prior to the period of European colonization, which eventually saw the British rule an empire bigger than any before or since. In certain lights, history looks like nothing more than a narrative of conquest and colonization.

The modern world is most obviously defined by the period of European empire building that began in the 15th century with colonization first of the New World, and subsequently of India and the East Indies. The so-called 'Scramble for Africa' in the late 19th century then divided that vast continent into spheres of European interest. In the 20th century, an unseemly jostle for international influence between the great European states culminated in the First World War, before the expansionist ambitions of, in particular, inter-war Germany brought about the Second World War, while post-Second World War Russian expansionism precipitated the Cold War. So imperialism has dictated the course of international politics.

There have been broadly four major justifications for imperialism. Firstly, there are arguments of an economic nature – that the colonizing country requires (or at least, desires) the resources of another country. Then there are strategic justifications – usually that an empire is required to protect the colonizing country's security. The Soviet Union, for instance, oversaw the Eastern Bloc in the twentieth century at least in part to have a succession of buffer states between itself and its Western enemies. Thirdly, empire has been seen as an expression of the natural order of the

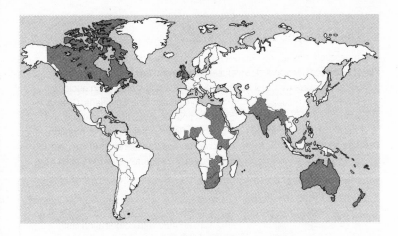

Map of the British Empire, 1914

world, in which some societies are inherently dominant over others. Julius Caesar exemplifies the idea when he is said to have coolly recorded: 'I came, I saw, I conquered.'

Finally, there is justification on moral grounds – for example, that the colonized people are being liberated from unjust rule or are being introduced to a better way of life.

The post-Second World War period saw the European empires recede from Africa and Asia, while the collapse of the Soviet Union seemed to confirm the arrival of what is sometimes called the 'post-colonial age'. Nonetheless, there are those who still see imperialism in action – from Russia's annexation of the Crimea to the West's economic and logistical support for particular regimes abroad, and even China's 'soft imperialism' as it heavily invests in Africa's economic development. But few world leaders now openly espouse imperialist ideology.

WAR

The historical record would suggest that warfare – armed conflict between two or more opposing groups – has been a fairly consistent feature of humanity's time on Earth. Its impact on our species is virtually incalculable, though conservative estimates put the combined death toll from war (and disease and famine resulting from it) at over 1.5 billion. Yet there has been a remarkable lack of consensus in regard to fundamental aspects of war – for instance, is it a natural and inevitable component of life, and is it ever morally justifiable? 'If you wish for peace,' the great military historian B. H. Liddell Hart once wrote, 'understand war.'

Lawrence H. Keeley, a professor of anthropology at the University of Illinois, has claimed that some 90–95 per cent of known societies throughout history have engaged in at least occasional warfare. The reasons for war are numerous but chief among them is the desire for territorial expansion (whereby one group or nation invades the territory of another), competition for control of resources, historical disputes over rights to land and resources, and ideological conflicts (as epitomized by the Crusades).

So, is war a natural state for a species that subdivides into competing social groups? This was the opinion of Thomas Hobbes, who famously depicted mankind in the 'state of nature' as 'in that condition which is called Warre; and such a warre, as is of every man, against every man.' It was a view echoed by Voltaire, who concluded: 'All animals are perpetually at war with each other . . . Air, earth and water are arenas of destruction.'

Plato regarded war as resulting from the abandonment of reason in favour of one's passions, fomenting political and moral discord. In *Phaedo*, he wrote: 'Wars and revolutions and battles are due simply and solely to the body and its desires. All wars are undertaken for the acquisition of wealth; and the reason why we have to acquire wealth is the body, because we are slaves in its service.'

Sigmund Freud, meanwhile, claimed Man is subject to a death instinct (sometimes called *Thanatos*), which leads 'organic life back into the inanimate state.' War, then, takes on the nature of a psychological compulsion.

The father of all things

Heraclitus described war as 'the father of all things'. Georg Hegel held a similar view, regarding it as a vital step on the path towards the 'Absolute Spirit' (the endpoint of civilization, knowledge and being). Each stage of world history is a necessary moment in the Idea of the World Spirit,' he argued, so that figures like Napoleon Bonaparte – the greatest military leader of the age – become the epitome of the *zeitgeist* (the 'spirit of the age') and drivers of progress. Spying the Frenchman in 1806 on the eve of the Battle of Jena, Hegel noted: 'I saw the Emperor – this world-soul – riding out of the city on reconnaissance. It is indeed a wonderful sensation to see such an individual, who, concentrated here at a single point, astride a horse, reaches out over the world and masters it . . . this extraordinary man, whom it is impossible not to admire.'

In the 19th century, Karl von Clausewitz established himself as perhaps the single greatest philosopher of war, and it was his contention that: 'War is not merely a political act but a real political instrument, a continuation of political intercourse, a carrying out of the same by other means.'

PACIFISM

Pacifism is the view that war is morally unacceptable and unjustifiable. While there are few who would argue that war is ever a wholly good thing, pacifism is nonetheless often subject to a criticism that it does not acknowledge that some wars are a 'necessary evil'.

In a pacifist clarion call just as the Second World War was about to take hold, Vera Brittain elegantly expressed her pacifist philosophy thus: 'All that a pacifist can undertake – but it is a very great deal – is to refuse to kill, injure or otherwise cause suffering to another human creature, and untiringly to order his life by the rule of love though others may be captured by hate.' The war that followed proved an ideological battleground for those in favour and against the pacifist ideal. To many observers, Hitler had created just the kind of regime that rendered pacifism untenable and demanded a military response.

For example, in 1941 George Orwell wrote: 'Since pacifists have more freedom of action in countries where traces of democracy survive,

The father of pacifism

Gautama Buddha (c. 6th century BCE) arguably founded the first expressly pacifist movement, demanding that his followers abstain from inflicting violence on any living creature. However, pacifism as an active political ideology took on a modern guise around the 18th century as part of a general call for the democratization of states – a process some hoped would transfer power away from bellicose monarchs to a peace-loving populace. During the 19th century, over which war continued to cast its shadow, there was a surge in membership of national and international pacifist organizations. Yet, in terms of absolute numbers, the 20th century saw the most war-related deaths of any century.

pacifism can act more effectively against democracy than for it. Objectively the pacifist is pro-Nazi.' Pacifism, though, is a nuanced philosophy. While the absolute pacifist believes that no war may ever be justified, there are many other 'conditional pacifists' who accept that war is inevitable under certain circumstances. Some may even agree to take a role in a war effort in a non-fighting capacity (such as serving as stretcher-bearers).

In the face of the existential risk posed by nuclear weapons, pacifism found a new relevance. Albert Einstein was prominent among them, making a strong case for pacifism even as his scientific discoveries made possible the theoretical development of the atom bomb. Pacifism also found powerful new adherents in, variously, Gandhi as leader of the Indian independence movement and Martin Luther King as spiritual figurehead of the US civil rights movement. Both would have felt sympathy with the words of the great Renaissance humanist Desiderius Erasmus from 1515:

> *If there is any human activity which should be approached with caution, or rather which should be avoided by all possible means, resisted and shunned, that activity is war, for there is nothing more wicked, more disastrous, more widely destructive, more persistently ingrained, more hateful, more unworthy in every respect of a man . . .*

DEMOCRACY

Democracy is a form of government whereby the entire population (or, at least, all eligible members of a society) participate in making decisions, usually through elected representatives. Over 85 per cent of the world's nations are now considered to be formal democracies. It is an ideal enshrined in the United Nations' Universal Declaration

of Human Rights, which states that 'the will of the people shall be the basis of the authority of government.'

The world's oldest extant democratically elected parliament is Iceland's *Alþingi*, which came into being around 930 CE. Although the reach of democracy has waxed and waned over time, its values blossomed among Enlightenment thinkers; it was profoundly influential in revolutionary France as well as underpinning the United States' constitution ('government of the people, by the people, for the people', in the words of Abraham Lincoln). While nations have experimented – and continue to do so – with alternative governmental systems, representative democracy is today the pre-eminent model, with India and its 800-million-plus eligible voters comprising the world's largest functioning democracy.

As with any system, democracy is not without its flaws and is too easily open to abuse. Nonetheless, it has proven the most resilient of political philosophies. Speaking in the House of Commons in 1947, as the world reconfigured itself in the aftermath of war, Winston Churchill was moved to remark: 'Many forms of Government have been tried, and will be tried in this world of sin and woe. No one pretends that democracy is perfect or all-wise. Indeed, it has been said that democracy is the worst form of government except all those other forms that have been tried from time to time.'

The birth of democracy

The introduction of democracy – literally 'rule by the people' – was arguably the crowning achievement of ancient Greek civilization. It is generally considered to have been born in Athens around 508 BCE under Cleisthenes, 'the father of Athenian democracy'. By the time Athenian democracy collapsed in the 4th century BCE under pressure from foreign invaders, Athens had enjoyed an unparalleled social and cultural golden age, during which time it became home to many of the ideas that would mould Western thought over the coming centuries and beyond.

AUTOCRACY

A system of government in which one person holds absolute power, autocracy overlaps with a number of other political concepts, including dictatorship (where power is commonly taken by force), despotism (in which absolute power is typically wielded cruelly and oppressively) and totalitarianism (where complete subservience to the state and its government is demanded). Autocracy is, in many respects, the counterpoint to democracy.

Absolutism, and especially absolute monarchy, has a long tradition. The pharaohs of ancient Egypt, for instance, were considered absolute rulers, able to exercise supreme authority while themselves being above the law and beyond reproach. Indeed, the pharaohs were able to consolidate their grip on power by taking on a quasi-divine status – a tactic used repeatedly in cultures across the globe throughout history.

Absolutism was also practised, for instance, by the civilizations of ancient Mesopotamia and India, while in the West Julius Caesar effectively ruled Rome as an absolute leader. The latter was, however, savagely dispatched by political enemies unsatisfied by his rule – an event proving Ambrose Bierce's pithy observation: 'An absolute monarchy is one in which the sovereign does as he pleases so long as he pleases the assassins.'

Despite the obvious dangers of investing unfettered power in a single individual, the Enlightenment saw a number of so-called 'Enlightened despots' – among them Catherine the Great in Russia and Frederick I in Prussia – who used their supreme power to introduce social reforms, such as the abolition of serfdom.

Absolutism seemed to have had its day by the 19th century. Yet the autocrat has proved a particularly resistant breed. The 20th century was scarred by the rise of numerous destructive despots – most notably

Hitler, Stalin and Mao Zedong – and today several absolute leaders remain in power, including Kim Jong-un in North Korea.

The absolute king

For many historians, absolutism was most fully realized in the person of Louis XIV of France (1643–1715). In 1661, aged twenty-three and already eighteen years into his reign, he dispensed with his prime minister to rule directly himself. In the belief that he operated under the 'divine right of kings' he set about centralizing power around himself, controlling all aspects of society including the army and the economy. It is fair to say that the excesses of his rule paved the way for the Revolution that swept through France in 1789 and brought about the end of the French monarchy for good.

MACHIAVELLIANISM

In 1513 Niccolò Machiavelli (1469–1527) wrote his landmark work, *Il Principe* (*The Prince*) – a guide to statecraft that he produced in the hope of currying favour with Florence's ruling family, the Medicis. Its central tenet – that the end justifies the means – has proved one of history's most enduring political doctrines.

A Florentine native, Machiavelli was a civil servant and diplomat whose personal fortunes ebbed and flowed with the fates of the city's ruling elite. In 1502, with his hometown in a state of flux, Machiavelli found himself sent on a diplomatic mission to Cesare Borgia, Duke of Valentinois and illegitimate son of Pope Alexander VI. Borgia was renowned for the ruthlessness of his rule, which he executed with energy, astuteness and great efficiency. Although Borgia was deemed an enemy of the Florentine state, Machiavelli was profoundly impressed by him. When he came to write *The Prince*, Borgia was the natural model for Machiavelli to reference.

For all its brevity, *The Prince* established itself as among the first rank of political philosophy. In wry and witty text, Machiavelli argued that the ruler must be totally ruthless in pursuing the success of his state, which in turn will secure his personal glory. Dispensing with traditional concepts of Christian morality (quite an approach in Catholic Renaissance Italy), he urged that the Prince must undertake whatever is required to meet his aims, however distasteful.

Deception, dishonesty and murder were all left on the table as the ruler seeks to weed out opposition in the interests of stability and security. Compassion and generosity were presented as means to stave off public hatred (and the attendant threat of rebellion) but Machiavelli argued that if one may not be both loved and feared, 'anyone compelled to choose will find greater security in being feared than in being loved . . . Love endures by a bond which men, being scoundrels, may break whenever it serves their advantage to do so; but fear is supported by the dread of pain, which is ever present.'

The threat of Machiavelli

The Prince was a comprehensive statement of *realpolitik* – politics based on practical objectives rather than ideals – long before that term was ever invented. It also served as a counterpoint to the idealism of such works as Plato's *Republic* and Thomas More's *Utopia*. So incendiary was it that the Catholic Church banned the book and it was only published five years after Machiavelli died.

THEOCRACY

Theocracy is the form of government in which all authority is believed to stem from a divine presence. In practical terms, power rests with a priestly figure ruling in the name of the deity. In such systems, officials (commonly members of the clergy) are considered to be operating under godly guidance, with the civic legal code accordingly rooted in religious law. Etymologically, *theocracy* comes from the Greek for 'rule by God'.

There are several modern examples, including the Islamic theocracy of Iran, with Saudi Arabia also widely regarded as a theocratic state. The Vatican City State, home of the papacy, is also sometimes considered a theocracy, although the Pope does not claim to be communicating divine will through civil law. To that extent, it may be regarded as being closer to an *ecclesiocracy*, where religious figures play a leading role in government without claiming the status of instruments of divine revelation.

It is thought that theocracy was originally conceptualized by the first-century historian Flavius Josephus as he sought to explain the workings of the Jewish commonwealth of that period. He wrote that Moses 'ordained our government to be what, by a strained expression, may be termed a theocracy, by ascribing the authority and power to God, and by persuading all the people to have a regard to him, as the author of all good things.'

Theocracies were reasonably common in the ancient world, and the Reformation saw attempts to reinstitute the system in Europe – with Girolamo Savonarola's reign in 1490s Florence a notable example. In modern times, the phenomenon has been more associated with Islam, as when the Ayatollah Khomeini seized power in Iran in 1979, organizing the state around the principles of sharia (Islamic religious law), and when the Taliban took control of Afghanistan in the late 1990s. Even more recently, the militant Islamist group known as ISIS has sought to establish a theocratic caliphate of its own.

For much of the world brought up on a tradition of secular government, theocracy is a highly problematic concept. Not least, the claim that theocracies operate under divine guidance leaves little room for dissent and opposition so treasured by adherents of democracy. C. S. Lewis, author of the *Narnia* novels and a noted Christian philosopher, put it in these terms:

> *Theocracy is the worst of all governments. If we must have a tyrant, a robber baron is far better than an inquisitor. The baron's cruelty may sometimes sleep, his cupidity at some point be sated; and since he dimly knows he is doing wrong he may possibly repent. But the inquisitor who mistakes his own cruelty and lust of power and fear for the voice of Heaven will torment us infinitely because he torments us with the approval of his own conscience and his better impulses appear to him as temptations.*

LIBERALISM

Liberalism is a wide-ranging political philosophy that prioritizes individual liberty by advocating equality of opportunity and recognizing individual rights. Liberalism is synonymous with such ideals as freedom of speech and conscience, democracy, limited government and (to varying extents) free-market economics.

Liberalism – which derives from the Latin for 'free' – has a long pedigree. Aristotle noted: 'Of all the varieties of virtues, liberalism is the most beloved.' However, modern liberalism grew out of Enlightenment thought and it was during the 17th and 18th centuries that many of its central tenets were established. One of its key founding texts was John Locke's *Two Treatises on Government* (1689; see The Social Contract on page 171), in which he outlined the individual's natural (i.e. human and inalienable) rights to life, liberty and property. The cause of liberalism was taken up by several prominent French philosophers of the age. The Baron de Montesquieu, for example, called for monarchs to be subject to legal constraints (not a popular idea with the Bourbon dynasty), as did Voltaire.

Jean-Jacques Rousseau, meanwhile, waged war on his contemporary society, famously noting that social convention stifles people's basic freedoms. 'Man is born free,' he wrote, 'and everywhere he is in chains.' He not only dismissed the notion of the divine right of monarchs but claimed that the people (by which he meant all citizens, including – remarkably for the age – women) were the only legitimate sovereign power.

In America, the War of Independence of 1775–83 was built around the Locke-esque credo of 'life, liberty and the pursuit of happiness', while the French Revolution was imbued with the liberal ideas of Voltaire and Rousseau (although the subsequent Terror and the substitution of the monarchy with the emperorship of Napoleon fatally undermined those values).

On Liberty

In 1859, John Stuart Mill wrote his masterpiece of liberalism, *On Liberty*, in which he examined the relationship between the individual and authority. He made a spirited defence of the rights of the individual in all circumstances except when they impinge on the rights of another: 'That the only purpose for which power can be rightfully exercised over any member of a civilised community, against his will, is to prevent harm to others. His own good, either physical or moral, is not a sufficient warrant . . . Over himself, over his body and mind, the individual is sovereign.'

Liberalism remained among the dominant philosophies of 20th- and 21st-century discourse – facing down, for instance, the rise of fascism and communism. In the words of the Austrian-American economist Ludwig von Mises: 'Against what is stupid, nonsensical, erroneous, and evil, liberalism fights with the weapons of the mind, and not with brute force and repression.'

CONSERVATISM

Conservatism is a political ideology that favours tradition and preservation of the status quo over radical change. That said, classical conservatism does not object to change *per se*, but considers that any reform should occur organically. Modern conservatism tends to be closely associated with free-market economic principles, the protection of private wealth and support for traditional social attitudes.

The beginnings of conservatism – the word stems from the Latin for 'to preserve' – are usually traced to the publication in 1790 of Edmund Burke's *Reflections on the Revolution in France*. The Irish-born Burke, a lawyer by training, entered parliament in London in 1765 as a member of the Whig Party – the forerunner of the Liberal Party.

As a good liberal, he believed in the right of the people to overthrow an unjust government. But as he set about writing *Reflections on the Revolution*, Louis XVI and Marie Antoinette were in prison in Paris and within three years each would have been sent to their death at the guillotine. His revulsion at these events saw him fundamentally reposition himself in the political array, signalling the birth of a new ideology. Burke believed that the revolution had been anchored in abstract philosophical conceits such as liberty and rights, with little relevance to the experiences of ordinary people. The French Revolution, he said, had left France 'a country undone'.

While he recognized the failings in the prior French system, he argued that it was far better to address social inequalities and constitutional failings through gradual reform than to invite the destructive chaos France was then experiencing. 'I cannot conceive,' he wrote, 'how any man can have brought himself to that pitch of presumption, to consider his country as nothing but carte blanche, upon which he may scribble whatever he pleases.' From such chaos, he warned (presciently, as it turned out), violence, tyranny and corruption would likely follow.

In calling for the stability inherent in keeping that which is already known (or at least changing it only slowly), Burke laid the roots of a conservative ethos that established itself as a major political force throughout much of the world over the next two centuries. Nonetheless, significant voices have been unconvinced by conservatism's tendency to preserve the status quo, warts and all. As the economist J. K. Galbraith once wryly noted: 'The modern conservative is engaged in one of man's oldest exercises in moral philosophy; that is, the search for a superior moral justification for selfishness.'

SOCIALISM

Socialism is a political and economic ideology that calls for the means of production, distribution and exchange (everything from raw materials and factories to transport infrastructure) to be owned and/or regulated by the whole of society. Seen as in opposition to capitalism, socialism aims to create more equitable societies by negating the influence of private wealth. The means of production includes all the facilities and resources for the production of goods and services.

Socialist-style models of government have been discussed for millennia. Some, for instance, cite Plato as espousing socialist ideals in *Republic*, with his call for an end to private families and limits on private property. In the 6th century CE, meanwhile, the Zoroastrian visionary

Mazdak instituted systems of communal ownership and social welfare in the Persian Sasanian Empire. However, modern socialist thought did not develop until the 18th century, in part inspired by the French Revolution. Towards the end of the century, Thomas Paine – future American Founding Father – was in England, arguing for new taxes on property to fund the welfare of the poor. By the 1820s and 30s, the first organized labour movements – such as the Chartists in Britain – were emerging, alongside cooperative movements (associations set up to meet the common economic and social needs of its members).

The father of socialism

By the mid-19th century socialism had gained a foothold across Europe. Its single most important voice was the German-born Karl Marx, who – often in partnership with Friedrich Engels – wrote the great philosophical masterpieces of socialism and what Marx considered its logical conclusion: communism. Marx and Engels published *The Communist Manifesto* in 1848. It envisaged humanity's fate as the culmination of economic and political factors played out over history. 'The history of all hitherto existing society is the history of class struggles,' he wrote. Marx traced a path from an ancient system of common ownership to one based on private property and slavery, which in turn led to feudalism, to be subsequently replaced by capitalism. Each system saw the domination of one social group by another until its own violent overthrow, and Marx predicted the next great transition – from capitalism to communism – was fast approaching.

Marx went on to argue that capitalism had seen wealth and privilege fall to a minority class of property owners (the *bourgeoisie*) at the expense of the mass of wage-labourers (the *proletariat*) as a result of exploitation. With technological advances and the further concentration of capital, he said, unemployment would swell the ranks of the disenchanted proletariat, precipitating inevitable revolution. Thus capitalism would bring about its own demise – another victim of the cycle of history. Moreover, he expected the resultant communist state to be the perfect realization of a society where everything is in common ownership, rendering crime and conflict redundant and government unnecessary. 'Let the ruling classes tremble at a Communistic revolution. The proletarians have nothing to lose but their chains,' concluded the *Manifesto*. 'They have a world to win.'

SOCIAL DEMOCRACY

Social democracy was birthed in the 19th century as a political, social and economic philosophy aiming for the gradual and peaceful transition from capitalism to socialism. However, it has evolved significantly so that today it is usually understood as aiming for a democratic state that melds both capitalist and socialist practices.

In Germany, for instance, the Social Democratic Workers' Party was established in 1869, before uniting with the General German Workers' Union to form the Social Democratic Party of Germany. By 1912 it was the largest party in the German parliament and at the forefront of a continent-wide social-democratic movement.

The philosophy won the support of numerous intellectuals – among them Eduard Bernstein, whose critique of Marxism was particularly influential in Germany, and the Polish-born Rosa Luxemburg (1871–1919), who, in the early part of the 20th century, proclaimed: 'The more that social democracy develops, grows, and becomes stronger, the more the enlightened masses of workers will take their own destinies, the leadership of their movement, and the determination of its direction into their own hands.'

The bloodshed associated with the Russian Revolution deepened the division between communist and social-democratic parties, the latter of which continued to grow in influence in northern and western Europe in particular. By 1940, for instance, George Orwell was writing of 'drifting definitely towards a world social democracy.' Sure enough, several social-democratic governments came to power in the aftermath of the war – for example, in West Germany, Sweden and the UK – and began to build modern welfare states. In Britain, for instance, the social-democratic Labour Party constructed a National Health Service, delivering healthcare to all free at the point of delivery.

Rather than transitioning towards socialism or even melding capitalist and socialist ideologies, many social-democratic parties settled instead for regulating state agencies and commercial enterprises with the aim of achieving greater social and economic equity. Essentially, social democracy had become shorthand for welfare provision and limited state intervention – a distance from the goals of its original adherents.

The third way

Social democracy adopted yet another guise in the 1990s – the so-called Third Way, which claimed to fuse traditional welfare policies with *laissez-faire* economics. Leading Third Way figures became major players on the world stage: Bill Clinton in the USA, Gerhard Schröder in Germany, Tony Blair in the UK and Romani Prodi in Italy. Blair told the Congress of European Socialist Parties in 1997: 'Our task is not to fight old battles, but to show there is a third way, a way of marrying together an open economy, a competitive and successful economy, with a just and humane society.'

ANARCHISM

Anarchism calls for the abolition of all government, instead envisaging a society devoid of any coercive force and arranged around principles of voluntary cooperation.

Anarchists – the word itself is derived from the Greek for 'without ruler' – reject the idea that any government or ruler can have moral legitimacy, so argue that no individual should be obliged to conform to a government's demands. In its emphasis on the individual's right to act independently, anarchy may be regarded as an extreme expression of liberalism, although certain branches of anarchist thought have more in common with socialism in their call for voluntary collectivism.

Several texts of antiquity may be read as expounding proto-anarchic ideas. The *Tao Te Ching*, a 6th-century Taoist text, for instance, rejects Confucian ideas of governance in favour of living in natural and spontaneous harmony. In ancient Greece, meanwhile, Zeno of Citium was among those who proffered the notion of a government-free society. As the great Russian anarchist philosopher, Peter Kropotkin, observed:

> *The best exponent of anarchist philosophy in ancient Greece was Zeno . . . who distinctly opposed his conception of a free community without government to the state-Utopia of Plato. He repudiated the omnipotence of the State, its intervention and regimentation, and proclaimed the sovereignty of the moral law of the individual . . .*

The era of modern philosophical anarchism is generally thought to have begun with English philosopher William Godwin (1756–1836). In his 1793 work, *An Enquiry Concerning Political Justice*, he depicted government as a corrupting force that keeps the population reliant upon it by perpetuating ignorance. However, he predicted that with the spread of knowledge, politics would give way to personal morality, bringing with it an end to social conventions such as law, marriage and private property.

All property is theft

Pierre-Joseph Proudhon (1809–65) in France was the first to identify himself as an anarchist, arguing that all property is theft and urging a new system that structures itself without a central authority or its attendant social institutions. 'To be governed is to be watched over,' he said, 'inspected, spied on, directed, legislated at, regulated, docketed, indoctrinated, preached at, controlled, assessed, weighed, censored, ordered about, by men who have neither the right, nor the knowledge, nor the virtue.'

By the late 19th century, there had been a synthesis of Marxist and anarchist ideas by the likes of Kropotkin and Mikhail Bakunin (1814–76), who argued that collective action and organization was necessary to preserve the rights of the individual. Sure enough, a great many anarchists played active roles in, for instance, the Russian Revolution of 1917.

Yet the anarchist view necessarily requires the goodwill of individuals in order that society may function – an assumption too far for some observers. In 1946, George Orwell commented: 'In a Society in which there is no law, and in theory no compulsion, the only arbiter of behaviour is public opinion. But public opinion, because of the tremendous urge to conformity in gregarious animals, is less tolerant than any system of law.'

NATIONALISM

Nationalism has several nuanced meanings, ranging from feelings of loyalty to one's nation and a sense of national consciousness to calls for political independence and even the belief than one nation's interests and culture are superior to all others. By extension, nationalism favours unilateral action on the international stage. It is related to but distinct from, at one end of the spectrum, patriotism (attachment to and support of one's homeland), and at the other end, jingoism (aggressive patriotism), xenophobia (prejudice against other countries), imperialism (see page 173) and, ultimately, fascism (see page 196).

The emergence of nationalism as a political philosophy is often considered to correspond to the rise of the European nation-states that resulted from the 1648 Treaty of Westphalia. Prior to that, it is generally assumed that most people's loyalties were directed to entities other than their nation – for instance, family, village, region, monarch or religious denomination.

By the 19th century nationalism had established itself as a potent doctrine, especially in Europe, although nationalist ideas also fuelled the American War of Independence against the British and a number of uprisings in South America in the period around this time. In Europe, Napoleon's territorial encroachments prompted a series of 'national awakenings'. In 1804, Serbian nationalists set the ball rolling with an uprising against their Ottoman overlords, while in the 1820s Greek nationalists also made an attempt to break free of Ottoman hegemony. There were, moreover, strong independence movements in Scandinavia in the early part of the century, but 1848 was perhaps nationalism's pinnacle year, with revolutions in Germany, Hungary, Italy and Poland (ultimately, none of which were effective). Italy was united into its modern nation-state form by 1861, with Germany following a decade later. Meanwhile,

The good and bad of nationalism

Amid the fallout of the First World War, nationalism showed its darker side in Europe, most obviously in the rise of fascist dictatorships in Italy and Germany. Extreme nationalist ideology was in large part responsible for creating the climate in which the Second World War became an inevitability. Nonetheless, the more moderate aspects of the philosophy retained their influence in the post-war world. In Africa, it fuelled the independence movements that brought an end to the years of dominion by European powers and saw the continent reconfigured into newly formed nation-states. Similarly, the age of empire was brought to an end across much of Asia. The collapse of the Soviet Union and its sphere of influence in the 1990s then brought about a new era of nationalism in Europe, as a plethora of newly independent countries established (or re-established) themselves out of the bones of the USSR, the Eastern Bloc and the collapsed Yugoslavia.

there was a growing clamour by Irish nationalists to remove the British from power there.

By the end of the First World War, the Ottoman and Austro-Hungarian Empires were in their death throes and Europe settled into a new system of nation-states. Nationalism had also started to spread to Asia, notably with the establishment of the Chinese Republic following the overthrow of the imperial dynasty in 1911 and the 'exceptionalist' philosophy that permeated Japanese society. In India, meanwhile, a sense of national identity developed as Mahatma Gandhi led the independence movement that would see the British surrender their interest in the imperial 'jewel in the crown' in 1947.

FASCISM

Fascism is a political ideology in which society is based on authoritarianism and nationalism, typically accompanied by aggressive militarism. In fascist societies, the rights and interests of the individual and specific social groups are considered secondary to the needs of the state. Government is typically centred on a dictator who demands adherence to strict social and economic organization, with opposition ruthlessly suppressed.

Fascism emerged in the early 20th century, in large part a response to the rise of both socialism and liberal democracy. Profoundly reactionary, fascism claimed to offer hope of national rebirth. Economically, fascism treads a path between free-market capitalism, on the one hand, and government control of certain industries along with large-scale public spending, on the other.

Fascism took hold in Europe in the aftermath of the First World War and the Russian Revolution of 1917. With Europe's economies ravaged and facing the threat of communist takeover, fascism's message of national regeneration was eagerly received by many. While Italy was first to come under fascist rule, the movement's most infamous figure was Adolf Hitler, who took the National Socialist German Workers' (Nazi) Party to power in Germany in 1933.

With the German economy experiencing hyperinflation – the result of the punitive Versailles Treaty that followed German defeat in the First World War – Hitler played on widespread social discontent with his credo of national recovery and expansionism. In 1937, he described the 'main plank' of the National Socialist programme with these words: 'to abolish the liberalistic concept of the individual and the Marxist concept of humanity and to substitute therefore the folk community, rooted in the soil and bound together by the bond of its common blood.' The

The coining of fascism

Benito Mussolini, Italy's fascist dictator from 1922 until 1943, originated the term *Fascismo*, which has its roots in a Latin word describing a traditional symbol of ancient Rome: rods tied round an axe – an image denoting 'strength through unity'. Along with Giovanni Gentile, the self-proclaimed 'philosopher of Fascism', Mussolini attempted to create an intellectual basis for the movement in 1932's *The Doctrine of Fascism*. 'The keystone of the Fascist doctrine,' Mussolini said, 'is its conception of the State, of its essence, its functions, and its aims. For Fascism the State is absolute, individuals and groups relative.'

results, as is well recorded, were disastrous – from domestic oppression and militaristic muscle-flexing sprang world war and mass murder on an unprecedented scale.

INTERNATIONALISM

Internationalism may be regarded as the philosophical antidote to nationalism, promoting not narrow national interests but greater co-operation (cultural, political and/or economic) between nations.

In some respects, internationalism was born out of the liberal, *laissez-faire* economic philosophy of Adam Smith (see page 220), David Ricardo and their ilk. In 1843, for instance, Richard Cobden – a noted campaigner against the protectionist Corn Laws in the UK – said:

Free Trade! What is it? Why, breaking down the barriers that separate nations; those barriers, behind which nestle the feelings of pride, revenge, hatred, and jealousy, which every now and then burst their bounds, and deluge whole countries with blood; those feelings which nourish the poison of war and conquest, which assert that without conquest we can have no trade, which foster that lust for conquest and dominion which sends forth your warrior chiefs to scatter devastation through other lands, and then calls them back that they may be enthroned securely in your passions, but only to harass and oppress you at home.

However, internationalism became more associated with socialism over the course of the 19th century. Leading socialist thinkers including Karl Marx, Friedrich Engels and Vladimir Lenin all saw their struggle as that of working people across boundaries – a class war, not a nationalist one. The International Workingmen's Association (also known as the First International) was founded in London in 1864 to bring together left-wing groups from numerous countries, and claimed a membership of some eight million at its peak.

In the 20th century, internationalism took a new course, in part a response to the conflicts that marred the era. A desire for peaceful cooperation, rather than the dissemination of socialist ideals, became the driving force of internationalists. As early as 1889 the Frenchman Frédéric Passy (who in 1868 had co-founded the International and Permanent League of Peace) and a Briton, William Randal Cremer, set up the Inter-Parliamentary Union, with an initial aim of arbitrating in transnational conflicts. Then, in the aftermath of the First World War, the League of Nations was established with the remit to maintain world peace. Largely toothless at critical moments, it was subsequently replaced by the United Nations in 1945.

<hr>

The era of European cohesion

In 1945, the Bretton Woods system was activated, with organizations including the World Bank and International Monetary Fund brought into being to regulate and mediate economic relations between nations. The precursors of the European Union first appeared in the 1950s, ushering in a new era of unprecedented – if sometimes rocky – European cohesion. Today, few nations operate in isolation, instead opting to join international organizations that promote trade, foster cultural cooperation, pursue common defence policies, sponsor scientific endeavours and rule on matters of international law.

<hr>

UNIVERSAL SUFFRAGE

Universal suffrage is the granting of voting rights to all adult citizens in a society – an idea essential to the full achievement of representative democracy. Where universal suffrage applies, no adult is barred from voting on the basis of race, gender, wealth, education, social position or beliefs. However, some countries operate universal suffrage with a few exceptions, such as those who are in prison or who are deemed mentally incapable.

Given its significance to our modern understanding of what democracy is, universal suffrage is a relatively new phenomenon. In the cradle of democracy, ancient Athens, women, slaves and foreign nationals were all denied the vote and typically no more than about 20 per cent of the population were permitted to take part at the polls. Things would not greatly improve for over two thousand years, during which time most nations operated systems in which only men could vote, and then only those of requisite wealth and status and with acceptable religious affiliations. Unified Germany's first Chancellor from 1871 until 1890, Otto von Bismarck, showed his distaste for the concept when describing

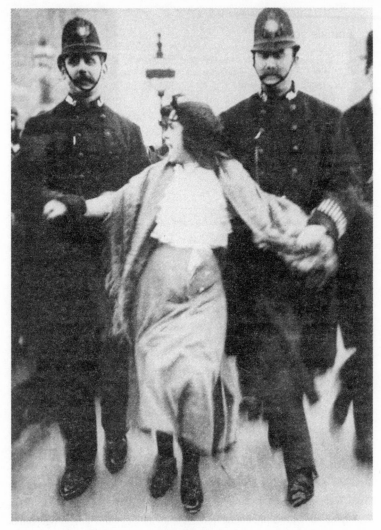

Female Suffrage

Female suffrage

The arrival of female suffrage was much delayed, and often came only after concerted campaigning – as epitomized by the Suffragette movements in the US and UK in the late 19th and early 20th centuries. As one of the British movement's key figures, Emmeline Pankhurst, noted: 'If it is right for men to fight for their freedom, and God knows what the human race would be like today if men had not, since time began, fought for their freedom, then it is right for women to fight for their freedom and the freedom of the children they bear.'

New Zealand was to grant universal female suffrage in 1893. Having eliminated racial criteria and extended the vote to all men over the previous decade and a half, it was thus also the first country that could claim truly universal suffrage. By contrast, some otherwise developed and progressive countries continued to block the female vote. Switzerland – an early adopter of universal male suffrage back in 1848 – held out on granting full voting rights for women at federal and cantonal elections until 1990. Meanwhile, the fight for female suffrage continues to be fought in various parts of the world, notably in the Middle East and parts of Asia.

universal suffrage as 'government of a house by its nursery'.

It was only in 1792 that post-Revolution France became the first nation to adopt universal male suffrage regardless of wealth or property ownership, to be permanently enshrined in French law in 1848. That year was a pivotal one for suffrage, with several European nations extending the vote in the aftermath of widespread revolution. The United States, meanwhile, adopted theoretical universal male suffrage in 1870 when black people were granted the vote after the American Civil War, but it was more theoretical than real.

Ulysses S. Grant, president from 1869 to 1877, said that 'suffrage once given can never be taken away.' However, that is what happened in much of the American South via the introduction of state property and literacy qualifications that effectively ruled out much of the black population. Only with the Voting Rights Act of 1965 did the USA – widely regarded as the world's leading democracy – institutionalize universal male suffrage. Infamously, South Africa denied the vote to its majority black population until 1994.

CIVIL SOCIETY

The term 'civil society' has evolved and changed greatly since Classical times but today may be broadly understood as that part of society representing a community of citizens pursuing common interests and undertaking common activities. In its modern guise, this equates to all those non-governmental organizations and institutions – distinct from government and corporate entities – that represent the desires and interests of citizens (what might be termed 'civic values'). In the modern age, civil society has played a vital role in the rebuilding of post-communist Eastern Europe and in the battle against globalization.

The civil society and enlightenment

By the medieval period, ideas about participatory society had changed dramatically. The social idealism of Plato and Aristotle had little relevance to vast swathes of the global population who lived under the unfettered rule of all-powerful monarchs, and who eked out an existence within the constraints of serfdom. It was only with the Enlightenment that the idea of civil society re-entered political discourse in any meaningful way. Philosophers and political theorists sought new ways to reconfigure the power imbalance that had grown between the Church and state on the one hand and the citizenry on the other. It was a subject notably explored by, among others, John Locke and Thomas Hobbes (see entry on The Social Contract on page 171).

Yet when the Greek philosophers first spoke of civil society, their terms of reference were quite different. For Plato, the civil society and the state were one and the same thing, striving for virtue, wisdom and the common good – in other words, civility. Aristotle, meanwhile, regarded the state as an amalgamation of civic associations, a grand framework in which the citizenry may actively participate in the virtuous running of the whole.

In the late 18th and early 19th centuries, the German philosopher Hegel changed the terms of the debate again. He regarded civil society as that part of society that intervenes between family and state, and he saw it as a distinctly economic entity governed by a civic code. This was a view notably followed by Karl Marx and Alexis de Tocqueville, the latter of whom believed that associations of citizens with a mutual purpose would ensure that selfish desires were kept in check and would also guarantee the health of political society.

By the 1980s and 90s, civil society had come to be seen as an agent of rebirth and regeneration in many of the post-Soviet states, where the rapid demise of communism had created a vacuum in the spheres of government and commerce. At around the same time, it was also held up as a paragon of anti-globalization, whereby local interests could find a voice in the institutions of civil society.

However, civil society is not without its critics. Some have pointed to its fundamentally undemocratic nature – its leading figures unelected and, opponents suggest, answerable to no one but a small coterie of their supporters – while others have suggested that the rise of international non-governmental organizations (arguably the ultimate expression of civil society) has been instrumental in the imposition of homogenised ideas and strategies that have fostered globalization.

FEMINISM

Feminism today means many things to many people, with differing interpretations often clashing. Women's rights to vote, to have an abortion, to be paid equally to men, to be allowed time off to have children and to dress without fear of judgement or expectation – all these (and much else besides) may be regarded as expressions of feminism. At its heart, though, is the idea that the sexes are equal and that women should not face discrimination on the basis of their gender.

It is widely accepted that men have enjoyed a privileged position throughout history, commanding the reins of power and wielding it often at the expense of women. Of course, there have been figures who have bucked the trend, like Hatshepsut and Cleopatra in ancient Egypt, Empress Wu Zetian of China, Byzantine Empress Theodora, Elizabeth I in England, Maria Theresa of Austria and Catherine the Great in Russia. But over the broad sweep of time, they have been the exceptions. Furthermore, there was little in the way of a concerted effort to change the situation until the 19th century.

The great 20th-century feminist, Simone de Beauvoir, identified the French writer Christine de Pizan (1364–*c*. 1430) as the first female explicitly to decry misogyny.

Others look to Mary Wollstonecraft's *A Vindication of the Rights of Woman* (1792) as the first consciously feminist work of literature. Her core theme was that men and women are capable of equal rationality and moral judgement when educated to the same level. While stopping short of expressing a 'wish to invert the order of things', her message to 'Let woman share the rights and she will emulate the virtues of men' was nonetheless new and powerful.

But it would not be until late the next century that feminism enjoyed its so-called First Wave. This was characterized by a demand for women's rights and social emancipation – as epitomized by the Suffragists who demanded women get the vote. There were also calls for better working and property rights, as well as protection against sexual violence within marriage. The term 'feminism' first came into popular usage in the 1880s but, after the eventual granting of certain legal concessions in much of the developed world over the ensuing decades, feminism's Second Wave did not arrive until the 1950s.

Feminism's Second Wave

Arguably beginning with the publication of Simone de Beauvoir's *The Second Sex* (in which she proclaimed the existentialist view that 'One is not born but becomes a woman'), this phase was led by figures including social and political activist and feminist, Gloria Steinem, Betty Friedan (author of *The Feminine Mystique*), Germaine Greer and Kate Millett. As well as seeking greater equality across all aspects of society, there was a push for sexual liberation, which seemed even more achievable with the introduction of the contraceptive pill that gave women new levels of control over their reproductive lives.

The Second Wave had subsided by the 1980s amid claims that the big arguments had now been won, but a Third Wave appeared in the 1990s. It sought to resolve issues emerging from the previous waves – including arguments that issues of class and race had not been sufficiently addressed by classical feminism. Into the 21st century, where gender identity is ever more fluid and the rise of social media has stoked a feminist backlash, the idea that feminism's job is done seems more far-fetched than ever.

ENVIRONMENTALISM

Environmentalism is a social and political ideology that seeks to protect the natural environment in the face of human activity. By the end of the 20th century many countries counted environmentalist parties among their political establishments, usually operating under the banner of 'green politics'.

Environmentalism argues that protecting the natural environment is in our long-term interests, promoting the ecological balance of the planet, better health and social justice, as well as preserving natural resources for future generations. Most environmentalists demand action from the level of the individual all the way up to inter-governmental cooperation. Classic environmentalist policy ideas include reducing consumption, recycling, using clean energy sources (such as wind and tidal power, rather than fossil fuels) investing in environmentally friendly technologies, protecting endangered animal species and nurturing natural environments (for example, the Amazon rainforest).

Although there were a few instances of environmental activism in centuries past, the history of mankind has been distinguished by accelerating use of natural resources. In terms of environmental politics, concern in the 19th century over urban air pollution prompted the first explicit activism. Meanwhile, the Romantics gave cultural impetus to the idea that the natural environment should be treasured. William Wordsworth, for instance, described his beloved Lake District as a 'sort of national property in which every man has a right and interest who has an eye to perceive and a heart to enjoy.'

'Education, if it means anything, should not take people away from the land, but instil in them even more respect for it, because educated people are in a position to understand what is being lost. The future of the planet concerns all of us, and all of us should do what we can to protect it.'

Wangari Maathai, Kenyan environmental activist

In 1962, Rachel Carson published *Silent Spring*, detailing the damage wrought by the use of the insecticide DDT. It prompted massive public interest in the USA and was in part responsible for the creation of the US Environmental Protection Agency. The 1970s then saw the creation of political parties campaigning principally on environmental issues – firstly in Australia and New Zealand and then in Europe. Meanwhile, in 1972 the United Nations held its first conference on the human environment, marking a sea change in the methods of dealing with environmental challenges at the international level.

The environmental sceptics

There has been a backlash from those who see environmentalist policies as putting a brake on human development. The world is more robust than it seems, goes one theory, and technological advances will counter the effects of environmental degradation. Developing nations, meanwhile, argue that it is unfair to stall their industrial development after the developed world has reaped the rewards of years of environmentally damaging activities. Others say that environmentalist 'red tape' threatens economic growth and jobs. In 2012, for example, the future US President Donald Trump asserted: 'The concept of global warming was created by and for the Chinese in order to make US manufacturing non-competitive.' While few serious scientists give any credence to such claims, it is indicative of the hostility environmentalism can encounter.

PART SEVEN

ECONOMICS

'The art of economics consists in looking not merely at the immediate but at the longer effects of any act or policy; it consists in tracing the consequences of that policy not merely for one group but for all groups.'

Henry Hazlitt

Economics studies how we distribute scarce resources to best satisfy our limitless list of wants and needs. As such, economics is also the study of human behaviour – what drives us to we act as we do, how we organize as societies and how we seek to meet our present desires within a long-term strategy. Yet it is a discipline that can be enormously frustrating, its big ideas often seeming to contradict one another, or else proving highly fallible or inexact. US President Harry S. Truman once pleaded: 'Give me a one-handed economist. All my economists say, on the one hand . . . on the other . . .' But economics impacts on our lives in the most fundamental ways on a daily basis. In the words of

John Maynard Keynes: 'The ideas of economists and political philosophers, both when they are right and when they are wrong, are more powerful than is commonly understood. Indeed, the world is ruled by little else.'

SCARCITY

Scarcity is the driving idea behind all economic thought. The more scarce a product in relation to the demand for it, the more it is likely to cost. The British economist Lionel Robbins defined economics as follows in 1932: 'the science which studies human behaviour as a relationship between ends and scarce means which have alternative uses'.

Humanity has long understood that demand for scarce resources is a source of tension. Gautama Buddha went so far as to suggest that desire and greed (*tanha*) are the root of all suffering (*dukkha*), and that personal happiness is achieved by the limiting of our wants and needs. Come the early 19th century, the Scottish economist David Ricardo set out to explain how scarcity influences value. He observed: 'Gold and silver, like other commodities, have an intrinsic value, which is not arbitrary, but is dependent on their scarcity, the quantity of labour bestowed in procuring them, and the value of the capital employed in the mines which produce them.' Note that scarcity tops the list of determining factors.

In more recent times, the Indian-born economist Amartya Sen has suggested that the mechanisms of the market economy can actually aggravate problems of scarcity. In a 1981 analysis of several African and Asian famines (including the Bengal famine of the 1940s, in which some 3 million people died), he concluded that death was often not the result of non-availability of food but rather arose from inequalities in the food supply chain.

In Bengal, for example, he noted that food production had declined

'Living with Scarcity'

year on year leading up to the onset of famine in 1943, but was still higher than it had been in earlier, famine-free years. However, landless, rural farmworkers and the urban poor died in unprecedented numbers. With India assisting colonial British rule in its war effort, money directed from London gravitated towards India's major cities – Calcutta (now Kolkata), in the case of Bengal. This drove up prices, leaving rural labourers and the urban poor unable to command high enough wages to enter the market. Although there was food to be had, they could not afford to buy it.

Scarcity, thus, is only half of the economist's conundrum, with the question of how to secure fair allocation being the other half. Furthermore, scarcity is not limited to physical resources. Shortfalls in technology, for instance, can also skew our ability to make the best use of resources – think of the farmer in Africa who lacks access to the tools that would allow him to move beyond a subsistence existence.

And there are those who argue that time is our most significant 'scarce resource', forcing us to make economic decisions at every turn. As Nobel laureate Paul Samuelson (1915–2009) once put it: 'Time is our ultimate scarcity... And so we're constantly having to sacrifice alternate activities to get the one that pleases us most.'

UTILITY

Utility, in an economic sense, relates to the amount of satisfaction or pleasure that is derived from consuming a particular item of goods, or a service. It is considered one of the driving forces of consumer behaviour since individuals are customarily assumed to make decisions on the basis of what will make them most happy under any particular set of circumstances.

While utility has clearly influenced consumer behaviour since the beginnings of time, its recognition as a substantive factor in how and what people consume is of much more recent vintage.

A calculus of pleasure

Several leading economists of the 19th century seized on the idea. William Stanley Jevons, for example, introduced his 1888 work, *The Theory of Political Economy*, with the words: 'In this work I have attempted to treat Economy as a Calculus of Pleasure and Pain.' Francis Edgeworth, meanwhile, suggested the development of a 'hedonimeter' – 'an ideally perfect instrument, a psychophysical machine, continually registering the height of pleasure experienced by an individual'. In its absence, Edgeworth and Jevons were forced to rely on subjective analysis of marketplace behaviour. As Jevons, again, wrote:

A unit of pleasure or pain is difficult even to conceive; but it is the amount of these feelings which is continually prompting us to buying and selling, borrowing and lending, labouring and resting, producing and consuming; and it is from the quantitative effects of the feelings that we must estimate their comparative amounts.

Attempting to measure happiness is a fraught business. What is happiness, anyway? Why does it feel so different to different people?

Notwithstanding such philosophical imponderables, classical economics suggests that the market provides those things that bring most people the most happiness – thus making best use of limited resources. Yet there are evident problems. We may enjoy eating chocolate cake, but if we buy and consume ten each day, we will likely end up chronically obese and unwell. So has all that cake really made us happy?

In such a light, it is difficult to see that our consumption of chocolate cake has resulted in our optimum utility or in the best use of limited resources. Therefore, economists since Friedrich von Wieser (1851–1926) have taken into consideration the attendant notion of marginal utility, which says that our levels of happiness are affected by how much of something we consume. A slice of cake a day or a week might increase our utility, but ten slices a day will lead to diminishing marginal utility – in other words, the more we consume of some things, the less benefit we get with each additional unit of consumption.

MONEY

The primary role of money is as a medium of exchange – that is to say, it is anything that is mutually recognized by both buyer and seller as a suitable method of payment when buying goods and services (for instance, coins, notes, credit cards). It also has a number of historical, subsidiary roles, including serving as a standardized measure of value and a store of value.

When humans gave up their hunter-gatherer existence and began to participate in trade (a hundred thousand or more years ago), they were forced to conduct business by exchanging one good or service for another. However, as trades became more complex, the barter system began to struggle. What if you wanted some wine that a villager had produced, but he did not at that time want the wheat you proposed to swap? And how could you know that you were swapping the same volume of wheat for, say, a leg of lamb as your neighbour was? Moreover, how much wheat is a fair exchange for a leg of lamb, or a litre of wine?

It became apparent that trade would work better if there were fixed tokens of value that allowed trade between multiple partners and ensured a fair system of price. A token of value that could be used to buy the wine, for example. In turn, the wine-maker could use the same token to buy whatever he desired. It is thought the first currency, the *shekel*, originated in Mesopotamia around 3000 BCE, its value fixed to a quantity of barley. Other ancient cultures used alternative tokens including shells.

Physical money

By around the 7th century BCE, currencies were increasingly based on precious metals such as gold and silver – commodities that were limited in quantity and of commonly accepted value. Under the wide-ranging reach of the Greco-Roman world in the 1st century BCE, money became increasingly standardized and regulated so that it could be used by ever-growing numbers of people, even across borders. It is thought paper money – essentially, promises to pay on demand a specific quantity of commodity money (e.g. gold coins) – was introduced into Chinese society around the 7th century CE, only being adopted in Europe some thousand years later.

In the modern world, while banknotes, coins, debit and credit cards remain important, most money today is 'bank money', such as cheques, drafts and bank credits. For much of history, gold has been the premium measure of value and it was only in the 20th century that leading economic powerhouses discarded the so-called Gold Standard, linking national currencies to the value of gold. The subsequent absence of physical resources (in the form of gold deposits) to support specific currencies has been blamed by assorted analysts for fostering a lack of trust in the international finance system, precipitating regular economic crises. Nonetheless, money continues to make the world of commerce go round, and in doing so it has helped shape cultures for thousands of years.

'Annual income twenty pounds, annual expenditure nineteen six, result happiness. Annual income twenty pounds, annual expenditure twenty pound ought and six, result misery.'

Charles Dickens

TAXATION

Taxation is the primary method by which governments finance themselves. Taxes are compulsory payments to government, levied against individuals and businesses. Most governments strive to keep the tax burden – the total cost to a country of paying taxes (including not just the taxes themselves, but the cost of administering and collecting them) – at the minimum level necessary to raise sufficient funds to carry out its obligations.

It has been said that there are but two certainties in this world – death and taxes. Certainly, tax has been with us for a long time – the ancient Egyptians, Greeks and Romans all had highly developed systems in place, often to support military endeavours. Indeed, income tax was invented by the British government to raise funds to fight Napoleon. And tax has never been popular. In 60 CE, Boadicea, leader of the Iceni, led an uprising in England against its Roman occupiers, at least in part inspired by corrupt tax collectors. Disputes over tax would subsequently lead to such landmark events as the drawing up of the Magna Carta and the onset of both the English Civil War and the American War of Independence. As

J. K. Galbraith would later observe: 'The American colonies, all know, were greatly opposed to taxation without representation. They were also, a less celebrated quality, equally opposed to taxation with representation.'

Progressive taxes require those with the most to pay a greater proportion. Income tax is, typically, a progressive tax, charged at a lower rate for those with a lower income, and increasing incrementally for incomes above certain thresholds. Other taxes, such as sales taxes, are charged at a flat rate regardless of personal circumstances. While it is generally accepted that progressive taxes are more socially equitable, there are those who argue that a system deemed to unfairly tax the rich risks losing its wealthiest members to more sympathetic tax regimes, with knock-on effects for the economy as a whole. For instance, in the aftermath of the global economic slowdown in the noughties it was suggested that banks should be subject to punitive charges, while others warned that bankers would respond by taking their business elsewhere, costing jobs and reducing the total volume of wealth in the economy.

Tax avoidance

Others unsatisfied at the tax demands upon them (and rich enough to employ someone to navigate loopholes for them) can attempt to reduce what they have to pay by practising tax avoidance. This is a legal – if morally suspect – strategy that can involve, for example, setting up companies in low-tax offshore jurisdictions, establishing shell companies (i.e. companies with legal status but not actively trading, through which to funnel money) and moving to a tax haven. Tax evasion, meanwhile, is any illegal attempt to shirk one's tax bill (for example, by misrepresenting income).

SUPPLY AND DEMAND

At the heart of all markets is the concept of supply and demand. This is true for a local fruit and veg market as much as a stock exchange, an online shopping platform or even the all-encompassing abstract market that governs the full gamut of humanity's transactions. The market strives to balance the types and volumes of goods and services provided by suppliers against the goods and services demanded by consumers – a relationship in fairly constant flux.

Demand, in simple terms, relates to the quantity of goods or service that consumers want at a certain price. *Supply*, on the other hand, is concerned with the quantity of goods or service that producers make available at a given price. Both consumers and suppliers face key questions as they approach a transaction from their opposing positions. Firstly, the consumer must decide whether they want a particular product, and then whether they are prepared to pay the price being asked by the supplier. They must also consider the question of opportunity cost: that which is given up in the process of making a particular economic decision. For instance, if I pay for a holiday, I won't be able to afford a new car. The supplier, meanwhile, faces different but related questions. How great is the demand for what I am offering? How large a price will the market bear? Is it enough for me to turn a profit?

At the end of the 19th century, Alfred Marshall popularized the standard model of supply and demand. He created a simple graph in which supply and demand are shown to be inversely proportional to each other in relation to price. In other words, as price increases, demand broadly declines and supply grows, while a price decrease sees supply fall and demand grow. By plotting their relative trajectories, he established the point at which they cross as signifying market equilibrium – the holy grail of the market, where supply exactly matches demand.

The seesaw of supply and demand

The general law of supply and demand is straightforward: if all other factors remain the same, the lower the price of a good or service, the more people will demand it; on the other hand, as demand grows, suppliers will seek to provide more and at a greater price, so maximizing their profit. The 14th-century Syrian academic, Ibn Taymiyyah, was among the first to put the idea into words: 'If desire for goods increases while its availability decreases, its price rises. On the other hand, if availability of the good increases and the desire for it decreases, the price comes down.'

Of course, levels of supply and demand are subject to many disparate and unpredictable factors – climate change, for example, may lead to a long-term upsurge in demand for sun-protection, while prompting a downturn in the supply of bread as a result of higher volumes of failing crops. Yet the fundamental law continues to wield enormous influence on the markets – and on our everyday lives too.

CAPITALISM

Capitalism is a system of economic organization in which private individuals or private organizations predominantly own the means of production, distribution and exchange of goods and services. Capitalism favours the free market (in which buyers and sellers trade independently of third-party – typically government – interference), with private profit a driving force in decision-making in everything, from investment and wages to production levels and pricing. The theory goes that the capitalist desirous of maximizing his profit will supply the market with what it most wants in the most efficient way.

The decline of feudalism and mercantilism

Many societies had incorporated aspects of capitalism into their economies since ancient times but until the medieval ages, feudalism dominated European society. This was a system in which most land was owned by the crown and the noble classes. They permitted the populace to live on the land, typically as serfs scratching a meagre existence from farming and in return paying homage and owing a certain amount of labour and produce to the landlord, as well as military allegiance. With the decline of feudalism from the 15th century and the rise of the nation-state – and with it liberal politics and *laissez-faire* trade – capitalism gradually became the most common mode of economic organization, firstly in Europe and then across the globe.

With the coming of the Industrial Revolution and the decline of mercantilism (see Protectionism on page 221), capitalism was enshrined as the prevailing economic orthodoxy in the 18th and 19th centuries by the likes of Adam Smith and David Ricardo. Where once wealth had gravitated to a small group based on their noble birth or military prowess, the economic behemoths of the capitalist world were entrepreneurial 'captains of industry' and financiers. Where feudalism had preserved old wealth, now anybody could make it rich – although in reality only a few did.

Some have argued that capitalism merely replaces one method of wealth ring-fencing with another. Among the system's fiercest critics were Karl Marx and Friedrich Engels, who declared that the pursuit of individual self-interest is ultimately injurious to the common good. Furthermore, they suggested, the capitalist exploits his workers, ensuring a long-term disparity in wealth distribution, while the system as a whole is prone to peaks and troughs, causing damaging waves of first over-production and then shortages and unemployment.

For all its undeniable faults, capitalism has dominated the global economic picture for some two hundred years. Today, most of the developed world operates a system of mixed economies, in which capitalism rubs up alongside state intervention in certain sectors, such as health and education.

Ludwig von Mises said: 'All people, however fanatical they may be in their zeal to disparage and to fight capitalism, implicitly pay homage to it by passionately clamouring for the products it turns out.'

THE INVISIBLE HAND

In raw terms, a free market is one where the prices for goods and services are determined by the forces of supply and demand without intervention from any external agency, such as a government or a monopoly. Although free markets have existed since one human first started trading with another, it was not until the 18th century that their mechanics were subjected to serious academic scrutiny. The most important free-market theoretician of his age was the Scottish economist, Adam Smith.

Smith (1723–90) was a moral philosopher and logician by training, and was heavily influenced by Enlightenment thought. His most famous work, *An Inquiry into the Nature and Causes of the Wealth of Nations* appeared in 1776 and contained many of his most important ideas, including that of the 'invisible hand', which he claimed guides the free market. It is, he suggested, the unseen force that ensures free-market economic activity is coordinated notwithstanding the absence of a centralized, organizing agent. To put it another way, the market provides those goods and services that society requires most efficiently when left to its own devices.

Writing at a time when mercantilism (see page 219) still held significant sway, Smith's ideas were striking. He contended that the free market is driven towards optimum distribution by self-interest – the suppliers' desire for enrichment through sales and the consumers' desire to enjoy particular goods and services. Thus, suppliers will provide for consumers that they do not necessarily know or have goodwill towards, and similarly consumers will gravitate towards suppliers with whom they have no personal connection. Smith described the situation like this:

> *Every individual necessarily labours to render the annual revenue of the society as great as he can. Generally, indeed, neither intends to promote the public interest, nor knows how much he is promoting it . . . by directing that industry in such a manner as its produce may be of the greatest value, he intends only his own gain, and he is in this, as in many other cases, led by an invisible hand to promote an end which was no part of his intention.*

Smith did see some instances where government intervention was desirable – such as in the provision of health and education, where he feared supply might falter in the hands of private enterprise – but his idea of the 'invisible hand' has been pivotal to the intellectual establishment of modern, free-market economics.

PROTECTIONISM

Protectionism is the economic philosophy that a government ought to shield its domestic industries from foreign competition by imposing regulations or offering incentives that skew international trade. While the incentives to protect one's own industries are obvious (particularly in periods of economic hardship), many economists argue that protectionism causes long-term problems both for the protectionist government and for the international trade system as a whole.

The end of protectionism

By the mid-19th century, Britain felt confident enough as a global industrial powerhouse to do away with many of the remnants of its protectionist past, including repeal of the Corn Laws that regulated imports of grain. Protectionism persisted throughout the 20th century, practised by an array of nations big and small, not least when facing pricy wars and sharp depressions. However, after the Second World War, the prevailing economic orthodoxy was that free trade benefits us all much more than protectionism. Whether that orthodoxy holds as the world attempts to recoup the losses incurred during the Great Recession that struck in 2007 remains to be seen.

A form of protectionism known as mercantilism was the preferred economic strategy of most of the leading European nations between the 16th and 18th centuries. This was a doctrine rooted in the idea that the volume of global trade was broadly static. Therefore, the theory went, a nation's wealth was reliant on ensuring less money flowed out of the economy than came in. This was most easily achieved by imposing tariffs to deter imports while enacting regulations that promoted exports. However, with Adam Smith and David Ricardo revolutionizing economic thought some two centuries later, mercantilism was steadily giving way to a more *laissez-faire* viewpoint.

There are a number of weapons in the protectionist's armoury. Among them are: tariffs (taxes on imported goods), which may be targeted at specific goods in the hope of encouraging purchases from local suppliers instead; subsidies (government payments to businesses to help increase their competitiveness); import quotas (limits on the volume of certain goods that may be imported); and export subsidies (government payments to encourage increased levels of exports). A government may also implement 'red tape' (e.g. safety standard requirements) to deter importers, or else enact patent laws designed to exclude foreign competition, or even manipulate the exchange rate in favour of exports over imports.

But critics argue few winners emerge from such tactics. Consumers are faced with less choice and potentially higher prices, while companies have no incentive to innovate and improve to see off foreign competition. Moreover, it does little to foster good relations between nations, either economically or politically.

In 2009 the G20 group of advanced nations seemed to acquiesce as they pledged: 'We will not repeat the historic mistakes of protectionism of previous eras.' Nonetheless, protectionism remains an influential doctrine. In the 21st century, the USA and China have freely accused each other of protectionism, prompting a series of cat-and-mouse retaliatory measures.

COMPARATIVE ADVANTAGE

Comparative advantage, a subject famously explored by the Scottish economist David Ricardo (1772–1823), is a key tenet of international trade. It explains why it makes sense for particular countries to produce and export certain products and import others.

As already mentioned, Ricardo worked in the period when mercantilism was still widespread – a practice that he considered resulted in inefficient use of resources over the long term and held back wealth-generation. Like his close contemporary, Adam Smith (see page 220), Ricardo believed that free trade between nations was the way forward. Smith had already elucidated the idea of absolute advantage – the ability of one country to carry out a particular economic activity more efficiently than another. For instance, it makes more sense for France – blessed with an ideal climate – to produce wine and export it to, say, Russia, than for Russia to attempt to produce its own wine while lacking the appropriate conditions.

Ricardo, though, took things a step further by developing the theory of comparative advantage. He showed that international trade can be beneficial to all participating countries even where one nation has an absolute advantage in all products. Even though this 'golden nation' may theoretically produce everything itself, Ricardo argued that it makes sense for it to specialize in certain goods and services (those at which it is very best) and import the rest.

Take an imaginary nation, Country A, and its potential trading partner, Z. Both countries want bread to eat and clothes to wear. Country A can produce 1,000 loaves of bread using fifty hours of labour and 1,000 garments using sixty hours of labour. Z, meanwhile, takes eighty hours to produce 1,000 loaves and seventy hours for 1,000 garments. According to the model of absolute advantage, A ought to produce everything, but that's before considering the opportunity cost. We see that the labour used in A to produce the clothes costs 6/5 units of bread, while in Z the opportunity cost is 7/5 units of bread.

In other words, it takes A 110 hours to produce 1,000 loaves and 1,000 garments, while it takes Z 150 hours. Their combined 260 hours result in 2,000 loaves and 2,000 garments. But if A specialized in bread-making, it could produce 2,200 loaves in its 110 hours, while Z could produce 2,143 garments in its 150 hours. Overall production will be increased despite no extra labour, even though Z is the less efficient producer per unit. Therefore, according to Ricardo, it is logical for A to specialize in bread production and Z in clothes-making. The theory of comparative advantage thus drives international trade towards best serving everyone's interests.

THE MALTHUSIAN PROBLEM

Thomas Malthus (1766–1834) was an English clergyman and political economist who introduced the so-called 'Malthusian Problem' in his *Essay on the Principle of Population* (1798). He summarized his central argument thus: 'The power of population is indefinitely greater than the power in the earth to produce subsistence for man.' His pessimistic conclusion was that population levels remain fairly constant in the long term because the planet is unable to sustain significant increases for more than short periods. In other words, economic stagnation will always rein in population growth. Although the global population has given the lie to his assumptions, his ideas continue to resonate with economists and, increasingly, environmentalists.

When Malthus wrote his treatise, he was swimming against the tide of opinion that held humanity was locked into a march of progress (see page 145). His central idea was that while population has a tendency to grow in rapid bursts, food production expands at a more constant rate as a result of the law of diminishing returns – there is a finite amount of land on which to grow food and increasing the labour supply results in increasingly smaller output gains. Therefore, Malthus contended, food shortages are inevitable since population growth outstrips growth in the food supply.

The resultant malnutrition leads, he said, to an increased death rate, accompanied by a dip in the birth rate as families regulate their reproduction in accordance to the food they have available to feed themselves. The population thus enters a period of 'natural wastage', resulting in more food being available to share around and a general spike in living conditions. But then the wheel turns again, since these improved conditions lead to fewer deaths and provide encouragement to have more children, raising the population level until lack of resources brings it back in line again. This 'Malthusian trap' – as it became known – goes hand in hand with a cycle of economic stagnation, in which the population makes do on just enough as they await the next inevitable wave of starvation, disease or other calamity that will bring the population back down to size. 'To prevent the recurrence of misery is, alas! beyond the power of man,' he declared.

Malthus offered no easy solution – even government welfare would only encourage an expansion of population size, hastening the onset of shortages, he suggested. However, he failed to take account of the technological advances (notably in agricultural production) that have propelled some 200 years of rapid global population growth, so that now we add about a billion people to the planet every decade. Nonetheless, his arguments have had profound influence on figures as diverse as Charles Darwin and John Maynard Keynes. Furthermore, as modern geographers, environmentalists and economists confront the idea that the planet might be nearing capacity – with battles for such basic resources as water becoming a genuine threat – there is a tide of opinion that Malthus may have had it about right all along.

MARXIAN ECONOMICS

Marxism has already been featured in this book, in the 'Socialism' section in the part on 'Politics'. However, there is a distinction – admittedly sometimes blurry – between Karl Marx's economic analysis and his political philosophy, so his economics warrants separate discussion here. After all, while he may have died penniless and largely unsung, his ideas were to have a profound effect on the planet in the century after his death.

As previously discussed, Marx saw human history as defined by a succession of economic systems, each new one replacing an older

The labour theory of value

Key for Marx was his idea of the labour theory of value. He was not the first to come up with such a theory (Ricardo, for instance, devised a thesis of his own) but Marx's was distinctively new. He argued that the bourgeoisie (the capital-owning class) profit by fixing prices to take account of the cost of raw materials plus the cost of wages and then adding a profit margin. It is the worker, he contended, who creates the added value (the profit margin) by turning the raw materials into something else, yet they are deprived of any cut of profit (the gap between the worker's wage and the value they produce being termed 'surplus value'). Indeed, Marx argued, capitalism encourages the consumer to think about the abstract commodity they are buying without considering the labour required to produce it – a process he called commodity fetishism. Moreover, the capitalist actively seeks to keep labour costs low (easily achievable where there is an expanding population and, thus, a supply of labour competing for a finite number of jobs). The search for profit also encourages technological innovation and job specialization that traps workers into low-paid and unsatisfying jobs.

dominant order. He believed capitalism pitted the bourgeoisie against the proletariat in a conflict that would culminate in a full-blown class war, paving the way for communism. But what were the economic underpinnings of his theories? He explored them in his *magnum opus*, *Capital: A Critique of Political Economy* (commonly known by its German title, *Das Kapital*), which appeared in three volumes, the first in 1867 and the others posthumously in 1885 and 1894.

Marx is credited as being among the first to recognize that the capitalist system is inherently prone to crisis, which he related to the tendency of the rate of profit to fall (what Marx would call 'the most important law of political economy'). He was attuned to the cycle of boom and bust that has marked out capitalism while most of his contemporaries had not yet begun to conjure with the notion.

Though Marx's status as an economist is hotly disputed, his significance is undeniable. Without Marxian economics, there would have been no Lenin and no USSR, no Stalin and his disastrous policy of forced collectivization, no Mao and his equally devastating Great Leap Forward.

KEYNESIANISM

Keynesianism is the term used to describe the philosophy of British economist John Maynard Keynes (1883–1946). He believed that government interventions in the economy could bolster overall spending levels and so ignite economic recovery in times of stagnation and recession. A hugely influential thesis, Keynesianism was adopted by governments impacted by the Great Depression of the 1930s and was a formative influence in the post-Second World War development of welfare states across Europe.

In 1929 the Wall Street Crash prompted the Great Depression, which quickly spread from the United States across the globe, bringing with it prolonged and painful mass unemployment and poverty. The Depression was a major shock to the system for many economists of the hitherto dominant Classical school. Economic orthodoxy had until then held that rises in unemployment and declines in economic output were a natural part of the economic cycle, with these respective peaks and troughs small enough to be brought back into line by the normal workings of the free market. But with the arrival of the Great Depression, all such bets were off.

Working against this backdrop, Keynes became convinced that it was unreasonable to expect that the markets alone could restore economic calm. In his most famous work, *The General Theory of Employment, Interest and Money* (1936), he critiqued many of the prevalent theses of the age.

John Maynard Keynes

It was widely thought, for example, that declines in demand for goods and services prompt a decline in production (since fewer goods and services are wanted) and an attendant increase in unemployment. This in turn leads to a climate of low wages and low inflation, under which circumstances, so the theory went, businesses are tempted to invest in new capital and labour, bringing about a surge in demand and restoring growth. In other words, market mechanisms maintain broad economic equilibrium.

However, Keynes argued that when demand sinks to a certain level, businesses are reluctant to employ new labour (even when it is cheap) to produce goods and services for which there is no market. Similarly, he suggested it was a fiction that firms took advantage of low prices to make capital investments. Instead, he argued, companies are as reluctant to spend in economic slumps as consumers, perpetuating the cycle of low demand and rising unemployment.

Keynes suggested that in such a scenario, the government should intervene to boost demand by pumping money into public works. In other words, a government can spend its way out of recession, while the nation also benefits from, for instance, new infrastructure. It was a remedy warmly received by world governments facing an apparently endless downturn. Keynesianism was an equally popular credo in the post-Second World War period, when the need to rebuild and kick-start economies was never greater. Keynes's standing was reflected in his selection to lead the British delegation at the 1944 Bretton Woods Conference that established both the International Monetary Fund and the World Bank. However, his ideas had largely fallen out of favour by the 1970s, when they were deemed ineffectual in dealing with the phenomenon of 'stagflation' – high inflation in concert with high unemployment and stagnant demand.

SPONTANEOUS ORDER

In general philosophical terms, spontaneous order refers to the spontaneous emergence of order from apparent chaos. It is a powerful and controversial idea within the realm of economics, most famously advocated by Friedrich Hayek.

Austrian-born Hayek (1899–1992) was a leading figure of the Austrian school of economics. This loose affiliation of thinkers covered a wide gamut of opinion but was broadly unified around the belief that the free market, despite its imperfections, is the best method of allocating resources. This was an idea shared with the so-called Classical and Neoclassical schools, but with one crucial difference – whereas Classical economists saw all the agents within the economy as 'rational players' making informed decisions on the basis of shared information, Hayek and his followers instead believed suppliers and consumers were rational only to the extent that they acted solely on information directly relevant to themselves. In other words, the market as a whole is left to look after itself, assimilating information linked to every separate transaction to establish the extent of supply and the correct price. From the chaos of a multitude of economic interactions, spontaneous order emerges.

With this in mind, Hayek argued against the prevailing trend among his contemporary economists for Keynesian policies, instead claiming that government intervention in economic matters posed a threat to spontaneous order. In his masterpiece, 1944's *The Road to Serfdom*, he outlined his conviction that government policy (which might come from just one individual in a totalitarian state, and at best is guided by but a small group of experts) is not equipped to take account of the huge quantity of information necessary to make wise economic choices. As a result, he argued, governments often turn to coercion to impose economic policy, moving even liberal, democratic governments towards totalitarian strategies.

Hayek believed the state should act to preserve free-market mechanisms (for instance, by protecting private property, enforcing the legality of contracts and generally ensuring the rule of law) but should intervene no further. Regarded as an exponent of heterodox (as opposed to mainstream, orthodox) economics for most of his lifetime, Hayek and his ideas found support from the 1970s onwards among fellow economists such as Milton Friedman (see page 233), as well as world figures including Ronald Reagan in the USA and Margaret Thatcher in the UK. Suddenly the once *outré* ideas of spontaneous order entered the economic mainstream.

CREATIVE DESTRUCTION

The theory of creative destruction – an idea elucidated by the Czech-born Joseph Schumpeter (1883–1950) – holds that the entrepreneur is the key figure in nurturing economic progress. Schumpeter promoted the counter-intuitive idea that economic recessions are forces for good, since they clear the market of inefficient agencies and leave space for growth. It is an argument that has held great sway among those who believe in minimal intervention in the markets.

Schumpeter introduced his theory in *Capitalism, Socialism and Democracy* (1942), where he described the process of creative destruction as 'the essential fact about capitalism'. He grew the idea out of the work of Karl Marx (see page 226), but where Marx considered that capitalism created economic crises through its need to overturn the existing economic order so as to produce new wealth, Schumpeter argued that the cycle of creative destruction is key to human progress.

For all his commendation of creative destruction, Schumpeter feared it contained the kernel of its own self-destruction by ultimately tearing down the institutional framework that upholds it. This was, he

> ### The power of ideas
>
> There are plentiful examples of creative destruction throughout history. Take, for example, the Industrial Revolution, when innovations including the steam engine and factory production reshaped the way people worked and lived. A similar upheaval is being brought about by the Internet, which has changed the way many older businesses operate – from record companies to newspapers and high-street retailers – and created entirely new types of business in the process. Schumpeter emphasized that creative destruction relies not only on technological innovation, but also on the introduction of new types of commercial models, methods of production and ways of doing business. For Schumpeter, the entrepreneur is every bit as important as the inventor, since it is their ideas that make new markets and propel capitalism.

suggested, the likely punchline to the 'process of industrial mutation that incessantly revolutionizes the economic structure from within, incessantly destroying the old one, incessantly creating a new one.'

MONETARISM

Monetarism – whose chief architect was the American Milton Friedman (1912–2006) – states that governments should make minimal interventions in the economy aside from taking measures to control the money supply. Born out of a rejection of Keynesianism (see page 228), monetarism became the prevailing economic orthodoxy in much of the developed world during the 1970s and 80s.

The origins of monetarism may be traced to the 16th century, when the quantity theory of money was developed. This theory is summed up by the equation $MV=PT$, where M = the amount of money in circulation over a defined time period, V = the velocity of money (i.e. how often it is

Stagflation

Monetarism's central tenet is that while governments may look after money supply, the markets can deal with inflation and unemployment. Whereas many governments sought to lower unemployment by spending more and accepting the resultant inflation, Friedman suggested that inflation pushes up wage demands so that employers are forced to cut jobs. Therefore, he argued, a government might end up with the worst of all worlds – high inflation and high unemployment. Indeed, this situation – known as stagflation – took a grip in several major economies in the 1970s.

Friedman also warned against excessive tinkering with the money supply – one of the leading causes, he suggested, of the Great Depression. Governments should instead merely focus on making sure there is enough money in the system to meet consumer demand for it. A good rule of thumb for central banks, he contended, is to increase money supply roughly in line with GDP growth. Then let the markets take care of everything else.

spent in that period), P = the average price level and T = the volume of transactions. It is generally acknowledged that the velocity of money is relatively constant over the long term; thus it is increases in the amount of money in circulation that result in increases in price. To put it another way, the more money that goes into the economy, the higher inflation will be over the long run, with knock-on effects for wages.

From the 1950s, Friedman challenged many of the underlying assumptions of Keynesianism, namely that individuals alter their patterns of consumption to fit with their current income. Friedman insisted that in fact individuals recognize a difference between their secure, long-term income streams and their less stable, transitory income. It is their secure income, he said, that determines their spending habits in the long term. So while, say, government expenditure on a new infrastructure project may boost levels of transitory income for a while, it has limited effect in boosting the overall economy for any significant period of time. Much better, Friedman said, for governments to focus on controlling the money supply in order to have an influence on the level of long-term incomes and, as a result, expenditure, too.

Today, there is a perhaps more nuanced approach to the theory, given its failure to bring the equitable prosperity its adherents had hoped for. Nonetheless, it remains a key component in the macroeconomic strategies of many governments.

GLOBALIZATION

Globalization describes the growing interconnectedness of the world as a result of increasing commercial and cultural exchange, often in tandem with technological innovation (such as the development of the Internet). It is customarily spurred by economic motivations, such as the desire of a Hollywood studio to capture new audiences abroad or the hope of a worker in one country of finding better-paid employment in another. The commercial symbol of globalization is the multinational company, offering homogenized products in markets around the planet.

In the 20th century, increased levels of international trade coupled with more efficient methods of transporting goods and people – along with a desire to foster greater interconnectedness as a brake on hostilities in the aftermath of two world wars – saw an explosion in globalization. The mass adoption of the Internet has been another key component of the phenomenon, connecting individuals with each other and with businesses in a way hitherto unimaginable. Whether this is for good or bad is very much up for debate.

The obvious winners are big businesses, which access huge new markets and reap the financial rewards. In return, globalization advocates argue that multinationals create new jobs, bolster local tax revenues and spread commercial and technological know-how. Furthermore, barriers are broken down between different cultures and nations, even to the extent that rogue governments are compelled to adhere to international standards.

Globalization and individuality

Others, though, are less convinced. Seeing a burger chain selling virtually the same meal in London, Lisbon, Lima and Lagos does little for cultural diversity, instead imposing a 'one-size-fits-all' template on the world. Furthermore, the appearance of a multinational in a market often spells doom for small local businesses and can skew the labour market, too. And while globalization may force some regimes into international line, others are accused of adopting policy stances more suited to the needs of big business than of the local population, as when drinks companies are given access to scarce water supplies in preference to the native population. As former United Nations Secretary-General Kofi Annan wrote in 2002: 'If globalization is to succeed, it must succeed for poor and rich alike. It must deliver rights no less than riches. It must provide social justice and equity no less than economic prosperity and enhanced communication.'

What is beyond doubt is that globalization is inescapable. Francis Fukuyama has said:

Today, no country can ever truly cut itself off from the global media or from external sources of information; trends that start in one corner of the world are rapidly replicated thousands of miles away . . .

The trick is to make it work for everyone. As economist Amartya Sen has said: 'Globalization is not in itself a folly: it has enriched the world scientifically and culturally and benefited many people economically as well.'

CONSPICUOUS CONSUMPTION

Conspicuous consumption describes the phenomenon whereby goods and services may be purchased for the principal purpose of emphasizing the buyer's wealth and social position. It is an idea popularized by the American economist and sociologist, Thorstein Veblen, in his 1899 work, *The Theory of the Leisure Class*.

Veblen wrote his most famous work during America's Gilded Age, when rapid industrialization had created a new class of the super-rich. It was the age of Rockefeller and Carnegie, Mellon, Guggenheim and Vanderbilt – 'robber barons' to some, 'captains of industry' to others. They and their families enjoyed fabulous lifestyles, their ostentatious spending gaining notoriety across the globe. Consider, for instance, the extraordinary parade of Newport Mansions on Rhode Island, monuments to the desire of one affluent family to outdo another in opulence.

While conspicuous consumption is most obviously expressed in the decadence of the wealthy, it is not restricted to the rich. The poor may engage in it just as easily, as long as there is someone else whose relative social position may be suppressed as theirs is elevated. These were significant insights in an age when economists worked on the basis that consumers are entirely rational. Veblen showed how we are, in fact, subject to a host of social and psychological factors when we make economic decisions. Whether we actually want or need a good or service is just part of the picture.

Out of Veblen's ideas arises the concept of 'Veblen goods' – usually luxury items (such as high-end jewellery and supercars) that are subject to increased demand as their price rises, in contravention of normal market rules. The high price tag is integral to exhibiting social status, so that a reduction in price reduces the satisfaction obtained by purchasing them. Veblen warned against fostering a 'relative consumption trap' where a nation's production capacity is excessively focused on that which is glamorous and desirable at the expense of that which is necessary.

Veblen has been the focus of renewed interest in recent years. In light of the global economic downturn caused in part by the accumulation of high levels of personal debt, his notion of conspicuous consumption – 'a means of reputability to the gentleman of leisure' – feels more vital than ever.

Consumerism and egoism

Traditional economic thought suggests consumers buy out of a desire to feel the satisfaction of consuming a particular product. Veblen, though, saw something else in the growing tide of consumerism. Utility plays a part in consumption, of course, but also important is the desire to emphasize one's elevated social status (and by extension, the lower status of others). 'The possession of wealth', Veblen wrote, 'confers honour; it is an invidious distinction.' Consumption thus becomes in part an act of egoism: 'So soon as the possession of property becomes the basis of popular esteem . . . it becomes also a requisite to the complacency which we call self-respect.'

GAME THEORY

Game theory is the analysis of how people make decisions in competitive situations, where the outcome of a participant's choice depends upon the actions of other participants. It explores how we model our behaviour when considering how another person's actions might

affect our potential gains and losses. It is a topic with relevance in fields as disparate as sociology, political science and war strategy, and is now understood to have a profound effect on the economic choices we make.

The Prisoner's Dilemma

The most famous game theory scenario is 'The Prisoner's Dilemma', which was created by Merrill Flood and Melvin Dresher. In its simplest form, two criminals are under arrest and unable to communicate with each other. Each must choose whether to testify against their associate or not, having been informed that if they both testify against each other, they will get a mid-level sentence, but if both stay silent, each will receive a shorter sentence (say one year). However, if one testifies but the other doesn't, the testifier will be set free and the other will be punished with a longer sentence (say ten years). Since they cannot act together, their self-interest is logically best served by choosing to betray, since they will each have a preferential outcome no matter what the other does. For example, if Prisoner X betrays while Prisoner Y stays silent, Prisoner X is set free. But if Y also betrays, X still receives a shorter sentence than if he keeps quiet.

If they could confer, each would stay silent to serve the shortest cumulative sentence, but it is not the best course of action for two information-deprived individuals. Similarly, in economic situations where we don't know how other parties are going to behave, our logical 'best course' may be different to that were we to know what everyone else is planning to do.

Game theory as a component of economic theory only emerged in the 1940s, when two American mathematicians, Oskar Morgenstern and John von Neumann, published *Theory of Games and Economic Behavior.* They looked at how economic behaviour can be moulded by the activities of a few 'economic players', such as governments or market-dominating companies. They examined a series of hypothetical zero-sum games (mathematical representations of a situation in which each participant's gain or loss of utility is exactly balanced by the losses or gains of the utility of the other participants) and examined how we incorporate consideration of the actions of others into our decision-making.

In the following decade, John Nash took their work a stage further. Where Morgenstern and von Neumann had considered situations in which participants were able to confer so as to decide on the most beneficial course of action, Nash's agents were forced to make decisions entirely independently – a situation more akin to real-life economic situations.

Game theory remains a vibrant field of investigation, looking at, for example, how our behaviour changes with repetition of certain scenarios and how negative-sum games (in which the act of playing the game can diminish the resources to be allocated) play out differently to zero-sum games.

PHILANTHROPY

Philanthropy is a concept of fluid meaning but in general terms refers to the promotion of others' welfare, most commonly by donating significant sums of money. In some definitions, charity is linked to alleviating the symptoms of a problem, while philanthropy tends towards addressing its root cause. For instance, to give a hungry man a fish is charity but to give him a rod and teach him to fish is philanthropy. There are three principal mechanisms for enabling the philanthropist to put their money to work: by giving it to a third party to use; by establishing an endowment (a financial gift administered by a charity for a specific purpose, like funding a scholarship); or to establish a foundation of their own to focus on their chosen projects.

Philanthropy is nothing new. In 347 BCE, for instance, we know that Plato bequeathed his worldly goods to a nephew with the express

Modern philanthropy

In the late 20th and early 21st centuries, philanthropy has been given an overhaul, spearheaded by two of the richest individuals in the world, the American investor Warren Buffett and the founder of Microsoft, Bill Gates. 'If you're in the luckiest 1 per cent of humanity,' Buffett has said, 'you owe it to the rest of humanity to think about the other 99 per cent.' The Bill and Melinda Gates Foundation, meanwhile, has pledged billions of dollars to initiatives such as the global eradication of polio. They have also done much to secure the future of philanthropy through the 'Giving Pledge', which calls on billionaires to give away at least half of their fortune. As of 2016, approaching 150 billionaires had taken the pledge.

intention of providing funds for the ongoing support of the academy Plato had founded. Later, Aristotle wrestled with what we might consider the philanthropist's fundamental conundrum: 'To give away money is an easy matter and in any man's power. But to decide to whom to give it and how large and when, and for what purpose and how, is neither in every man's power nor an easy matter.'

From the West to the East, there are long traditions of charitable giving, along with state and privately sponsored initiatives to help the poor and needy. However, philanthropy as we know it today can be said to date from the 19th century. As President Lyndon Johnson's Secretary of Health, Education, and Welfare, John Gardner, once observed: 'Wealth is not new. Neither is charity. But the idea of using private wealth imaginatively, constructively, and systematically to attack the fundamental problems of mankind is new.'

Philanthropy became associated with distinct political causes, such as the slavery abolition movement. It was also boosted by an array of industrial trailblazers who opted to use their wealth for the general good. The likes of George Cadbury, Andrew Carnegie, Henry Dunant,

John Paul Getty, W. K. Kellogg, George Peabody, J. D. Rockefeller and Joseph Rowntree accumulated huge riches before re-disbursing them, driven by such noble aims as to promote 'the well-being of mankind throughout the world' (Rockefeller) and 'the advancement and diffusion of knowledge and understanding' (Carnegie). The latter believed that 'he who dies rich dies disgraced'.

PART EIGHT

ARTS, ARCHITECTURE AND MUSIC

'Art is the signature of civilizations.'

Beverly Sills

The arts are sometimes thought of in terms of entertainment and certainly that is one of the roles they fulfil. However, they reveal much more about human nature than that and help us to examine our world in all its detail, as well as better comprehend our relationship with it. To the American novelist, John Cheever, art is nothing less than 'the triumph over chaos' while Leo Tolstoy said: 'Art is a human activity having for its purpose the transmission to others of the highest and best feelings to which men have risen.' Of course, such claims may not be true of all art, but even that which might be regarded as the most trivial product of 'low culture' can shed light upon the human condition. Perhaps it is more useful to think of art rather in terms of that which is good and that which is not. Leonard Bernstein had this to say: 'Any great work of art . . . revives and readapts time and space, and the measure of its success is the extent to which it makes you an inhabitant of that world – the extent to which it invites you in and lets you breathe its strange, special air.'

CLASSICAL ART AND THE RENAISSANCE

In terms of cultural production, the Classical period refers to that of the ancient Greek and Roman civilizations. Classicism and Neoclassicism, meanwhile, denote later revivals based on the philosophical and aesthetic principles of those ancient traditions. The most famous of these revivals is the Renaissance (literally, *rebirth*) that stretched roughly from the beginning of the 15th to the end of the 16th century.

The Classical era lasted approximately from 1000 BCE to the mid-5th century CE, when the Roman Empire was approaching its end. As such, it encompasses a great many styles, traditions and regional influences. Nonetheless, it is possible to draw out some general features. For instance, classical painters and sculptors tended to value harmony, proportion and balance. They also developed a highly naturalistic style, in contrast to the stylized images of, say, the ancient Egyptians or the medieval religious painters who worked after the end of the classical period. However, while the classical tradition prized naturalist depictions, it also specialized in idealized forms and well-defined notions of beauty – the men typically muscle-bound, full-lipped and virile, the women curvaceous and, custom often had it, red-headed. Many classical artists became experts in the study of human anatomy. It is said that Michelangelo refused Pope Julius II's request that he add limbs and a head to the then recently discovered 'Belvedere torso' – the remains of a *circa* first-century-BCE seated, marble, male nude – on the grounds that it was too beautiful to be adapted.

Classical architecture

In architecture, themes of balance and proportion again reigned. Important buildings were typically adorned with columns and capitals, all built on the basis of exacting mathematical principles. For instance, pillars were customarily fatter in the middle so as to appear to better conform to the principles of perspective. Among the finest extant examples of classical-era buildings are the Parthenon in Athens (featuring the work of the architects Iktinos and Kallikrates as well as the sculptor Pheidias) and the Pantheon in Rome.

Revivals of classical styles were not long in coming after the fall of Rome – the 'Carolingian Renaissance' extended from *c.* 750–900, while the Romanesque architectural style found favour in the 11th century. But Italy was the focal point of the greatest revival – the Renaissance that began in the early 15th century when the values of the classical age were reconstituted and built upon in remarkable ways. The result was a body of cultural production almost without rival. Figures such as the architects Filippo Brunelleschi (whose work includes the Duomo in Florence) and Andrea Palladio, along with an array of artists, such as Donatello, Raphael, Michelangelo and Leonardo da Vinci, redefined the boundaries of artistic possibility. Indeed, their combined work is still regarded by many as the high point of human cultural endeavour.

THE MUSIC OF THE SPHERES

Music – that is to say, vocal and/or instrumental sounds that combine to produce recognizable form, harmony and emotional expression – has provided the soundtrack to civilization. From ancient tribal music to sacred choral music, music to inspire soldiers in battle and the music of high opera and the great composers, through to the popular forms of jazz, rock, pop, rap and dance – it is an extraordinarily democratic art form and one that often defies intellectual analysis. Nonetheless, the idea of the Music of the Spheres (or *Musica universalis*) has proved an enduringly appealing way to attempt to understand the pull that music has over us.

It is likely that humanity's relationship with music began via drum-like percussive instruments, which were probably used in rituals. But by 4000 BCE the Egyptians were playing music on harps and flutes, with the trumpet following about 1,500 years later, and the guitar (invented by the Hittites) about another thousand years on.

Celestial bodies and musicality

The idea of the Music of the Spheres suggests that there is a relationship between the movement of celestial bodies and musicality. Specifically, the proportionality of their movement has a mathematical correlation to the production of perfectly harmonious 'tones' inaudible on Earth. The idea stems from the work of Pythagoras in the 6th century BCE, among whose achievements was establishing that the relationship between the pitch of a note and the length of a string that produces it may be represented as a ratio of whole numbers. He came to regard music as one of the universal ordering principles, believing that the Sun, Moon and planets each emit a unique hum related to their movement in orbit, which in turn impacts on our experience of life on Earth even as we are unaware of it.

Human-made music, Pythagoras thought, was a sort of approximation of the Music of the Spheres and also an audible manifestation of number – number being that which defines the universe and everything within it. The idea of music as an expression of the universal was a potent one, prompting Plato to observe that 'rhythm and harmony find their way into the inward places of the soul, on which they mightily fasten, imparting grace, and making the soul of him who is rightly educated graceful'.

In the 6th century CE, the philosopher Boethius arrived at three classifications of music in his *De Musica*. The first of these was the Music of the Spheres, the second the harmonious internal music of the human body, and third the music of singers and instruments. Music, he said, is 'so naturally united with us that we cannot be free from it even if we so desired.' His ideas proved influential through to the Renaissance and beyond. Even now, there is a sense that what makes great music so profoundly affecting cannot be decoded and replicated, since it is hardwired into something elusively fundamental. Arthur Schopenhauer put it in these terms: 'The effect of music is so very much more powerful and penetrating than is that of the other arts, for these others speak only of the shadow, but music of the essence.'

POETRY

Poetry is a literary form that seeks to heighten the expression of ideas or feelings through the use of distinctive rhythms and other poetic devices. A popular form since antiquity when it was traditionally an oral format, poetry is often regarded as the most elevated mode of literary expression.

> *'Poetry is simply the most beautiful, impressive, and widely effective mode of saying things, and hence its importance.'*
>
> Matthew Arnold

Evolving poetry

Poetry has constantly adapted and evolved to cater for the demands of new generations of poets and their audiences. These include formal innovations – such as the fourteen-line sonnet beloved of Petrarch and Shakespeare – as well as original treatments of subject matter, whether the natural landscapes beloved of the Romantics, the nonsense verse of Edward Lear or the reality of urban existence depicted in rap lyrics. Poetry, though, has proved resilient because of its consistent ability to touch the reader, or listener, in a profound way. As the great Romantic poet William Wordsworth had it, 'Poetry is the spontaneous overflow of powerful feelings . . .'

Aside from rhythm (the repetitive beat or metre of a poem), other weapons in the poet's armoury include alliteration (in which the first letter of a word is repeated in the following words), dissonance (a combination of discordant sounds), imagery (including similes, metaphors and personification), symbolism, onomatopoeia (where a word sounds like the noise it is describing), repetition, rhyme and tone (i.e. the mood of a piece). This, though, is far from an exhaustive list.

The word *poetry* comes from the Greek for 'making', and poetry probably emerged in prehistoric communities as a way to share stories and recall events. The oldest known poem is the *Epic of Gilgamesh*, the story of King Gilgamesh written in Mesopotamia sometime around 3000 BCE. The theory of poetry, meanwhile, was first investigated in Aristotle's *Poetics* (which is, in fact, a 4th-century-BCE treatise on drama, an art form closely connected with poetry in ancient Greece).

Aristotle's ideas were of enormous influence right up to the modern age, by which time the major categories of poetry were usually defined as epic, lyric and dramatic (which included tragedy and comedy; see entry on Drama). An epic is essentially a lengthy narrative poem, often telling the story of a heroic figure or historical events – examples of which include Homer's *Iliad* and *Odyssey*, Virgil's *Aeneid* and Dante's *Divine Comedy*. Lyric poetry, by contrast, tends to be shorter and was traditionally intended to be sung (the custom of accompaniment by a lyre giving the genre its name).

DRAMA

Drama refers to the fictional representation of a story designed to be performed in front of an audience. From the theatre culture of ancient Greece, through Shakespeare, Molière, Ibsen and Chekhov to Wilde, Beckett and Stoppard, via opera and musical theatre to the latest cinema release, drama has proved an enduringly popular and powerful way of documenting and reflecting human experience over thousands of years. As Edward Albee, author of *Who's Afraid of Virginia Woolf?*, noted: 'A play is fiction – and fiction is fact distilled into truth.'

The word *drama* derives from the Greek for 'action', while the performance of drama has been described in terms of a 'play' (with its connotations of a game) since antiquity. Early technical innovations in the presentation of drama included the construction of raked auditoria to assist viewing. More importantly, in the 6th century BCE a performer called Thespis introduced spoken dialogue into proceedings, marking himself out as the first 'actor' (it is in honour of him that today we still refer to Thespians). Then, in the 4th century BCE, Aristotle wrote his *Poetics*, a work of literary theory that explored differences in the form and content of various types of play. While his thoughts on comedy have not survived, his ideas about the nature of tragedy have proved timeless through his elucidation of concepts such as *catharsis* (the purging of the emotions) and *hamartia* (a fatal flaw in character).

The fundamentals of drama have changed little since they were established by the ancient Greeks. Their theatre is epitomized by the

'Action'

Athens was the focal point of ancient Greek drama, with the earliest plays, put on by the followers of Dionysus, telling tales from mythology via song (delivered by a chorus who typically wore masks) and dance. Soon there were regular festivals and competitions centred upon the three main dramatic genres: tragedy, comedy and the satyr play. Satyr plays were saucy romps featuring mythical half-man/half-goat characters, but Greece's traditions in tragedy and comedy were to provide more lasting legacies. Among the most famous authors of tragedies – dramas dealing with unhappy events related to the downfall of a heroic character, along with grand themes including pride, love, greed and power – were the 5th-century-BCE authors Aeschylus, Sophocles (whose masterpiece was *Oedipus Rex*) and Euripides. Comedy, meanwhile, sought to satirize the foibles of the powerful and wealthy, with the genre's leading exponents arguably Aristophanes and, later, Menander.

image of a pair of masks, one joyful and the other in anguish – and still drama may be considered the art of making 'em laugh and making 'em cry.

Eugène Ionesco, one of the most celebrated playwrights of the 20th century, considered that drama 'lies in extreme exaggeration of the feelings, an exaggeration that dislocates flat everyday reality.' Alternatively, Sarah Bernhardt – a beloved actress of the late 19th and early 20th centuries – described theatre as 'the involuntary reflex of the ideas of the crowd.'

ARCHETYPAL STORIES

While our modern culture is replete with stories incorporating every imaginable setting, plot and character, the history of storytelling has been characterized by the retelling of a few basic stories, involving a selection of core character types. This has proved a durable way of exploring the human condition, with archetypes providing a shorthand for audiences to engage with universal themes, among them, love, death, tragedy, war, faith and death. The psychologist Carl Jung claimed that archetypes were the product of our 'collective unconscious'.

As is evident elsewhere in this book, ancient narratives such as creation myths reflected a fairly limited number of basic storylines. Aristotle's *Poetics* outlined a small pool of basic plots underpinning Greek mythology, while Greek performers used masks to hasten audience recognition of the archetype each character embodied. Similarly, most

The seven basic plots

Among the more celebrated attempts at specifying the extent of archetype in drama is Christopher Booker's 2004 book, *The Seven Basic Plots: Why We Tell Stories*, in which he identified the following recurring narratives: overcoming the monster; rags to riches; the quest; voyage and return; comedy; tragedy; and rebirth. Georges Polti (1867–1946) had earlier enumerated thirty-six basic 'dramatic situations'. As for identifying character archetypes, among the most famous attempts is Vladimir Propp's *Morphology of the Folktale* (1928), in which he identified seven basic figures: the dispatcher, the false hero, the helper, the hero, the princess and her father, the provider and the villain. Other critics have noted the absence from this list of the earth mother, the everyman, the *femme fatale*, the innocent, the mentor, the outcast and the scapegoat – to name just a few.

societies have developed canons of legends (often myths taken out of the world of the fantastical and recast in a more naturalistic setting) and folktales that deliver a notably consistent set of themes and character types.

While opinions differ on the specifics, there is nonetheless a general acceptance that archetypes have been a defining feature of our species' storytelling traditions. As recorded by James Boswell in his *The Life of Johnson*, Samuel Johnson once observed: 'how small a quantity of *real fiction* there is in the world; and that the same images, with very little variation, have served all the authors who have ever written.'

THE BAROQUE

The baroque, which encompassed art and architecture, was an important period of art and style in Europe from about 1600 until the early 18th century. It was often highly theatrical and emotionally engaging, and was partly a response to the stylized and intellectual Mannerist movement of the later Renaissance. Baroque artists employed a freer, more realistic style, which in turn was replaced by the more elaborate, frivolous and sometimes overblown Rococo style.

One of the driving forces of the baroque movement was the Roman Catholic Church, which used baroque artists as part of its Counter-Reformation offensive. Long an important patron of the arts, the Papacy pumped money into commissioning striking works of art and spectacular buildings. Paintings and sculptures, often within grandiose church or palace settings, were typically large-scale, while in architecture the straight lines of the Renaissance were replaced by curves. Everything was bigger and more impressive than what had gone before, and figures in the field, including Caravaggio, Annibale Carracci, Alessandro Algardi, Peter Paul Rubens and Gianlorenzo Bernini, became stars of the European art scene for their work in Rome and elsewhere.

In France, the baroque was characterized by the work of Nicolas Poussin, who in turn influenced Charles Le Brun, whose work would adorn the baroque masterpiece that is the Palace of Versailles, and whom Louis XIV called the greatest French artist of all time. However, the baroque took a different turn in the Netherlands (a Protestant country beyond the reach of the Vatican), where it manifested as a trend for smaller-scale genre paintings (portraiture, landscapes, still-lifes) aimed at well-to-do middle-class patrons. It was a style epitomized by Rembrandt and Vermeer, but also reflected in the work of Diego Velázquez in Spain. In Eng-land, the style is detectable in some of the great architectural projects of the era, including Christopher Wren's St Paul's Cathedral in London and John Vanbrugh's Castle Howard and Blenheim Palace.

Rarely understated, the baroque was described by Jorge Luis Borges, one of the most important figures of 20th-century Argentinian literature, thus: 'I would define the baroque as that style that deliberately exhausts (or tries to exhaust) its own possibilities, and that borders on self-caricature. The baroque is the final stage in all art, when art flaunts and squanders its resources.'

THE NOVEL

The novel, usually comprising a long, fictional prose narrative, has been the dominant literary form since the 18th century. Typified by relatable characters engaged in involved plots and normally in settings with at least parallels to the everyday world, the novel has served as a means of undertaking in-depth studies into the human condition free from the formal and thematic constraints of, say, epic poetry. In the words of Khaled Hosseini, author of *The Kite Runner*: 'Writing fiction is the act of weaving a series of lies to arrive at a greater truth.'

The great novelists

The roll call of great novelists is long, illustrious and indicative of the influence the novel has had on moulding our cultural identities. A hardly exhaustive list might include, for instance, Jane Austen, the Brontës, Agatha Christie, Joseph Conrad, Charles Dickens, William Faulkner, F. Scott Fitzgerald, E. M. Forster, Graham Greene, Dashiell Hammett, Thomas Hardy, Aldous Huxley, Henry James, James Joyce, Jack Kerouac, D. H. Lawrence, Harper Lee, Ian McEwan, Vladimir Nabokov, George Orwell, Philip Roth, J. D. Salinger, Vikram Seth, John Steinbeck, Evelyn Waugh, Edith Wharton and Virginia Woolf. It is an extraordinarily adaptable format too – Woolf called it 'this most pliable of all forms' – catering for genres as disparate as science fiction, the picaresque (i.e. episodic tales of roguish heroes) and gothic horror to crime fiction, Westerns and 'chick-lit'.

The origins of the novel are disputed. Some point to Petronius's *Satyricon*, written in the 1st century CE, and Lucius Apuleius's *Golden Ass* a century later as bearing many of the hallmarks of the novel – notably the use of prose and stories set in the 'ordinary' world and concerned with non-heroic themes. Others, however, regard it as having emerged from the tradition of medieval chivalric romances – with Thomas Malory's *Le Morte d'Arthur* (1470) considered an early candidate. Indeed, the word for novel in French is *roman*, and in Italian *romanzo*. Others alternatively cite publication of Miguel Cervantes' *Don Quixote* in the early 17th century as marking the start of the era of the novel, with the likes of John Bunyan, Aphra Behn and Daniel Defoe trailblazing the English-language variant.

By the 19th century, the novel had firmly superseded poetry in popularity if not respectability. Into the 20th century, modernism allowed novelists to reinvent the format again, moving it away from the formalist, realist approaches of the Victorian masters to render the novel essentially independent of rules – a fact most famously attested to by James Joyce's *Ulysses* (1922), the tale of a day in the life of a Dublin man told using such revolutionary techniques as stream-of-consciousness.

G. K. Chesterton once said: 'People wonder why the novel is the most popular form of literature; people wonder why it is read more than books of science or books of metaphysics. The reason is very simple; it is merely that the novel is more true than they are.'

AESTHETICISM

All art forms – whether visual, literary, musical, cinematic or something else altogether – serve to communicate ideas, engage an audience and elicit an emotional and/or intellectual response. As such, the aims and motivations of individual artists and artworks are manifold. A 19th-century sonata by Brahms clearly draws a different reaction to, say, a song by the Sex Pistols. Equally, a love sonnet by Browning has different intentions to a political allegory such as George Orwell's *1984*.

Yet, there are those who argue that no artwork need have a 'purpose' beyond itself. Or, as this idea is commonly summarized, 'art for art's sake'. This became the slogan of the Aesthetic movement that grew up in the 19th century. Aesthetics may be considered that area of thought that seeks to examine the nature and appreciation of beauty. In the words of one of aestheticism's chief spokespersons, Victor Cousin, 'the beautiful cannot be the way to what is useful, or to what is good, or to what is holy; it leads only to itself.'

It was a philosophy that arguably reached its peak in the visual arts with the great Pre-Raphaelites such as Dante Gabriel Rossetti, the pioneering symbolist and Art Nouveau works of Aubrey Beardsley, and the paintings of James Abbott McNeill Whistler, that giant of the American Gilded Age. On the literary front, its most celebrated voice was Oscar Wilde. As he wrote in *The Picture of Dorian Gray*: 'People say sometimes that Beauty is only superficial. That may be so. But at least it is not so superficial as Thought is. To me, Beauty is the wonder of wonders.'

Nonetheless, the very idea of what constitutes beauty changes and evolves over time and between cultures. The voluptuous beauty of a Rubens nude, for example, contrasts starkly with the ideal of feminine beauty found on your average contemporary Paris or Milan fashion-show catwalk.

So, can we reach any broad conclusions as to what constitutes beauty? Plenty have tried. Some evolutionists, for instance, argue that we tend to regard as beautiful that which signals the best chance of our key evolutionary goals – survival and reproduction. Therefore, it might be said, the curves of one of Ruben's women appeal because they speak of a healthy, nourished body, well poised for the task of childbearing.

Oscar Wilde

The golden ratio

The 'golden ratio' – a common mathematical ratio that can be used to create pleasing, natural-looking compositions and also known as the 'Golden Mean' – was first described by Euclid in the 3rd century BCE. It has been used by artists and architects (often unconsciously) for millennia and may also be found in nature, with some claiming that it underpins universal ideals of beauty. Salvador Dalí, for example, consciously echoed the so-called golden ratio in several of his works.

Beauty, perhaps, is best thought of as something we may hope to recognize but not to understand. As Pablo Picasso once noted: 'Beauty? To me it is a word without sense because I do not know where its meaning comes from nor where it leads to.'

ROMANTICISM

Romanticism was an artistic, intellectual and cultural movement that emerged in Europe in the late 18th century. It was in part a response to the intensely rationalist approach to life that had been championed by the Enlightenment. The nature of Romanticism took on distinct forms in different countries, although there were unifying features – most notably the privileging of subjectivity, inspiration and individualism over pure reason. In addition, whereas Enlightenment thinkers sought to establish universal truths, the Romantics were more interested in the relativist nature of personal truth.

In Great Britain, Romanticism was also seen as a response to the Industrial Revolution. Leading figures of the English Romantic movement – legendary names such as Byron and Keats, Shelley and Wordsworth – idealized the natural world and raised up the medieval period (a trend also reflected in Gothic Revival architecture that became popular from around the 1830s) that had been reviled by Enlightenment thinkers as 'the Dark Ages'. Industrialized, enlightened modernity, the Romantics suggested, was not the earthly paradise some had hoped for.

In both Britain and Germany, Romanticism served as something of an antidote to the cultural and military imperialism of Napoleonic France. Moreover, it proved highly influential in the evolution of America, where its individualist philosophy was warmly embraced. However, Romanticism had largely run its course by 1848, when a succession of failed revolutions across Europe extinguished the flame of Romantic nationalism, while exciting new artistic movements jostled to capture the public imagination.

The Storm and Stress movement

German Romanticism, meanwhile, could trace a path back to the *Sturm und Drang* ('Storm and Stress') movement that roughly stretched from the 1760s to the 1780s. Emotion and personal subjectivity were given free rein in the face of Enlightenment rationalism and reason, with figures including Friedrich Schiller, Karl Friedrich Schinkel, Johann Wolfgang von Goethe and G. W. F. Hegel contributing to the development of a powerful sense of national spirit. Romanticism thus came to have disparate political impacts in different countries. In Britain, it came to be seen as deeply conservative, yearning for a bygone past in which individuals wandered lonely as a cloud and factories did not chug out fumes and irreversibly scar the countryside. In Germany, though, it became a conduit for radical nationalist demands, and remained a potent cultural force even during the rise of Hitler almost a century after Romanticism had ceased to be a vital movement.

IMPRESSIONISM AND POST-IMPRESSIONISM

Today, the great masterpieces of the Impressionist movement – hugely familiar and often-reproduced works such as Monet's Water Lilies series – have something of a 'chocolate box' reputation. But when the movement first came on the scene, it quickly earned a reputation far removed from the sense of cosy recognition it has today.

Impressionism was born amid the cafés and studios of Paris in the 1860s, where a disparate community of artists and thinkers had grown tired of the pursuit of perfect naturalism and the preoccupation with historical and mythological subjects that had long been championed by the state-run academies and salons. The loose affiliation of artists who would come to sit under the umbrella term of Impressionism sensed the time was ripe to challenge the status quo.

With artists such as Édouard Manet, Claude Monet, Edgar Degas, Camille Pissarro, Pierre-Auguste Renoir and Alfred Sisley to the fore, the Impressionists sought to catch fleeting moments of reality. With bold use of colour and a disregard for the formalism of their predecessors and most of their contemporaries, they endeavoured to record the play of light, atmosphere and sense of movement in a spontaneous way. They wanted to paint the world as they saw it, not as it was expected to be.

Their pictures are characteristically loose in style – consider, for example, the way Monet extravagantly applied paint to the surface of his canvases as opposed to the almost photographic quality of brushwork practised by, say, Leonardo da Vinci. Yet at their best they capture a sensual reality that might have evaded a more naturalistic approach. As Monet put it: 'Impressionism is only direct sensation. All great painters were less or more impressionists. It is mainly a question of instinct.'

'Impression Sunrise'

As outsiders to the artistic establishment in Paris, the Impressionists began to exhibit together in 1874. At that show, Monet displayed a painting of the sun rising over the port of Le Havre. Called *Impression, Sunrise*, it was seized upon by the critic Louis Leroy as the epitome of all that was wrong with the show. By 1877, the group had taken his slur and turned it around, calling themselves the Impressionists. Their subject matter was wide-ranging, encompassing *plein air* studies, figurative works and cityscapes that captured Paris's urban development in the late 19th century. The last Impressionist show was held in 1886, by which time many of the key figures were going their separate ways and experimenting with new modes of painting.

Just as the Impressionists rebelled against what had gone before, so the movement inspired its own reaction – Post-Impressionism. Emerging in France in the latter decades of the 19th century, its disparate membership rejected Impressionism's dominant concern with the rendering of light and colour in moments of spontaneity. Instead, a more formal approach was favoured, even as its exponents implicitly acknowledged the artifice of the medium.

Counting such eminent practitioners among their ranks as Paul Cézanne, Paul Gauguin, Vincent van Gogh and Georges Seurat, the Post-Impressionists were also more interested in symbolism (see page 265). Where the Impressionist hoped to provide a window on to the world, the Post-Impressionists are sometimes regarded as revealing the soul of the artist himself as they plunder their memories and feelings for inspiration. As Edvard Munch, profoundly influenced by the Post-Impressionists, once said: 'Nature is not only all that is visible to the eye. . . It also includes the inner pictures of the soul.'

REALISM

Realism was an artistic and literary philosophy that emerged in France in the 19th century, championing engagement with more realistic subject matter. It should not be confused with naturalism – the pursuit of a more lifelike representation of a subject – although there is an overlap between the two. Realist artists attempted to capture scenes of 'real life' – for instance, urban street-life, the conditions of the working and rural classes, as well as more honest representations of nudity far removed from the idealized bodies long preferred in high art. Realism may be regarded as favouring subject matter that more truthfully reflected everyday, ordinary modern life in the post-industrial age.

Realism's chief exponents in the visual arts were Gustave Courbet (1819–77), Honoré Daumier (1808–79) and Jean-François Millet (1814–75). As Courbet once noted: 'Painting is an essentially concrete art and can only consist of the representation of real and existing things.' The influence of the Realists extended to artists in other styles, notably the

Realism in literature

In terms of literature, the Frenchman Honoré de Balzac is regularly cited as the first great realist writer, with George Eliot among the pioneers in the English language. Realism would also give rise to a number of sub-movements. For instance, the social realism of the 1920s and 30s aimed to reflect the realities of social hardship, reaching its zenith in Depression-era New York. Alternatively, magical realism combines elements of realism and fantasy, finding its ultimate expression as a literary mode in the works of Gabriel García Márquez and Salman Rushdie. Since the 1960s, meanwhile, photorealism has seen artists producing handcrafted works that are virtually indistinguishable from photographs.

Impressionist Edgar Degas. However, there was also an international aspect to the movement, notably in Germany, Russia and the USA, where its leading figures were Adolph von Menzel, Ilya Repin and Thomas Eakins, respectively.

Realism has had a mixed critical reception over the years. Edvard Munch took an overtly hostile position, criticizing those 'holier-than-thou honourable realists who walk around in the belief that they have accomplished something, simply because they tell you for the hundredth time that a field is green and a red-painted house is painted red'.

While naturalism may be regarded as a conservative style, realism was revolutionary in its own way, unshackling art from traditional notions of what constitutes acceptable subject matter for serious art.

ABSTRACT ART

The idea behind abstract art (sometimes also known as non-representational art) is that the artist need not strive to depict visual reality but may express deeper truths through the use of abstract shapes, colours and forms. It is a philosophy that has found expression in an array of genres, from Impressionism and Expressionism to Cubism, Surrealism, Op-Art (whose leading exponents included Victor Vasarely and Bridget Riley), Pop Art and Conceptual Art. In the words of the French artist, Robert Delaunay: 'As long as art cannot get free from the object, it will continue to be a description.'

In ancient times, figures as eminent as Plato had noted the intrinsic beauty in, for example, straight lines and circles, but for many hundreds of years leading up to the late 19th century, the orthodox view from the academies that ruled the European art scene was that the artist should strive to show something recognizable – a person, an object, a landscape or seascape – in their works.

Then came a succession of movements that began to question the notion that artistic worth was in direct relationship to a work's naturalistic nature. It is Maurice Denis who is generally thought of as the great philosopher of abstract art. In *New Theories of Modern and Sacred Art* (1922), he wrote: 'Remember that a picture, before being a battle horse, a nude, an anecdote or whatnot, is essentially a flat surface covered with colours assembled in a certain order.'

Not all were convinced by his arguments. Picasso, notably, never really accepted that there was such a thing as abstract art (despite others linking him with the movement). 'There is no abstract art,' he insisted. 'You always start with something. Afterward you can remove all traces of reality.' Yet the ideas of Denis would spread to many other movements over the ensuing decades. Among them were the abstract expressionists, who emerged from the 1940s and whose undoubted star was Jackson Pollock, famous for his vivid paint-spattered canvases that showed scant regard for anything approaching traditional form.

Another giant of abstract practice, the sculptor Barbara Hepworth, put it like this:

Working in the abstract way seems to release one's personality and sharpen the perceptions so that in the observation of humanity or landscape it is the wholeness of inner intention which moves one so profoundly. The components fall into place and one is no longer aware of the detail except as the necessary significance of wholeness and unity . . .

MODERNISM

Modernism is a term covering a wide-ranging movement that dominated Western culture from around the mid-19th century to roughly the mid-20th. Straddling many different art forms, its central credo was a rejection of traditional styles in favour of experimentation (with form, technique and materials) in an effort to better echo the conditions and characteristics of the modern world. Modernism was never afraid to challenge its audience, sometimes revelling in a reputation for being 'difficult'.

Modernist architecture

Modernism saw a redefinition of architecture, with architects focusing on functionality and simplicity of form. To this end, they were helped by technological innovations (such as the steel frame, the curtain wall and reinforced concrete). Arguably its greatest stars were Le Corbusier, Walter Gropius (founder of the hugely influential Bauhaus movement), Mies van der Rohe and Frank Lloyd Wright. Between them, they changed the look of the built world, eschewing ornament for clean lines. Modernism brought us the skyscraper – those era-defining monoliths of steel and glass – as well as the mass housing estates that moulded urban living around the world.

In the realm of the visual arts, it encompassed a number of other movements discussed elsewhere in this chapter – for example, Abstraction, Cubism, Expressionism, Impressionism and Surrealism – each of which experimented to create original visions of the world. In literature, meanwhile, modernism ushered in a prolonged period of formal innovation (such as stream-of-consciousness) and treatments of non-traditional subjects, with figures such as Joseph Conrad, T. S. Eliot, James Joyce and Virginia Woolf at the vanguard. Music, too, underwent a revolution, not least in the willingness of composers to challenge conventional tonal and structural patterns. The likes of Béla Bartók, Arnold Schoenberg and Igor Stravinsky collectively turned on its head the accepted rulebook of 'serious' music, while the spontaneity inherent in jazz redefined popular music for evermore.

By the 1960s and 70s, modernism no longer represented the revolutionary reaction to tradition but had instead become the new 'traditional'. Having been absorbed into the mainstream of culture, it inspired its own reactions. These took two distinct paths: on the one hand, a wistful nod to some of the past traditions that modernism had so ruthlessly swept away; and on the other, the emergence of postmodernism (see page 283), which urged a reappraisal of how we look at the world and made modernism seem decidedly old hat.

SYMBOLISM

Symbolism, which emerged in the late 19th century, was an artistic and literary movement that sought to express truths through the use of symbols that endowed particular images and objects with additional meaning. It dismissed many of the principles of traditional representational art (as well as those of its close antecedent, Impressionism), instead seeking to express the spiritual and psychological aspects that lie behind physical reality – as the symbolist poet Stéphane Mallarmé phrased it, 'to depict not the thing but the effect it produces.'

Other prominent symbolists working in the literary field included Paul Verlaine and Charles Baudelaire – whose *Les Fleurs du mal* (*The Flowers of Evil*, 1857) is regarded as a symbolist masterpiece – while among its leaders in the visual arts were Aubrey Beardsley, Paul Gauguin, Gustave

Objectifying the subjective

Symbolism believed the artist or writer as capable of revelation. The subject matter of much symbolist work was correspondingly challenging – from religious mysticism to dreamscapes, from death to decadence and highly charged eroticism. In 1886 Jean Moréas published the 'Symbolist Manifesto' in France, in which he outlined the movement's disdain for 'plain meanings, declamations, false sentimentality and matter-of-fact description.' Instead, Moréas wrote, symbolism aimed to 'clothe the Ideal in a perceptible form.' At around the same time, the French poet Gustave Kahn gave his own definition: 'The essential aim of our art is to objectify the subjective (the externalization of the Idea) instead of subjectifying the objective (nature seen through a temperament).'

Moreau, Odilon Redon and James Abbott McNeill Whistler. Oscar Wilde also flirted with symbolism, notably in *The Picture of Dorian Gray* and *Salomé*. The symbolist movement is seen by some critics as an expression of a *fin-de-siècle* desire to challenge the moralism and materialism that had become a feature of European life in the period. It may also be regarded as prefiguring some of the psychological insights with which Sigmund Freud became synonymous.

Symbolism was a relatively short-lived movement but significantly affected how audiences approached artworks, actively searching for the 'real meaning' behind sometimes quite incongruous images. The symbolists were unapologetic in making artworks that were not there to be merely looked at but to be investigated and understood.

EXPRESSIONISM

The idea of Expressionism, which emerged in Germany around the turn of the 20th century, is that the artist or writer communicates their inner emotional state, rather than representing the reality of the external world. Often seen as evincing anxiety in the face of modernity, it characteristically manifested itself in the visual arts in bold, swirling brushstrokes and daring use of colour.

The original Expressionist movement is generally regarded as having formed in Dresden in 1905, when Ernst Ludwig Kirchner, Fritz Bleyl, Karl Schmidt-Rottluff and Erich Heckel came together. A further group appeared in Munich in 1911, including such stellar names as Wassily Kandinsky, Paul Klee and August Macke. The term *expressionism* had been coined a year earlier by an art critic who used it to denote artists

The Scream

The Expressionists were heavily influenced by an earlier generation of painters including Vincent van Gogh, Gustav Klimt and Edvard Munch, whose *The Scream* is regarded by many as the first great Expressionist masterpiece, despite predating the emergence of the Dresden group by a decade. Munch would describe how the work began to form in his mind during a walk in Oslo when 'the sky turned as red as blood. I stopped and leaned against the fence . . . shivering with fear. Then I heard the enormous, infinite scream of nature.'

Like Munch, the Expressionists sought to elicit a guttural, emotional response from their audience. For instance, the Dresden painters created images of the urban underbelly that reeked of alienation and the commodification of society. Their Munich colleagues, meanwhile, employed unnatural colour tones and distorted images to discomfort the viewer. They also showed the profound influence of symbolism.

working in opposition to the values of impressionism (i.e. expressing their inner lives as opposed to celebrating the beauty of the natural world).

The First World War curtailed the Expressionist movement's momentum, with many of its chief exponents called up to fight and several losing their life. Kandinsky and some of his Russian colleagues, meanwhile, left Germany to return to their homeland. Nonetheless, this first phase of Expressionism carried on for a while after the war and achieved international reach through figures such as Marc Chagall. Later generations were heavily influenced by the Expressionist legacy, which birthed both Abstract Expressionism and a Neo-Expressionist school that achieved an international profile in the 1980s. As Ernst Ludwig Kirchner reflected on the original movement: 'The German artist creates out of his imagination, inner vision, the forms of visible nature are to him only a symbol.'

CUBISM

Cubism was a revolutionary movement that emerged at the end of the first decade of the 20th century and was most closely associated with Pablo Picasso and Georges Braque. It characteristically involved depicting subjects from multiple viewpoints within the same picture, replacing Western art's naturalist tendency with disjointed, fragmented and abstracted versions of reality.

In 1907, Picasso – under the influence of Cézanne and within a growing interest in non-Western art styles too – produced arguably the first great work of Cubism, *Les Desmoiselles d'Avignon*. This led to a collaboration with Braque that produced its most interesting results over the next decade or so. The critic Louis Vauxcelles is generally credited with coining the term *cubism* when he responded to Braque's paintings at an exhibition in Paris in 1908 with the observation that he reduced his subjects to 'geometric outlines, to cubes'.

Analytic cubism

The initial stage of Cubism began around 1907 and is known as Analytic Cubism. By abandoning the traditions of perspective in place since the Renaissance, its exponents explored new ways of interpreting space – often, for example, there was no clear delineation between foreground and background, and colour palettes were commonly muted. Many critics believe this was a response to how modernity – urbanization, industrialization, technological advancement – was altering perceptions of the world. As David Hockney noted: 'Cubism was an attack on the perspective that had been known and used for 500 years. It was the first big, big change. It confused people: they said, "Things don't look like that!"'

Picasso and Braque in turn inspired the 'Salon Cubists' (among them Robert Delaunay, Henri Le Fauconnier and Jean Metzinger), who brought the philosophy to a wider public. From around 1912, the second iteration of the movement – Synthetic Cubism – came to the fore, with the use of non-traditional art materials (such as newspapers, sometimes reflecting an active engagement with current affairs) a striking characteristic.

Cubism was one of the most influential movements of the 20th century, inspiring other avant-garde schools and entering the mainstream in, for example, Art Deco stylings. 'Cubism is not a reality you can take in your hand,' Picasso would say. 'It's more like a perfume, in front of you, behind you, to the sides, the scent is everywhere but you don't quite know where it comes from.'

FUTURISM

Born in early 20th-century Italy (and with parallel movements in other parts of Europe, from the UK and Belgium to Russia), Futurism was characterized by a passion for technology, youth (including a certain penchant for youthful violence) and urban modernity. Its passion for the new and its love of change and development were reflected in a wish to overturn the old order and establish new forms, although mainly within the traditional genres of painting, sculpture and, to a lesser extent, architecture.

In 1909 Italian writer Filippo Tommaso Marinetti published the 'Futurist Manifesto' in France's largest-circulation newspaper, *Le Figaro*. For a movement celebrating the modern, mass-production society, the choice of mass media to communicate its message was an obvious one. Marinetti wrote:

> *We want to fight ferociously against the fanatical, unconscious and snobbish religion of the past, which is nourished by the evil influence of museums. We rebel against the supine admiration of old canvases, old statues and old objects, and against the enthusiasm for all that is worm-eaten, dirty and corroded by time; we believe that the common contempt for everything young, new and palpitating with life is unjust and criminal.*

He found support from Italian artists including Umberto Boccioni, Giacomo Balla, Gino Severini and Carlo Carrà – all of whom wished to explore how the heat, space, speed, violence and excitement of modern, urban life might be captured in figurative art. After finding initial enclaves of support in Milan, Naples and Turin, Futurism soon became a national, and then an international, phenomenon, and had developed a clear style of its own by the early part of the 1910s. At a famous exhibition in Milan in 1911 perhaps the star piece was Boccioni's fragmented depiction of an urban landscape, *The City Rises*. He would also contribute important sculptural work such as 1913's *Unique Forms of Continuity in Space*. Other Futurists, meanwhile, adopted new technologies such as chrono-photography, which allowed for an animation-like treatment of images by projecting them across a series of frames.

The demise of futurism

Such was the Futurists' passion for the age of the machine and all that threatened the old order that many of them embraced the arrival of the First World War. As the true nature of that conflict became apparent, the passion for 'the new' diminished, as did the stature of the movement as a whole. What had once seemed avant-garde and vital now appeared frivolous and irrelevant. By the war's end, Futurism was all but dead.

ART DECO

Art Deco was a trend in the visual arts born in pre-First World War France, but by the 1930s it had spread throughout the Western world, finding expression in everything from painting, sculpture and fashion to type fonts, architecture and product design.

In many respects, Art Deco was a hotchpotch. In its early guise, it took inspiration from assorted exotic cultures, including North Africa and the East. It looked also to ancient cultures for inspiration, notably the ancient Egyptians and the Mayans. Then there were classical European influences – the flamboyant craftsmanship redolent of Louis XVI's reign, for instance. Also plundered were several more modern artistic movements, including

> ## *Streamline moderne*
>
> After the Exposition Internationale des Arts Décoratifs et Industriels Modernes exhibition of 1925, Art Deco found a new lease of life in America where it developed into *Streamline Moderne*, a look characterized by smooth, curving forms and shiny surfaces – as epitomized by New York's skyscrapers such as the Chrysler Building of William Van Alen. Where the European movement might have opted for extravagant colour palettes and materials such as gold, granite and mother-of-pearl, the sleeker American take instead chose chrome, concrete and Bakelite.

the geometric Cubist school and the Fauvists (epitomized by Matisse and renowned for a particularly vivid and colourful style of painting). It is also possible to track the influence of the groundbreaking Paris-based dance company, the Ballets Russes, in the development of the style.

The magpie movement thus combined the best of modernism and technological innovation with handpicked elements of classicism and a fascination with the exotic. It also demanded the highest quality of craftsmanship and was generally associated with expensive and luxuriant materials, such as ivory, ebony and marble. Art Deco, it may be said, brought together art, glamour and consumerism in a way never before seen.

The movement's name is a short form of *Arts Décoratifs*, which itself was the abbreviated title of the celebrated Exposition Internationale des Arts Décoratifs et Industriels Modernes (International Exhibition of Modern Decorative and Industrial Arts) hosted in 1925 in Paris. Showcased was work from over 15,000 artists, architects and designers who strove to create everyday and functional objects that were inherently beautiful (although in a slightly more pared-back style than the Art Nouveau and Arts and Crafts movements of recent vintage).

Art Deco had its critics, among them the famous architect and designer Le Corbusier, who critiqued the movement's reliance on excessive

The Construction of the Chrystler Building

ornamentation – ironically, given that his name came to be inextricably linked with the style. Among its leading exponents were René Lalique, Erté, Tamara de Lempicka, Émile-Jacques Ruhlmann and Cassandre.

The rise of Art Deco was halted by the Second World War, which made some of its excesses appear almost distasteful, and it has drifted in and out of fashion ever since. It remains, nonetheless, an enduringly influential movement, especially in furniture and commercial design.

SURREALISM

The Surrealist artists – among them André Breton, Salvador Dalí and René Magritte – turned their backs on the rationalism and realism of so much art, instead exploring the unconscious as a means of accessing their creative imaginations. They were greatly influenced by the rise of psychoanalysis spearheaded by Sigmund Freud in the early 20th century (see page 107). Magritte summed up the movement

like this: 'To be a surrealist . . . means barring from your mind all remembrance of what you have seen, and being always on the lookout for what has never been.'

Surrealism emerged out of the Dadaist movement, which was responsible for producing often incongruous works that challenged cultural and aesthetic assumptions – most notoriously, Marcel Duchamp's *Fountain* (see Conceptualism on page 281). However, the Surrealist emphasis on the imagination also recalled Romanticism, while its embracing of fantastical imagery was foreshadowed by the likes of Hieronymus Bosch (1450–1516).

The imagery employed by the Surrealists was, necessarily given its origins, disparate – from the bowler hats of Magritte to the melting clocks of Dalí and the birds of Max Ernst. Their works, though, could be at once playful and highly disconcerting. For Dalí, surrealism was 'destructive, but it destroys only what it considers to be shackles limiting our vision', while Breton claimed: 'The mind which plunges into Surrealism, relives with burning excitement the best part of childhood.'

There were also significant experiments in film – most famously Luis Bunuel's *Un Chien Andalou* (1929) – and the influence of the movement was widespread. Jackson Pollock, for instance, experimented with automatism, while in film David Lynch continues to carry the surrealist flame.

Art and the unconscious

The birth of Surrealism can be dated to 1924 when Breton wrote *The Surrealist Manifesto*. He described Surrealism as 'psychic automatism in its pure state, by which one proposes to express – verbally, by means of the written word, or in any other manner – the actual functioning of thought.' This was a call to create art by channelling the unconscious at the expense of conscious reason. His ideas sprang out of the theories of Freud, who in works such as *The Interpretation of Dreams* (1900) had argued that the unconscious is the seat of our true feelings and desires.

'Everything we see hides another thing, we always want to see what is hidden by what we see.'

René Magritte

STRUCTURALISM AND POST-STRUCTURALISM

At the heart of structuralism is the notion that all products of human activity – including ideas – are created and not naturally occurring. Their meaning and how they are understood derives from the language we use in relation to them – in other words, there is a complex underlying relationship between signifiers (i.e. words) and the signified (meaning). The study of these signs and symbols is known as semiotics. Post-structuralism, by contrast, comprises an array of philosophical and intellectual positions that broadly respond to what some regard as structuralism's inflexibility.

The founding father of structuralism was the Swiss linguistic theorist Ferdinand de Saussure (1857–1913), and his ideas would spill over from linguistics into other disciplines including philosophy, psychology, sociology and anthropology. Key to understanding structuralism is the idea that language itself does not have inherent meaning but achieves meaning within a complex linguistic code, in which we 'pick up' on prompts.

One of the key structuralist texts is Roland Barthes' *Mythologies* (1957), in which Barthes examined how societies create myths through the use of language (verbal and non-verbal) and to what end. He considered, for example, professional wrestling, arguing that its elaborate staging renders it unlike other sports where the primary goal is to find a winner or else exhibit excellence. Wrestling, Barthes said, instead mythologizes society's concern with concepts of good and evil, justice and retribution, all played out by a cast of social stereotypes. Wrestling, then, becomes not an expression of truth or reality, but a cultural product of a specific set of historic and cultural circumstances. And myth, he suggested, is a kind of propaganda that uses a discourse of widely accepted meanings to influence what we feel about ourselves and the world.

Post-structuralism and literature

In common with others such as Jacques Derrida and Michel Foucault, Roland Barthes is variously identified as a structuralist and a post-structuralist. Whereas structuralism argues that meaning is created within a fairly rigid system of coded interrelationships and through the manipulation of signifiers, post-structuralism is concerned with the idea of unfixed meaning. For the post-structuralists, meaning is not within the gift of the author. Instead it is created by the reader, who brings their own unique set of experiences and perceptions to a text, along with a set of assumptions rooted in the wider cultural and literary context.

Again, Barthes authored one of the key post-structural works, *The Death of the Author* (1967), in which he argued that the true meaning of a text is contained entirely within itself as interpreted by the reader. Knowledge of the author – their life, opinions and historical context – results only in imposing 'a limit on that text' – 'a text's unity,' he said, 'lies not in its origins but in its destination.' In *What is an Author?* (1969), Foucault made his own influential examination of how 'knowledge' and 'truth' are produced and communicated within specific historical contexts. Among his striking conclusions was that the idea of 'Man' (as a figure representing the eternal, fixed nature of humanity) dates only to the 19th century.

Structuralism and post-structuralism, with their often-overlapping cast of thinkers, revolutionized the way that we seek to find meaning in cultural productions – not only books, but also songs, films, paintings, sculptures, architecture and even computer games.

DECONSTRUCTIONISM

Deconstructionism, an intellectual movement spearheaded by Jacques Derrida in the 1960s, emerged out of the structural and post-structural movements. It is notorious for undermining the notion that language has any capacity to represent truth or reality. Deconstructionists believe that language is inherently unstable, since words only have meaning in reference to other words. Our attempts to discern meaning are thus doomed, since it may only ever be derived from language that itself has no inherent meaning. So a climate is created in which traditional ideas and beliefs simply cease to exist. Instead the reader must actively redefine the meaning of a text themselves.

The deconstructed cheescake

A hugely controversial idea, deconstructionism has nonetheless pervaded many areas of society. Consider, for instance, the deconstructed strawberry cheesecake that your local aspirational restaurant serves you – the strawberry gel, freeze-dried strawberry powder, the aerated cheese foam and the little trail of crumb across your expansive plate that seems to bear little resemblance to the delightful sweet treat of your childhood memory. But maybe, just maybe, you can gather the various components into a satisfying spoonful that brings the cheesecake to life in new ways for you. So too, perhaps, the works of Shakespeare or the movies of Orson Welles as viewed through the deconstructionist prism.

Indian scholar and literary theorist Gayatri Chakravorty Spivak, offered up this potential definition of deconstructionism in 1976: 'To locate the promising marginal text, to disclose the undecidable moment, to pry it loose with the positive lever of the signifier; to reverse the resident hierarchy, only to displace it; to dismantle in order to reconstitute what is always already inscribed. Deconstruction in a nutshell.'

Others, however, are resolutely convinced that deconstructionism does not get us very far. Take, for instance, the words of Mark Goldblatt in a 2004 article for *The American Spectator*:

> *Derrida's special significance lies not in the fact that he was subversive, but in the fact that he was an outright intellectual fraud – and that he managed to dupe a startling number of highly educated people into believing that he was onto something . . .*

POP ART

Pop Art reached its zenith in 1960s New York, where artists including Andy Warhol and Roy Lichtenstein created works that consciously sought to blur the distinction between traditional notions of 'high art' and 'low culture'. The movement became synonymous with youthful exuberance and 'cool', its refusal to comply with accepted ideas of what constitutes art finding popularity around the world. In Warhol's words: 'Art is what you can get away with.'

The origins of Pop Art may be traced to London in the early 1950s when the Independent Group – whose members included Edouardo Paolozzi, Richard Hamilton, and Alison and Peter Smithson – met to ruminate on the relationship between popular culture and fine art.

By the middle of the decade, the movement had spread across the Atlantic, where many of those who came to be most closely associated with Pop Art began to create work out of that which was familiar and commonplace – often using the mass media, popular culture and objects of mass production as their inspiration. It was a conscious move away from traditional artistic themes – such as mythology, history and nature – and an embracing of that which mattered to ordinary people in their everyday lives. In the words of Lichtenstein: 'Pop Art looks out into the world. It doesn't look like a painting of something, it looks like the thing itself.'

Tinned soup and Mickey Mouse

Warhol famously produced a series of works in 1962 based on Campbell's soup cans, thus elevating an apparently functional, commercial item into a piece of gallery art. He also appropriated the faces of global icons – Marilyn Monroe, Mao Zedong and Mickey Mouse among them – reproducing their images in series of often-garish prints. Lichtenstein, meanwhile, produced vast canvases in the style of comic-book pictures.

Compared to the highly commercialized feel of the New York movement's output, other places developed their own Pop Art styles. Los Angeles Pop, epitomized by Ed Ruscha, was less concerned with consumer products and more with combining incongruous images and mixing media to evoke a particular 'feel'. Germany's version, meanwhile, went by the name of Capitalist Realism and aimed to critique consumerist culture, while the French *Nouveau Réalisme* sought, according to critic Pierre Restany, 'poetic recycling of urban, industrial, and advertising reality'.

Warhol – above all the others – became an icon of mainstream celebrity culture himself, although the lustre of Pop Art faded somewhat in the 1970s. However, a Neo-Pop movement grew up in the following decade, spearheaded by Jeff Koons, whose subjects variously included Michael Jackson, vacuum cleaners and porn stars.

BRUTALISM

Brutalism is a style and philosophy of architecture that emerged out of the modernist tradition and found widespread expression in urban environments around the world from the 1950s until the 1970s. Stark and functionalist, it employed steel and concrete (pre-poured into huge blocks) as core building materials. Many of its leading exponents saw the style within the context of a broad socialist utopian philosophy, since it allowed for mass housing provision, often in high-rise blocks. The legacy of Brutalism, however, is disputed, with some accusing it of an impersonality that fostered social discord in those areas where it predominated.

As countries sought to rebuild in the aftermath of the Second World War, Brutalism found its niche because of its low costs, both to design and build. The style was typically adopted for government buildings, large-scale social housing developments, universities and shopping centres, everywhere from the USA and Europe to Brazil, Japan, the Philippines and Australia. Its rejection of bourgeois notions of elegance and its uncompromising, almost sculptural features also proved popular in Eastern Europe, where Brutalist buildings became synonymous with communism.

As concrete aged and the realities of high-rise living became apparent, Brutalism became a much-derided style. Prince Charles, for example, noted in 1987: 'You have to give this much to the Luftwaffe. When it knocked down our buildings, it didn't replace them with anything more offensive than rubble.' Nonetheless, it still claims fierce defenders. Buildings such as Ernő Goldfinger's Trellick Tower in London, for example – cited by some as the epitome of failed post-war planning – are to others masterpieces of honest, unpretentious civic-minded design.

The godfather of brutalism

Le Corbusier is often recognized as the godfather of Brutalism for his choice of raw cement (*béton brut*) in Marseille's 1940s' Unité d'Habitation housing project. However, it was Swedish architect Hans Asplund who first used the term 'brutalism' in relation to the Villa Göth in Uppsala (1949). The phrase soon entered popular discourse, with the British architectural partnership, Alison and Peter Smithson, and architectural historian Reyner Banham eager adopters.

CONCEPTUALISM

In conceptual art, the idea of the artwork is considered more important than its visual aspect or formal construction. In this respect, it is a profound challenge to long-held notions of what art is. Since its emergence in the 1960s, conceptual artists have kicked against the idea that an artwork should be a thing of aesthetic pleasure or even that the artist need be skilled in traditional modes of artistic expression. Nor does conceptualism accept that the financial value attributed to any given piece ought to be considered a reflection of its true worth. American artist Sol LeWitt (1928–2007) once noted of its impact: 'Conceptual art became the liberating idea that gave the art of the next forty years its real impetus.'

In 1967 LeWitt published 'Paragraphs on Conceptual Art', widely considered a manifesto for the movement. He wrote: 'What the work of art looks like isn't too important. It has to look like something if it has physical form. No matter what form it may finally have it must begin with an idea. It is the process of conception and realization with which the artist is concerned.'

Over the next couple of years, what had hitherto been an informal

The birth of conceptualism

The origins of conceptualism may be traced back to the controversial Dadaist, Marcel Duchamp (1887–1968). Works such as 1917's *Fountain* (a ready-made porcelain urinal that he signed and dated under an alias before putting it on display) demanded a reappraisal of what constitutes art – including whether the artist must display specific 'artistic skill'. Dadaist principles remained influential in the 1960s and combined with an appetite for using found objects in artworks, along with industrial fabrication, repetition and simplification. In short, much conceptualist art basked in being non-traditional.

grouping of artists grew in influence, so that in 1969 the Museum of Modern Art in New York held an exhibition of conceptualism. Soon it became commonplace to see non-traditional art forms such as installations, performance art, body art and 'happenings'. The philosophy that the idea is everything was notably explored by figures like Joseph Kosuth (in works such as *Three Chairs*) and Lawrence Weiner, who wrote: 'Art that imposes conditions – human or otherwise – on the receiver for its appreciation in my eyes constitutes aesthetic fascism.'

Conceptualism also played with the idea that an artwork is 'completed' by the setting in which it is shown – e.g. a museum or gallery – and also by the audience in their response to it. Considering its ability to alienate some viewers as much as it draws in others, conceptualism has been remarkably resilient. Some of the biggest names in contemporary art may be regarded as conceptualists, among them Ai Weiwei and Tracey Emin.

POSTMODERNISM

Postmodernism is a cultural philosophy and style that emerged in the late 20th century as a response to modernism (see page 264). The term came into popular usage in the 1970s in reference to artworks typified by self-consciousness and anti-authoritarianism. Postmodernism generally rejects the notion of certainty and fixed truth, so that the subjective experiences of each individual member of an artwork's audience becomes pivotal in making sense of a work.

Postmodernism in literature and film

Postmodernism is not restricted to the visual arts. Authors such as William Burroughs, Douglas Copeland, Umberto Eco, Don DeLillo, Thomas Pynchon, Hunter S. Thompson and Kurt Vonnegut are among those to have brought postmodernism to literature, while it is evident too in the films of, for example, Ridley Scott (especially *Blade Runner*), Quentin Tarantino, Pedro Almodóvar and David Lynch.

Given that postmodernism is characterized by a multiplicity of meanings, often contradictory, it is unsurprising that the movement itself is a tricky one to pin down. 'Simplifying to the extreme, I define postmodern as incredulity towards metanarratives', observed the French philosopher and literary theorist, Jean-François Lyotard. Nonetheless, there are certain characteristics that many postmodern works share. For instance, postmodernism often melds high and low culture and plunders different styles and media, as well as embracing technological innovation. In addition, postmodernism often shamelessly seeks to shock its audience – sometimes by creating works that are funny or ridiculous, or by being overtly political, sexual or otherwise controversial. It is also a philosophy rooted in self-awareness.

The Pop Artists (see page 278) may be regarded as at the forefront of postmodernism in their self-conscious eclecticism, but postmodernism has spread across genres, finding expression in, for example, conceptual art. Artists including the aforementioned Tracey Emin, Damien Hirst, Jeff Koons and Chris Ofili have become global stars of the postmodern age.

Influential even as some find it infuriating, postmodernism has been succinctly summed up by the Filipino writer Miguel Syjuco as follows: 'Postmodernism was a reaction to modernism. Where modernism was about objectivity, postmodernism was about subjectivity. Where modernism sought a singular truth, postmodernism sought the multiplicity of truths.'

PICTURE ACKNOWLEDGEMENTS

INDEX